I. M. PEI

A PROFILE IN AMERICAN ARCHITECTURE

I. M. PEI

A PROFILE IN AMERICAN ARCHITECTURE

CARTER WISEMAN

HARRY N. ABRAMS, INC., PUBLISHERS, NEW YORK

To my wife, Eileen, our children, Emma and Owen, and the memory of my father, Mark Wiseman

Editor: Margaret Donovan

Designer: Samuel N. Antupit

Design Assistants: Doris Leath Strugatz, Pamela Geismar

Rights, Reproductions and Photo Research: J. Susan Sherman

Library of Congress Cataloging-in-Publication Data
Wiseman, Carter.
   I.M. Pei: a profile in American architecture/by Carter Wiseman.
     p. cm.
  Includes bibliographical references.
  ISBN 0–8109–3709–3
  1. Pei, I. M., 1917– . 2. Architects—United States—Biography.
I. Title.
NA737.P365W57   1990
720'.92—dc20
[B]   90–30727
                                     CIP

Page 1: I. M. Pei in the East Building of the National Gallery of Art, Washington, D.C.

Page 2: Wall detail from the Fragrant Hill Hotel, Beijing

Page 3: Detail of the skylight of the East Building

Pages 4—5: Pei's pyramid for the Louvre, Paris

Page 6: Stairway at the Wiesner Building, MIT, Cambridge, Mass.

Page 7: Detail of balcony at the Morton H. Meyerson Symphony Center, Dallas

Pages 8—9: Staircase at the Meyerson Center

CONTENTS

INTRODUCTION

Asurprising number of people tend to assume that a work of architecture is entirely the product of an individual designer bent over a drawing board with T-square and triangle in an act of solitary inspiration. It is an image that many architects have encouraged, but it is never really the case. All architecture is a collaborative effort that involves artists, technicians, managers, and a host of other practitioners. This has been true throughout the history of architecture and has become steadily more so as buildings have grown larger and more technologically complex.

Nevertheless, the best architecture always bears the imprint of a single creative sensibility. I. M. Pei, the founding member of the architecture firm of Pei Cobb Freed & Partners, has, over his forty-year career, managed to combine the role of the individual with those of the larger architectural team in a unique way. He is an outstanding artist in his own right and has been involved to varying degrees in everything his firm has done. Yet like other architects, he has often served more as an executive—participating in the conceptual phase of a building and guiding its development, but leaving some design decisions, not to mention details, to collaborators. So effectively has Pei integrated his own artistic identity with that of his firm that outsiders often have difficulty identifying the hands most responsible for what is commonly thought of as an I. M. Pei building.

This book is an attempt to distill from the portfolio of work done by the Pei firm a sense of the man who established it and an understanding of his personal architectural vision.

The eight men currently listed as full partners of Pei Cobb Freed & Partners represent an extraordinary concentration of aesthetic and organizational talent. That firm—with the possible exception of McKim, Mead & White in the late-nineteenth and early-twentieth centuries and Skidmore, Owings & Merrill from the 1950s to the 70s—is alone in the history of American architecture in having produced such a large number of significant buildings of consistently high quality. It has become a model for combining corporate success and artistic excellence.

From the beginning, the firm has been what the writer and architect Peter Blake has called "a fellowship of artists and intellectuals."[1] In the years they have worked together, the partners (and their co-workers, whose number now fluctuates near 300) have created more than 100 major works, ranging from school buildings to skyscrapers, from museums to master plans for entire cities in the United States and abroad. That figure does not include the scores of proposals and schemes that for any number of reasons never made it into construction.

Nevertheless, the buildings for which Pei himself is primarily responsible are, as a group, the finest work the firm has produced. Moreover, they most clearly represent the aesthetic with which Pei, to a remarkable degree, has been able to suffuse those who work with and for him. Through the personal direction he has given his firm over the years, he has created a unique imprint on the face of American design.

Pei has known, studied, or taught with many of the great European and American figures of twentieth-century architecture, including, most significantly, Walter Gropius and Marcel Breuer. He has drawn on them and others in that tradition—especially Le Corbusier, Mies van der Rohe, and Louis Kahn—for inspiration in his own work. So, of course, have other members of Pei's generation, architects like Philip Johnson, Paul Rudolph, and Edward Larrabee Barnes. But Pei has brought to his mix the elusive ingredient of a sensibility formed during his upbringing in China. Trained in the largely antihistorical, form-follows-function tenets of Modernism, Pei has survived both its constrictions and the revivalist tendencies of Post-Modernism by insisting on a remarkably independent design course. He did not so totally embrace the philosophy of the Bauhaus as he learned it at Harvard's Graduate School of Design that he felt the need, as some of his colleagues did in the 1970s and 80s, to turn totally against it. And when the Post-Modernist countermovement (and its successor, Deconstructivism) began to stall, Pei found his aesthetic comfortably—and profitably—intact.

That aesthetic cannot be reduced to or defined by any particular style. Pei is widely known as a Late Modernist, but his works elude such simple categorization. As a result, while he has his imitators, there is no "school of Pei." In the Modernist tradition, he remains devoted to rigorous geometry and to the use of simple, often sculptural, forms. But having said that, one has to look more at the process by which Pei creates architecture than at the shape of the result in order to establish what he stands for as an artist. The key to that process is a willingness to examine a commission for what it has to offer rather than to impose upon it a rigidly formal preconception. Pei looks first at what exists and then turns to what might be made of it. He studies the site with care and seeks to relate what he puts upon it to the natural setting as well as to the buildings that may already stand nearby. The result may not resemble its neighbors (as some "contextualists" might wish), but it is almost always calculated to fit into a larger urban or landscape composition. More important, Pei approaches the intended use of the building as a guide to its formal expression. Beyond that, he focuses with a skill rare in his profession on how people will experience the building as they pass through and around it.

This approach—concentrating on the architectural and human environment of a building before arriving at an appropriate form—accounts for the remarkable variety of architectural shapes Pei has produced. The relentless geometry of the East Building of the National Gallery in Washington, D.C., would seem to have come from another hand than the one that designed the frankly ornamental Fragrant Hill Hotel outside Beijing, until one retraces the common analytical process by which Pei conceived them. That process, then, coupled with a reverence for high-quality materials and the way they are assembled, is what defines and unifies Pei's body of work.

Some of Pei's critics have attacked his architecture for what they see as an inhumane devotion to geometry. Others have felt that he has diluted his art through service to the rich and the powerful. Still others insist that what passes for architecture by I. M. Pei is in fact the work of talented collaborators led by a socially adept salesman.

There is some merit to each of these claims, but there is no question that Pei has emerged as the most durably creative of American architects working at the grand scale. His addition to the National Gallery became an instant classic. The controversial pyramid he designed for the Louvre in Paris is a unique combination of timeless form and high technology. And his seventy-one-story tower for the Bank of China in Hong Kong has helped redefine high-rise construction techniques while creating an urban sculpture of rare power.

For his myriad accomplishments, Pei has received virtually every professional tribute of any importance in his field. Among the most significant are the Arnold Brunner Award from the National Institute of Arts and Letters (1961), the Thomas Jefferson Memorial Medal for Architecture (1976), the Gold Medal for Architecture from the American Academy of Arts and Letters (1979), the Gold Medal of the American Institute of Architects (1979), La Grande Medaille d'Or from the French Academy of Architecture (1981), the Medal of Liberty (1986), the National Medal of Arts (1988), and the Japanese Praemium Imperiale, established in 1989 to honor lifetime achievement in the arts. The citation for the Pritzker Prize, generally considered to be the architectural equivalent of the Nobel and awarded to Pei in 1983, read in part: "Ieoh Ming Pei has given this century some of its most beautiful interior spaces and exterior forms."

Impressive as Pei's professional achievement may be, his personal story is no less compelling. Born in pre-Communist China, where his father was a leading banker, he came to the United States in 1935. After studies at the University of Pennsylvania, MIT, and Harvard and World War II service in weapons research, he was hired by William Zeckendorf, the most flamboyant of the period's real estate developers. The years with Zeckendorf gave Pei a taste of commercial realities and large-scale urban practice unlike any encountered by his design contemporaries.

The leadership of the firm since it became independent of Zeckendorf in 1960 has brought its senior partner, who is known to his friends, staff, and clients as "I. M." (and whose surname is pronounced "pay"), into contact with many of the most powerful financial, social, and political figures in the United States and, indeed, the world. His clients have ranged from a Chinese bank to Paul Mellon, from the Kennedy family to the government of France, from institutions of higher learning to a Japanese religious sect.

Pei's architecture could not be called revolutionary. It is fundamentally about the creative refinement of what has gone before. In pursuing that refinement, however, Pei has not only risen to the highest levels of his art, but in the process has embodied the classic American story of a foreign-born entrepreneur who attains great success through talent and industry.

In organizing this book, I have tried to isolate distinct periods in Pei's development as an architect as they have been expressed in a selection of outstanding buildings for which he, rather than his partners, has been most responsible. Where this is the case, those buildings have been made the center-pieces of chapters. In those chapters, related buildings done by Pei, his partners, and other architects are discussed to set the story of the individual work of architecture in a broader context. Any account of the East Building of the National Gallery, for example, would be incomplete without reference to Pei's Everson Museum of Art in Syracuse, the Johnson Museum of Art at Cornell, or the Paul Mellon Center for the Arts at Choate Rosemary Hall.

In two cases, that of the John Hancock Tower in Boston and the Jacob K. Javits Convention Center in New York City, it seemed appropriate to focus on buildings for which Pei's partners, rather than Pei himself, were the primary designers. The reason for the exceptions is that these buildings, while designed by other hands, were of major significance to the firm as a whole. And whatever the variety of talents within it, the firm of Pei Cobb Freed & Partners remains a unified enterprise whose overall health and ultimate importance are inseparable from the fortunes of its members.

The hazard of such selectivity is that many of the works produced by Pei himself and other members of the firm inevitably had to be given short shrift, or excluded altogether. It is hoped that the complete listing of the firm's works provided at the end of this volume will compensate to some degree for any imbalance by allowing readers a sense of the architects' daunting collective reach.

14

1. AN ORDERLY ENIGMA

Beyond his international distinction as an architect, I. M. Pei is known to the public as an elegant, charming, and thoroughly diplomatic individual. The publicity photograph released by his office shows him wearing an impeccably tailored double-breasted suit of nailhead tweed, round-rimmed tortoiseshell glasses in the traditional Chinese fashion, and a serenely engaging smile. Even at the end of a long day of work in his office, on New York City's Madison Avenue, Pei is likely to be wearing his jacket. He is not a shirt-sleeves sort of architect.

But on a sunny Saturday afternoon not long ago, I. M. Pei was sweating hard. He, several members of his family, and a number of friends had gathered at the summer house Pei built for his family in 1952 in the wooded hills of Katonah, some thirty miles northeast of New York. (The house, a one-story Modernist box whose formal severity is mitigated by distinctly Oriental details, was later expanded by blasting out the rock foundations to create two bedrooms for Pei's children.) The occasion was the installation of a sixteen-foot-high sculpture by Pei's weekend houseguest, the English artist Anthony Caro, who is a former student of Henry Moore's and a longtime Pei friend. The spindly abstraction of raw steel was being eased into place on a small promontory of rock not far from the house by a team of burly workmen.

Despite his years, the five-foot-seven-inch Pei—dressed in a faded pink polo shirt, khakis, and Tretorn tennis shoes—moved with a surprisingly youthful agility, darting up and down the outcropping to study the position of the sculpture. He and Caro, a craggy, taciturn man with a short white beard, would circle the piece, gesturing to the workmen as they struggled with the "legs" of the as-yet-untitled sculpture. Occasionally, the architect and the sculptor would

The official portrait of the architect in his headquarters at 600 Madison Avenue in New York City.

15

huddle, cock their heads to left or right, and signal the crew to move their burden slightly to one side or the other.

When the piece was settled to their satisfaction, Pei and Caro crouched with the engineer, who was overseeing the installation at the spot where one steel leg should have met the outcropping. The forward "foot" of the member was level with the rest of the piece, but was several inches short of the rock where it fell away toward the house, leaving a gap. There was a brief discussion about moving the entire piece back so that the steel would meet the level portion of rock, but Pei argued that it should stay where it was. "It just ought to be longer," he said, pointing at the ungrounded shaft of rust-stained steel. "It should reach down the slope so that the piece grips the rock—so that it has an *anchor*." The sculptor, who might have been forgiven for protesting the architect's editing of his work, nodded his assent.

A foot-long section of scrap beam was hurriedly cut with an acetylene torch and maneuvered into the gap. "I like the length now," said Pei, giving Caro an inquisitive glance. "I don't mind it," said Caro. Pei broke into a smile that virtually consumed his face, his eyes nearly shut behind his glasses, his teeth flashing with Cheshire-cat prominence.

The engineer, studying ways to attach the new piece, turned to Pei and began to sketch on a piece of cardboard. He showed how the steel could be joined to the original member with a bolt, or by welding it. "Are you ever going to remove this sculpture?" he asked. "No," replied the architect, again looking to Caro, who smiled. "Then we *weld*," declared the engineer, gesturing to his torch man.

The job done, there was much shaking of dirt-caked hands, and while the workmen began to clean up, the architect and the sculptor walked toward the porch for a lunch of salad and French wine. ("I don't spend as much time on wine as I do on architecture," the architect said with a laugh to a guest who admired the selection, "but I'd like to.") They were followed by the other members of the party, who were careful first to pack up their Nikons and Camcorders. This may have been a private ceremony, but it had an air of public import; the guests had evidently been given to feel in advance that it would be appropriate to record the occasion for posterity.

The installation of the Caro sculpture said much about I. M. Pei as an artist and as a man. He has an intense dedication to art, both his own and that of others. (He has confessed privately that, in another life, he might have chosen to be a sculptor himself.) He also has a steely determination that is unfailingly deferential and an uncanny appreciation of how to influence even the most apparently spontaneous of events.

People who have worked with Pei often mention the fondness he has for the high and the mighty. A former associate once said, "I. M. is able to tell within minutes of entering a room who is important." Another recalled that during their years together, Pei displayed "a superior sense of who the influential people are and which are the key occasions. He has a gift with the powerful." The trait is apparent even to sensitive strangers. During a working trip to Iran in the 1970s, Pei and a number of associates were persuaded to seek out a local fortune teller. Everyone considered the visit a lark, but the fortune teller rapidly impressed the Americans with some piercingly accurate observations. His assessment of Pei: "He is very interested in meeting kings and queens." To at least one former collaborator, who has the highest respect for him as a person and an architect, Pei can be "something of a social and cultural snob." The man was quick to explain that he did not mean his remark as a criticism, but as a tribute. An architect who has worked with Pei for nearly twenty years ascribes the affinity for the influential to the simple fact that Pei was born among such people and understands them. "Imagine having grown up as the son of one of the most important men in one of the world's oldest cultures," he said. "Seeking out the top people just comes naturally to Pei."

It is, however, less the prominence of the clients than their willingness to share in an intense dialogue about the creation of architecture that has produced Pei's best work. Where such a relationship was missing, the work has suffered.

Theodore Musho, a senior member of the firm who has worked on many of its best-known buildings, including the John F. Kennedy Library in Boston and the Dallas City Hall, described the demands of the relationship simply. Pei, he said, "has an *idée fixe* about priorities, about what the building is supposed to be and what it is supposed to do to its surroundings. If he can't have a conversation with the client about such things at the beginning, before the designing starts, the job is probably not worth doing. I. M. wouldn't say it, but his attitude is: 'If you want to do a piece of junk, I'm not your architect.'"

If a client *can* have the sort of conversation Musho described, he is likely to get more than he bargained for and, usually, like it. Pei is well known for making the balkiest client feel that the project he is paying for has greater artistic potential than he had dreamed of—and will be worth the additional cost. William Walton, President John F. Kennedy's arts adviser and a major participant in the extended drama of Pei's Kennedy Library, wrote in 1981 that the architect combines his knowledge of the setting of a building and the people involved in it, "along with immense gifts of persuasion, to guide them down paths which they subsequently think they invented themselves. He shows them the need for a park here, or a new highway there, or some other device for improving the quality of life that seems to connect only indirectly with the building that he has been commissioned to design."[1]

So skilled is Pei at the subtleties of working with clients that, according to one of his close friends, "it's conceivable there are some who feel they've been had—but not until afterwards." Pei is, said a former collaborator, "a master of marketing, a magician." Said another, "He is a genius as a salesman of design."

An alumnus of the Pei firm explained the phenomenon by comparing the architect's approach to that of one of his former collaborators. During work on a building in Boston, that architect (who subsequently left the firm) presented the client with a design for a conference table. The client was clearly unhappy with the material, which was to be a rare granite. But rather than reject it out of hand, the client began gently pointing out how cold the stone would be to the touch and how unyielding it would be to write on. At each objection, Pei's associate, rather than taking the hint, would offer a solution: the table could be heated electrically; leather panels could be added to provide softer writing surfaces. But he was unbending about the stone. Finally, the frustrated client declared testily that he just didn't like the table and ordered the architect and his drawings out of the room.

Pei, speculates the observer of this scene, would have asked the client what material he would prefer, putting him in the awkward position of advising an expert. "The owner might have suggested wood or glass, to which I. M. would have said, 'Of course! And it will be the most beautiful thing of its kind ever made!' It would also probably have been twice as expensive. Pei's goal would have been to do a beautiful table; the material would have been secondary. I. M. will give in on the small stuff, but never on the really important issues. If he weren't an architect, he could be the CEO of any corporation in the country."

It is a measure of Pei's special relationships with his best clients that many of them have become lifelong friends.

Although Pei's face is marked by the spotting of age now, it still has a boyish quality, and when he is excited about a subject, he can become almost childlike. "Vivacious" is a word that recurs frequently when people talk about Pei, but it does not sum up the energy he conveys. Explaining the complex use of multiple vanishing points in his design for the East Building of the National Gallery, he will thrust his small hands out before him and hunch his shoulders as if to urge his point physically forward. Presenting a design for an elaborate light fixture for a symphony hall in Dallas, he will start to blink even more rapidly than usual, as if blinded by the anticipated glitter.

Pei laughs easily, but occasionally seems to miss the point of others' humor. Once, some members of his staff were chiding him about how much of his designing he did in his head, rather than on paper. (He has never put much trust in drawing, saying it is too slow.) They suggested that if the Library of Congress were ever to ask for his archives, the office would have to send his head instead of drawings. The response was a quizzical look and a change of the subject.

Despite more than half a century in the United States, Pei still speaks with a slight Chinese accent and occasionally makes minor grammatical mistakes. The definite article is frequently dropped: people long dead are sometimes described as acting in the present: the word "subsequently" is pronounced "sub-*see*-quently." The combined traces of exoticism and linguistic uncertainty seem only to add to Pei's charm and credibility.

From the beginning, Pei has been drawn to controversy, whether it involved the size and site (and, ultimately, the fragile windows) of the John Hancock Tower in Boston, the political jockeying in New York City over the Javits Convention Center, or the critical storm that greeted his plan for the pyramid for the Louvre. "He loves impossible challenges," said Araldo Cossutta, a former partner. "He makes very personal commitments." Those commitments have seen him and his firm through crises that would have crushed a less determined man.

Whatever the impact of the crises, even the successes have produced some strain. Invitations to parties and ceremonies flood Pei's mailroom, but he prefers to spend most of his off-duty time with his wife and a few friends or members of his family having quiet dinners at home or at Gino's, an Italian restaurant on Lexington Avenue not far from his office. Pei's wife, Eileen, noted that the "star" circuit to which her husband has risen can make such moments rare. (She has dealt with the pressure by recalling something her mother said to her while she was still a girl in China, "Remember, no matter how tired you may be, your husband may be even more tired.")

Through it all, Pei has maintained with colleagues, clients, and the public a level of pragmatism that is rare among his fellow architects. In an era when many of them have built entire reputations on the skill with which they can discuss their work in polysyllabic abstractions, Pei is remarkably grounded in results. What a colleague once called an "aedicular indication of a room," Pei would more likely describe as a window. A young associate once suggested to Pei that his work reflected a sensitivity to "the dialectics of form." As the associate recalled the exchange, Pei's first response was "puzzlement." When he recovered, "the conversation went nowhere. I think I. M. is oblivious to the meaning of his architecture at an abstract level."

That fact—combined with his manifest success—has made Pei few friends among academic architects and students, who are often more interested in theory than in built work. Indeed, he is widely considered standoffish and unchic by the architectural avant-garde. He has chosen not to teach in architecture schools, as many of his colleagues (including his partners) do, preferring to instruct by example within the confines of his own firm. A prominent professor of architectural history at Yale could always count on a laugh from his students when he described how Pei, during work on a proposal for downtown New Haven, emphasized the importance of space for parking.

With his immediate staff, Pei is invariably polite. Some years ago, an assistant put him on the wrong plane for the opening ceremonies at one of his buildings. She got a brief talking-to after he got back, but the slip was not mentioned after that. His personal secretary of thirty years, a diminutive Vermonter named Leicia Black, once confessed that she had heard Pei swear "exactly once" in that period, and the oath was "dammit." According to another longtime member of the office staff, "I. M. almost never criticized and never overpraised, but you always felt his reactions." He is not the sort to pass on his worries to those around him. "At the peak of frustration," said an architect who worked closely

The architect has never put much faith in drawing, finding it too slow. He prefers to initiate a design with a simple sketch and then develop it in steadily more detailed discussions and "editing" sessions among the members of his design team.

with Pei for five years, "he can be almost icy." When the pressure in the office is particularly heavy, the only indication that Pei is feeling it is likely to be a slight tremor of his hands as he rearranges the papers in front of him. But when things are going well, he is able through the sheer force of his own involvement in his work to create an atmosphere that, as a member of his staff has described it, "crackles and pops."

Pei's design process is, said a veteran associate, "rather haphazard." But, the same associate added, "when you analyze the thought, it turns out to be highly rational." Design changes that are made late in a project are rarely afterthoughts; they have simply been put off while more important decisions were being made. One of Pei's secretaries said that she could always tell when he was designing instead of following what she was saying. "He got a strange look on his face," she noted, "but then he would come right back to the same place in the conversation." Pei does not give orders; he leads by suggestion. A former employee remembered with some pain Pei's provocative comment on a presentation that had been struggled over for weeks: "Well, we're not quite there yet." Many of his people have worked with him for so long that simple exchanges are instantly interpreted as if they were in code. Discussing refinements on the facade of the bell tower he was designing for a religious group in Japan, Pei listened intently to the options presented by an associate, then proposed moving one element slightly, and concluded with, "This may require some further thought." Although meaning-less to an outsider, the message implicit in that apparently cryptic exchange was sufficient for his co-worker to proceed without any doubt about what Pei intended.

In recent years, as his firm has grown and prospered, Pei has eased away from overseeing its entire production and has involved himself more deeply with individual designs, leaving his partners to operate with steadily growing auton-omy. In doing so, Pei has assembled teams of young associates, who seem fired by the contact with the senior partner and grateful for the independence he has given them. Arriving early at the office, he is likely to drop in on a young designer to chat before continuing to his own desk. If he and his people are working through the weekend, which they often do, Pei will from time to time gather up a group of associates for an impromptu lunch at Gino's. There is almost never an agenda, just conversation, during which, according to one former employee, Pei can make even a green recruit feel like the most knowledgeable person at the table.

As was the case forty years ago, Pei's working technique is to encourage competition among his subordinates, eliciting a number of alternatives and then,

as one put it, "clarifying and directing" their interpretations of his instructions. "There is a degree to which art cannot be owned," commented a close collaborator of recent years, "and I. M. acknowledges that shared quality. He is able to step back from a project and let others step in. He doesn't hog the design. But he is very preemptive and has always thought the thing out. The one with the most athletic mind will dominate the result, and it is usually I. M."

Pei tends to have a special relationship with his designers, and the ones he most favors often describe him as something of a father figure. The bond can create conflict. Because the firm is so dominated by the senior partners, the chances of rising past a certain level are remote. Many young employees with ambition have decided that the chances of making their own marks would be better if they left the firm, a process that often proves painful to the ones who are moving on. A number of those who have done it have confessed to feeling that they were betraying Pei's faith in them. "I felt like a son to him," said one. "It was very difficult to leave."

Those in the firm who are not highly favored may feel frustrated at being relegated to less responsible positions. If they complain, they are likely to be reassigned to more challenging work. But according to an architect who saw it happen more than once, the malcontents, after savoring their triumph, are likely some months later to be gradually shifted back toward designing relatively minor details. "Pei sizes his people up very fast," said the former associate. "But then he tends to have them fixed in his mind."

Even when physically and mentally drained by weeks of uninterrupted work and intercontinental travel, Pei will rarely, even if provoked, speak ill of his adversaries or competitors. His wife explains: "Life is too short, and carping doesn't really gain you anything. I. M. feels that what you do should speak for you, not what you say about other architects."

Despite his star status, Pei is able to make a first-time visitor, a workman on a construction site, or even a stranger paying his respects from the next table at a restaurant, feel as if the architect is the one being honored by the attention. When talking with a guest in his office, Pei will rarely be the one to end the conversation. The result is that other visitors with appointments will be kept waiting. But with an apologetic smile and outstretched arms, Pei is able to make them feel grateful for even a portion of the remaining hour. While working with Pei on the expansion of the Louvre, the museum's director—himself a busy man—confessed his amazement that Pei, "an even busier man," always seemed to have time for people. He is, as a result, often late. Pei's wife confessed that

From the early days with Zeckendorf, Pei and his colleagues made especially effective use of site models, which showed clients exactly how their projects would fit into the larger urban or landscape scheme. Here, during a presentation in 1967, Pei makes a point with the help of a detailed model of midtown Manhattan.

traveling with her husband can be a challenge. "We are always running for planes," she said, "because he is always squeezing in one more person to talk to."

To close friends, Pei can be extraordinarily generous and hospitable. Eileen Pei tells the story of the welcome her husband gave a Japanese friend, a gallery owner who was visiting New York. Pei knew that his friend was an ardent golfer, and while he himself has no use for the game (although he has been given several sets of clubs over the years), he arranged with a golf club near the Katonah house to reserve a weekend slot. "I. M. just walked around with them while they played," Eileen said. "They're good friends, but that wasn't necessary."

For all his storied charm and public warmth, there is a level past which I. M. Pei does not invite, or indeed permit, intimacy. People in his office will often mention how like a family the Pei firm seems (until recently, the office public address system announced fresh popcorn weekly; the practice was suspended when clients began to comment on the odor). But Pei himself rarely speaks of his parents or his siblings. His wife and four children (three boys, one girl) are mentioned only occasionally. He rarely volunteers opinions on politics, the changing times, or the state of his art. He is clearly consumed by the architecture at hand. "I know the man, but I don't know him," said a secretary. "He gives a great deal of himself, but far from all." Added an architect friend of nearly forty years: "He is the most inscrutable man I know, and I know him very well." At times, Pei seems burdened by his own reserve. One of the qualities that attracted him to his wife, he once said to a television interviewer, was that she was "so straightforward."[2]

Although the door to Pei's office is almost always open, people with business to transact, including close associates, rarely burst in unannounced. The office itself suggests a man highly concerned with order. The palette is black, white, and gray, matching an enormous Al Held abstraction that covers an entire wall. The books on the shelf behind the chrome-legged stone table that serves as a desk include cloth-bound catalogues of his work, a book on the Bauhaus, and a three-volume edition on the architectural history of Rome. Neither the books nor their positions change much from year to year: the shelf in 1990 bore almost the same selection that appears in a photograph of the office taken in 1973, except for the addition of a book on American architects and one about Disneyland. After absences during which the office cleaning crew regularly moves a miniature of Picasso's *Bust of Sylvette* (the full version of which stands amid the towers of Pei's University Plaza complex in New York) by only an inch or so from its customary place on his office windowsill, Pei will replace it in its original location with an almost ritualistic precision. The wastebasket in his office is built flush into the bookcase and must be tilted outward for use. There is rarely more than a single crumpled piece of paper in it.

Pei's four-story townhouse on Sutton Place, on Manhattan's East Side, is similarly correct for a man whose taste in art has always tended to the Modernist classics. The living room, which overlooks a small garden facing the East River, is embellished with works of art by Dubuffet, Morris Louis, Lipchitz, and De Kooning, among other artists of their generation. The paintings and sculptures are there not for effect, but because they are loved and understood. (Pei delights in telling how he pointed out to Dubuffet the similarity between his sculptures and the ornamental rocks favored by the designers of classical Chinese gardens.) The room is kept immaculately clean, and every piece of furniture is obviously arranged with a larger composition in mind; there is no stack of old magazines or Sunday papers. The house is overseen with quiet authority by Pei's wife, a pertly elegant woman whom Pei met shortly after she arrived in the United States from China. If a picture frame should be left askew by the cleaning woman, Eileen is likely to excuse herself from a conversation to straighten it.

Pei's small study, which contains neither desk nor drawing board, is as tidy as the living room. It is dominated by a wall of ceiling-high bookcases that contain relatively few volumes on architecture; those that are there range from *The Plan of St. Gall* to works on Marcel Breuer and Le Corbusier. Most of the rest of the books are about art: monographs on Noguchi, Magritte, and Rembrandt and *Old Master Drawings from the Albertina*. There is a worn copy of Henry Adams's *Mont-Saint-Michel and Chartres*, which was given to Pei as one of the many prizes he won as a student at MIT. There is little fiction; he says he doesn't have time for it (although he occasionally returns to Antoine de Saint Exupéry's *Wind, Sand, and Stars*). He prefers verse, much of it Chinese. His favorite American poet is Whitman.

Pei's taste in poetry is significant. Nature is an important part of his life and his architecture. When he decided to thin out some of the overgrown property near his country house, he found the process surprisingly painful. The land was covered with large trees, some of them quite old. "The hardest part of the task," Pei said, "was deciding which of the trees should be cut down to allow the others to flourish." He decided not to remove the three Chinese pines he had planted when he built the house, although they had grown tall enough to block the view from the porch of the valley beyond. He hoped that they would eventually grow high enough so that he could see the view under the branches.

Pei's relationship with his children is clearly warm, but somewhat distant. His youngest son, Li Chung, known as Sandi, who along with an older brother, Chien Chung, is now an architect in the Pei firm, remembered that while he was growing up, he was more of "an observer than a participant" in his father's life. Even when times were bad, as they frequently were during the saga of the Kennedy Library and the crisis over the Hancock Tower, and Pei was clearly affected, Sandi said that he "never saw it." Although Sandi was one of the architects working on the earliest stages of the Bank of China, his father never mentioned the striking family symmetry represented by the fact that his own father had once been an officer of the same bank. In the end, said the son, "my mother was there to bring us up. My father set the standards, which were always the highest. It was daunting."

Pleased as he manifestly is to have two of his sons working with him, Pei once confessed that he would have liked them to try their wings on their own. "They are trapped," he said with some gravity. "How can a son go somewhere else after working on the Louvre?" Pei's wife sees the situation from another perspective. "Their father is proud that they wanted to do the same thing he does, and wants them to do well," she said, "and they don't want to let him down. The trouble is that they will often demand too much of themselves. Fathers and sons are like that."

It is tempting to suggest that there is an Oriental dimension to Pei's pervasive aura of order and formality. But people close to him point out that

Pei with his wife, Eileen, in the living room of their Manhattan townhouse, which overlooks the East River.

behind the smilingly elegant Chinese, there is a "very Western, very pragmatic mind clicking away." A consultant to the firm has described Pei as possessing "a golden tongue and a titanium spine." From his earliest professional days working for William Zeckendorf to his present associations with the most prominent clients in the United States and abroad, I. M. Pei has been as much in control of his passage through life as he has of the exquisite details of his best buildings. Peter Blake has described him—fondly—as "a Chinese Metternich."[3]

Nevertheless, there are moments when I. M. Pei is capable of betraying an almost sentimental streak. With a glass or two of Bordeaux behind him, he turns almost impish, gripping a friend's arm, throwing back his head, and laughing rapidly, frequently at rather simple jokes. After winning the Medal of Liberty, awarded on the centennial of the Statue of Liberty to twelve foreign-born Americans who had made major contributions to American life, he was asked at a lunch what the event had meant to him. He said that while he had never suffered from racial discrimination in the United States, he had, at least in the early days, sometimes felt like "an outsider." Even though he has been an American citizen since 1955 (he was sworn in along with some 10,000 others in a mass ceremony at New York's Polo Grounds), his eyes suddenly grew moist as he described how important the medal was to him as a symbol that he had been accepted by the American people. (He rated it above all of his professional honors.)

But perhaps the most striking quality about the architect today is a sense he communicates that he must get on with his work. While Pei is a patient man, willing to wait out the most exasperating delays if he feels the goal is worth it, he also exhibits something bordering on anxiety about the next phase of his career. After more than four decades of prodigious feats of organizing the work of others, whether in the service of William Zeckendorf or his own firm, he is clearly eager to leave a deeper mark as an autonomous designer. This underlying sense of being in a hurry expresses itself in indirect ways. In the course of explaining the geometry he was exploring in his design for the Dallas symphony hall, he became increasingly agitated, leaning forward and stabbing with both hands at a pile of correspondence on his desk. Placing a phone call about a detail of the construction of the Louvre, he would say, "It is a matter of some urgency." I. M. Pei seems to feel that he is freer now than ever before, but that there is only limited time to do what he intends to be his best work. Discussing his hopes for the future, he invoked the Russian-born American architect Louis Kahn, whose first major building was not finished until he was fifty-two and who died in 1974 at the age of seventy-four: "Look at the burst of energy in his last ten years."

The Pei family on a 1964 trip to Venice. From left: Chien Chung, T'ing Chung, Li Chung, Eileen, Liane, and I. M.

2. CHINA, MIT, AND HARVARD (1917–48): THE SHAPING OF AN ARCHITECT

Although he has made his name as an architect primarily in the United States, I. M. Pei has never abandoned his Chinese heritage. Indeed, he is insistent about having come to America not as an immigrant, but as a student. And any close study of his architecture reveals inescapable traces of an enduring Chinese sensibility in both approach and form. Despite the upheavals that have overtaken his homeland since he left, he has remained deeply loyal to a timeless China that remains, for him, beyond politics. In 1979, not long after the celebrated "opening" of China to the West, Pei was offered—and eagerly accepted—a commission to design a hotel outside Beijing; the tallest of his several tall buildings is one for the Bank of China in Hong Kong, finished in 1990. Pei's interest in the commission for the Fragrant Hill Hotel, in an ancient hunting preserve not far from the Chinese capital, was based very much on a desire to find a new and appropriate architectural form for his native land at a time when it was seeking a new cultural identity. His interest in building a skyscraper for a Communist bank had less to do with diplomacy than with the fact that his father had been general manager of the same branch before the revolution.

Art and commerce were both ingrained in Pei's upbringing. His family had lived for more than 600 years in Suzhou (formerly Soochow), a city in the Yangtze basin northwest of Shanghai. The history of Suzhou goes back some 2,500 years, but it became prominent during the Sui Dynasty (A.D. 581–618) with the completion of the Grand Canal, which linked several major trading cities along a line running northwest from Hangzhou to Beijing. In addition to its prominence in the rice and silk trades, Suzhou became known for its craftsmen, artists, and scholars. So prosperous and refined was Suzhou in the public

A formal portrait of the Pei family in the 1920s. I. M. is seated at the extreme left. His father, Tsuyee, is standing, left of center. Pei's mother, Lien Kwun, is holding one of his brothers.

imagination that a saying grew up around it and its neighboring city, "In Heaven there is Paradise, on earth Suzhou and Hangzhou."

Pei's father, Tsuyee Pei, was born in Suzhou in 1893 to a well-to-do landowning family. He met his wife, Lien Kwun, while he was a student at the local university, from which he graduated in 1911. After further studies, in mining (at Tongshan University in northern China), he took a job with the Bank of China's main office, in Beijing. Before long, he was transferred to the Shanghai branch.

During the period the elder Pei and his wife were in Shanghai, the city was fertile ground for traders and entrepreneurs, many of them Europeans and Americans, who could operate freely there, engaging in trade with a minimum of controls and taxes. This internationalist atmosphere made Shanghai a center of financial activity and a heady place for bankers, like Pei's father, who had an interest in the world beyond China. Rising rapidly in the city's superheated environment, Tsuyee Pei was soon promoted and, in 1914, he was assigned to open a new branch of the bank in Canton, now Guangzhou. The branch prospered, as did the family. The Pei family already included a daughter, Yuen

A 1930s view of the Shanghai waterfront. At the time, the bustling port city was dominated by foreign traders and entrepreneurs, who made it a center for international commerce.

Hua; the couple's second child, Ieoh Ming, was born on April 26, 1917.

The country at the time was wracked by fighting among local warlords. The strife was making any sort of civic order in China all but impossible. The countryside was devastated, bringing famine to the peasants along with outrageous profits to hoarders and other profiteers. Thousands of people starved to death, and it was common to see corpses lying in the gutters of city streets.[1]

When, in 1918, Pei's father came under pressure from warlords who were eager to take over his branch office, the bank headquarters instructed him to leave Canton with the family for the Hong Kong branch. Pei recalled that part of the journey was spent on the back of his "amah," or nursemaid. In Hong Kong, the senior Pei's reputation grew on the strength of his knowledge of foreign exchange, a new area for Chinese banking. When the country adopted the silver standard, the bank briefly sent their talented young foreign-exchange expert to Mexico to buy up stores of the precious metal. During the years spent in Hong Kong, the Pei family grew to include three more children, a girl, Wei, and two boys, Kwun and Chung.

In 1927, Pei's father was made manager of the Bank of China's headquarters office in Shanghai. Despite Tsuyee Pei's growing success in his profession, banking was not something his firstborn son learned much about. "The Chinese father-son relationship was based on respect," Pei said. It was also distant. According to the son, the elder Pei "was not the sort of man to pat a son on the back, or hug a daughter." The father never discussed his business affairs with his children, regardless of whether things were going well or badly. Pei recalled that he "never felt a need to express affection openly" to his father.

Pei's bearing and obvious taste lead many Westerners who meet him to take him for an aristocrat. It is an impression he does not discourage, but it is not quite accurate. Over the centuries, Pei's family had had its share of calligraphers and winners of the all-important imperial examinations, which marked a Chinese as a member of the highest ranks of traditional society. But it was with a trace of reluctance that, while Pei described his father as "an educated man," he added that he was "not cultivated in the ways of the arts." Although men of his father's generation frequently collected art, Pei's father did not. The son was emphatic that his own interest in the arts derived not so much from his family upbringing as from his later experience in the United States. "I have cultivated myself," he said.

In contrast to the respectful and somewhat distant relationship with his father, Pei's relationship with his mother was extremely close. An accomplished flute player and a devout Buddhist, she was, according to Pei, "someone I would

Pei as a young boy poses in traditional upper-class garb with an aunt.

go to for advice." She twice took him on religious retreats. (Pei's brothers and sisters were not so honored.) On one of those trips, while savoring the total silence that enveloped the serene mountaintop community where they were staying (and suffering from the pains of the kneeling position he was obliged to assume), the young Pei became convinced that he could hear the bamboo growing in the groves nearby.

Pei's mother died after a long illness during which she was given opium to ease her pain. It was a common medical prescription at the time in China, and Pei was responsible for preparing his mother's regular opium pipe. He was thirteen at the time of her death, but even for a boy of that age, there was little room for grieving. "As the oldest son," Pei recalled, "I was supposed to understand." Pei's father remarried three years later, but the boy never had the devoted relationship with his stepmother that he had had with his own mother. (Although he chose long ago to accommodate the political changes of the 1940s, and in fact concluded that much of what was done by the Communists was necessary, Pei said that the one thing for which he could not forgive them was destroying his mother's grave, outside Shanghai; it was bulldozed during the Cultural Revolution to create farmland.)

In the summers, the Peis would leave Shanghai for weekends and vacations in Suzhou, where many of their family members had homes. A shrine to their ancestors lay in the hills not far away, and from time to time the family would make pilgrimages to it, leaving the city by car and continuing over the rough ground by rickshaw, on foot, or, in the case of the older relatives, in sedan chairs. Pei remembered that everyone—himself included—made the journey dressed in the long silk gowns that were worn on such occasions by members of the upper classes. It was an idyllic period during which, Pei recalled, "I had the impression that anything I wanted, I could get." (After the Communist victory in 1949, the area around the shrine was used by the military for artillery practice. In the late 1980s, having completed the Fragrant Hill Hotel, Pei asked the Chinese government to have the family remains moved to a more tranquil spot, which was done, evidently in gratitude for his architectural contribution.)

A good part of Suzhou's reputation for art and culture was based on the ornate family retreats that had been built there over the centuries. They were not really meant to be lived in full-time, but were instead places where the well-to-do could gather for holidays and refined entertainment, to enjoy poetry and painting, and to reflect in the ornamental gardens designed as miniature evocations of the larger natural landscape. The Pei retreat, known as the Garden of the Lion Forest, had changed hands many times over the centuries and was in Pei's youth owned by a granduncle, who had made extensive renovations.

Pei spent many hours in the Lion Forest with other young family members studying under the tutor who had been retained to see to their off-season education. The infinitely complex design of the garden, and the others like it in the city, was to make a lasting impression on the future architect. He was most deeply affected by the ways in which architectural and natural forms were combined in the gardens in an almost inextricable fashion and by how light and shadow were manipulated as elements in the overall composition. Pei was to return to the gardens in the late 1970s to refresh his memory in preparation for the design of the Fragrant Hill Hotel.

During the academic year, which was spent in Shanghai, Pei went to Saint John's Middle School, studying under Protestant missionaries, who at the time were at the height of their influence in China, turning the eyes of many young Chinese toward Europe and the United States. Indeed, from the early years of the century, it was becoming increasingly common for sons of prominent Chinese families to spend several years studying abroad so that they might return as part of an educated cadre to help in China's modernization. Saint John's was accustomed to caring for this youthful elite: among Pei's predecessors at the school was T. V. Soong, the brother of Madame Chiang Kai-shek, who went on to Harvard and returned to China to become one of the world's richest men, one of Chiang's key financiers, and a banking associate of Tsuyee Pei's.[2] A classmate remembered that Pei's father's signature was at the time printed on the notes issued by the Bank of China and that the younger Pei was sometimes ribbed about how similar his own signature was to the one on the national currency.

Saint John's was a demanding institution, granting its students only a half day a month away for their own amusement. (Pei and a few friends were able to fit in enough billiards in local halls to become accomplished players.) The teaching was carried on in Chinese, but Pei, who was one of the better students, and his fellow pupils read the Bible and some of Dickens in English. Nevertheless, his command of the language was still shaky when in 1935, at the age of seventeen, he prepared to leave for the United States.

Pei's father, who had made a number of English and Scottish friends through his banking activities (the British dominated banking in China at the time), had wanted his son to study in England. But American movies were arriving in China to an enthusiastic audience. Although Pei was a major fan of Betty Grable's pictures, he remembered in particular a film starring Bing Crosby

The carefully framed views and studied irregularities of the Suzhou gardens, in which Pei played as a child, proved a stylistic source to which he would often refer as a mature architect.

as a college hero. "It was an idyllic image of American university life," recalled Pei. "But I sensed a certain vitality in what I was seeing."

Pei's father had little use for the United States as a place to educate his son and was no more interested in France, another country Pei had considered. ("It's the last place I would send you," the son remembered the father declaring. "Paris is not a place for serious study.") Given the traditional nature of his relationship with his father, Pei's response to his family's intentions about his education was relatively bold. He agreed to take the examinations for Oxford, but only if he could then be allowed to make his own choice of where to study. He passed the examinations and afterwards announced to his father that he intended to study not at Oxford, but at the University of Pennsylvania in Philadelphia.

Disappointed as Pei's father may have been by that news, he had further cause for concern in his son's choice of career. While family background and contacts would have made banking an obvious possibility, Pei was not much interested in the field. "I had already sensed that the life of a banker was not ideal," Pei recalled. "I had seen from my father's experience that bankers were constantly under political pressure. He was not entirely happy."

Pei's selection of a career was not quite as casual as his choice of a place to study. During his schooling in Shanghai, he had spent many hours in the library poring over the catalogues of European and American universities. "I could as easily have been a doctor or a lawyer," he said years later. "It was the descriptions of the architecture courses at Penn that did it." Of course, there had to have been a predilection. Pei said he was fascinated by the sight of an unprecedented twenty-three-story building, the Park Hotel, going up across the street from the movie theater in Shanghai where he had got his first glimpse of American university life.

Pei traveled to the United States by boat, landing in San Francisco. From there, he took a train to Philadelphia, via Chicago, which he had come to know not as the premier city of American architecture, but as the hometown of the gangsters Al Capone and John Dillinger. Pei's experience in Philadelphia was brief. The prevailing architectural philosophy at Penn—and at most other American architecture schools at the time—was based on that of the Ecole des Beaux-Arts in Paris, a strict course of study that relied heavily on the great monuments of Greece and Rome and was taught largely through drawing from plaster casts of the Classical orders. Pei found the dean of the architecture school particularly intimidating. ("He scared hell out of me," said Pei.) And he found the training and imagination of his fellow students daunting. What most concerned him was the quality of their draftsmanship. Shortly after arriving at Penn, Pei was

Growing up in Shanghai, Pei was able to watch the progress of construction on the Park Hotel. Although hardly exceptional by Western standards, the building—at twenty-three stories—was unprecedented in China and made a deep impression on the young Pei, who later cited it as one of the reasons he chose architecture as a career.

climbing a staircase at the school when he came upon a colored-ink rendering in the Beaux-Arts style of a Tibetan monastery done by a student as a class exercise. "I was crushed," recalled Pei. "How, I thought, could I, as an Asian myself, and with no artistic training, become an architect if I had to go up against such things?" After only two weeks, Pei was convinced that such emphasis on drawing was neither what he wanted, nor what he was likely to excel at. In what seems in retrospect to have been either a rare display of discouragement or a characteristically efficient cutting of losses, he gave up the idea of becoming an architect and transferred to the Massachusetts Institute of Technology to study engineering.

Despite Pei's bruising experience with drawing at Penn, the faculty at MIT, where he arrived in the fall of 1935, detected more than an engineer in their transfer student. The dean of the architecture school, William Emerson, recognized Pei's design talent and urged him to enter the architecture department (taking him to his Brattle Street home for Thanksgiving to press the case). Recalling his experience at Penn, Pei protested that he was no draftsman, to which Emerson replied, "Nonsense, I don't know any Chinese who can't draw." And so Pei switched back to his original subject.

Put off by his brief experience at the University of Pennsylvania's architecture school, Pei transferred to the Massachusetts Institute of Technology (above, in the 1930s), where he studied engineering.

During the summer vacation of 1938, Pei, who had that year been introduced through his reading to the architecture of Frank Lloyd Wright, embarked on a trip west in hopes of meeting the great man. "I wasn't comfortable writing him letters," Pei recalled, "so I just went." Arriving in a well-worn Chevrolet at Taliesin, Wright's shrine in Spring Green, Wisconsin, Pei was disappointed to find him away. Wright's presence, however, was palpable. "The people there treated him like a god," Pei remembered. "I admired him, but I wouldn't have treated even my father that way." After a fruitless two-hour wait (accompanied by the aggressive yapping of two large dogs who left their claw marks on the Chevy), the would-be disciple left. "I wasn't interested in worshiping at Wright's feet," he said. (Pei later conceded, however, that Wright's work— particularly his free-flowing manipulation of horizontal spaces and his unorthodox combination of materials—had had a considerable influence on his own architecture. If the influence was not greater, he said, it was because Wright concentrated so heavily on private houses, of which Pei was to design only one.)

Following the abortive visit to Spring Green, Pei decided to see some more of the United States. The rest of the trip took him to Los Angeles, where he worked briefly for a local architecture firm (on the design of a prison). On his way back to the East Coast, he drove through the Grand Canyon, but even that all-American natural wonder failed to shake what was still a stand-offish attitude toward the United States. "I was not a typical immigrant," he insisted later. "I had come to this country to study, and I had no real interest in breaking into American society."

A slightly airy assumption that other Chinese in America had come for similar reasons made it hard to accept what he saw of his countrymen's condition in Boston and Cambridge. Most were running laundries or restaurants, and Pei was surprised that they were not better off. At the same time, he remembered being impressed that while some of the seventy-odd Chinese who were studying at MIT with him had, like him, come from privileged backgrounds, others had come to the university from far humbler origins, including those very laundries and restaurants.

For all the enthusiasm shown to Pei by Dean Emerson, the new student was not yet sure he wanted to be an architect. The MIT program was, like Penn's, anchored in the Beaux-Arts tradition, and even MIT's more hospitable reception wasn't enough to elicit much passion. "I still wasn't excited by design, and there was something lacking in the teaching," Pei said. "I spent most of my time in the library looking at the latest work from Europe, especially what Le Corbusier was

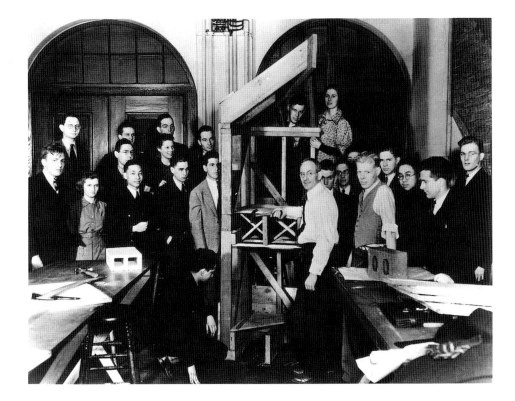

doing. It was the library that saved me." Nevertheless, he absorbed a great deal that was to be of enormous value later in his career. "MIT taught me something for which I will always be grateful," Pei told an interviewer in 1985, "and that is a real understanding of what technology stands for—to know really that what technologists and scientists are looking for is very much the same as what architects are looking for."[3]

Pei's interest in design began to develop in earnest when he won a joint competition held for MIT and Harvard students for a weekend sketch problem. "I was aware that something was happening at Harvard," Pei said, "but Dean Emerson was against the place." Walter Gropius, the former head of the Bauhaus, the seminal German design school which had been closed by the Nazis, had recently arrived as chairman of the architecture department at Harvard's Graduate School of Design following an invitation from the dean, Joseph Hudnut. But according to Pei, MIT's hostility to the heretical European was so great that "you couldn't even mention Gropius's name in Emerson's presence."

While Pei was still at MIT, a chance meeting during a trip to New York brought something of his homeland to his doorstep. Eileen Loo (she had

At MIT, Pei was persuaded by the dean to return to his original ambition of becoming an architect. Opposite, at his drawing board; above (front row, third from left), in his sophomore year, 1936–37.

Anglicized her Chinese name, Ai-ling) had come to the United States in 1938 from China to study at Wellesley College, a popular choice for prominent Chinese, including Madame Chiang, who as May-ling Soong had graduated in 1917. (Eileen had asked her father, who had studied engineering at MIT, if she could do the same, but he recommended Wellesley as "a nice girls' school nearby.") Having landed in San Francisco after the ocean voyage from Hong Kong, she was traveling by train to New York before going on to Boston. As it turned out, a friend of Eileen's who was also a member of "FF," the Chinese fraternity to which Pei belonged at MIT, was on the same train. Pei had arranged to meet him on arrival at Grand Central Terminal. When the train pulled in, Pei's classmate introduced him to Eileen. Since she had a long wait before making the connection to Boston, Pei offered her a lift in his car. She already had her ticket and turned him down, but when he later heard that the train had been held up in Hartford by a hurricane, he used the news as an excuse to call her for a date. According to Eileen, he announced on the phone: "See, you should have come with me!"

Pei was an outstanding student at MIT, and along with his Bachelor of Architecture degree, which he received in 1940 (his thesis project was entitled "Standardized Propaganda Units for the Chinese Government"), he won the American Institute of Architects Medal and the MIT Traveling Fellowship. (Despite his impatience with some of its offerings, Pei was to maintain a lifelong affection for MIT, an affection expressed in four buildings he later designed for the school.)

Pei had been planning to return to China as soon as possible after his graduation. By that time, however, the Japanese had invaded, forcing Pei's father to move his banking operations to Chunking. Tsuyee Pei wrote to his son advising him to stay on in the United States until things improved. (While in Chunking, the elder Pei endured repeated attacks by Japanese bombers, but made things slightly more bearable by selecting a bomb shelter that, while somewhat less safe than the others, had a resident chef of high renown.) When the Japanese attacked Pearl Harbor, Pei, who heard the report on the Chevy's radio, "almost danced a jig to know that America was going to be on China's side." Nevertheless, it was clear to him that any return to his own country would have to be put off for the foreseeable future.

To earn some money and gain some practical experience after finishing at MIT, Pei took a job with the Boston engineering firm of Stone & Webster, where he worked on a variety of engineering projects. It turned out to be an important, if brief, experience, giving him an introduction to the concrete technology that was to become such a crucial ingredient in his own early architecture. Meanwhile,

Pei and Eileen Loo were married in the spring of 1942, after Eileen's graduation from Wellesley. The rising tide of the Second World War interfered with their plans to return to China.

Pei's relationship with Eileen Loo had blossomed, and they were married in the spring of 1942, shortly after she finished at Wellesley. Pursuing a long-standing interest, Eileen was planning to enroll the following fall in the landscape architecture program at Harvard.

Pei had been drawn to the activities at Harvard ever since the joint MIT-Harvard sketch problem, and Eileen's involvement with the Graduate School of Design increased his exposure to what was going on there. In the early fall, Eileen and her husband invited one of her professors to dinner at their apartment. The lively conversation (which included the news that a fellowship was available at the GSD) convinced Pei that Harvard was indeed a place he wanted to know more about. "The next morning," remembered Eileen, her husband was "off to Dean Hudnut's office."

Pei enrolled at the GSD in December of 1942 for a master's degree in architecture. After the dry fare at MIT, Harvard was, Pei recalled, "a breath of fresh air. It was closer to what I understood architecture to be." But with wartime demands on manpower growing, Pei in early January of 1943 suspended his studies and volunteered for work at the National Defense Research Committee in Princeton, New Jersey. Ironically, the young man who had been talked back into architecture from a course in engineering was put to work developing new methods of destruction. "If you know how to build a building," Pei recalled his superiors telling him, "you know how to destroy it."

The early focus of Pei's work was the bombing of bridges in Germany and Italy. Later, he was assigned to similar work on the destruction of Japanese cities. Since Japanese architecture at the time was constructed primarily of wood and paper, the sort of high explosives used to blast the masonry buildings of Europe were not the most efficient. Fire, rather than simple explosive force, was deemed the best way to level urban Japan, and Pei was put to work on a fusing device for incendiary bombs.

He still intended to return to China after the war, but his father, who by then saw the inevitability of the Communist victory, wrote him saying he should again extend his stay in the United States. Pei did so, working briefly in the architectural office of Hugh Stubbins, Jr., in Boston. In the summer of 1945, Pei and his wife, who had decided to give up her landscape studies after the birth of their first son, T'ing Chung, stayed for a period in the house Walter Gropius had built for himself and his family in the elegant Boston suburb of Lincoln. While housesitting, Pei spent a good deal of time designing a temporary rope net that would prevent the infant T'ing from falling off the stairs.

An aerial view of Harvard University (above), where in the 1940s Walter Gropius (opposite) was transforming the Graduate School of Design along the Modernist lines of the Bauhaus.

Pei returned to Harvard in the fall of 1945 to resume his architectural education. Even though his degree requirements were not yet satisfied, he was offered a post as an assistant professor of design on the strength of his MIT record and the short period he had already spent at the GSD. Although from what Pei had seen in the MIT library, Le Corbusier might have been preferable as a mentor, he found Gropius a worthy substitute. With Gropius as chairman and Marcel Breuer, another Bauhaus refugee, on the faculty, the Graduate School of Design had become the most forward-looking architecture school in the United States, offering to a country still steeped in the Beaux-Arts tradition all the innovative and optimistic thinking of the European Modern movement.

While Gropius and Breuer did not arrive at Harvard until 1937, the philosophy of which they were key advocates had been introduced forcefully to the American avant-garde in 1932 by a show at New York's Museum of Modern Art entitled "The International Style: Architecture Since 1922." (It was organized by Henry-Russell Hitchcock and Philip Johnson, who was then at the museum but would later enroll at Harvard to study design.) The impact of the show was enormous, helping to draw the attention of the best of America's architectural talent and patronage to the developments that had been remaking architecture in Europe.

As the founder, in 1919, of the Bauhaus, Gropius had created an institution intended to bring together artists, craftsmen, and architects as equal collaborators, but he also strove for an intimate alliance of art and technology. At its heart, the curriculum was intended to instill in its students a single methodology for solving design problems in a variety of media. Whenever possible, those solutions were to be arrived at through team effort, so that, in the case of architecture, the students would be prepared for what Gropius saw as their vital task of co-ordinating the many individuals involved in all phases of a project. (It may not be too farfetched to suggest that this emphasis on group effort was later to become especially helpful to Pei, whose professional career was to be marked by a rare ability to integrate his own talents with those of his collaborators.)

The entire Bauhaus enterprise was fueled by a conviction that its followers could have a major impact on the lives of the people they touched. Indeed, although the Bauhaus architectural aesthetic—with its flat roofs, white walls, and strip windows—has since become all but synonymous with architectural sterility, it was in its youth deeply idealistic, moved by a faith that art and the machine, if properly combined, could make the world a better place by creating a more efficient and humane built environment.[+]

Gropius quickly made the GSD the best place to be for students frustrated by the insistent symmetry and rigid Classicism of the Beaux-Arts style. In short order, he instituted major revisions in the Harvard architecture curriculum, bringing landscape architecture, design, and planning together as an integrated course of study in an updated version of the Bauhaus regimen. Significantly, architectural history was dropped from the core curriculum and offered only as an elective.

It is hard now to recapture the excitement of those days at Harvard. Modern architecture has been so thoroughly discredited in recent years that the term has become one of opprobrium in some circles, especially those traveled by the Post-Modernists, who feel that the Modernists' rejection of architectural history was a fatal misstep. Much of the criticism is well deserved, to be sure. Terrible damage has been done to cities in this country and abroad by architects serving under the Modernist banner who have deposited all too many faceless office towers in all too many barren plazas. But in the 1940s, Modernism meant to young students of architecture like Pei all that was hopeful for the future of design. And under Gropius, they could expect to get it at its most inspirational.

In an *Architectural Record* article that appeared shortly after he became chairman at Harvard, Gropius announced: "I want a young architect to be able

to find his way in whatever circumstances; I want him independently to create true, genuine forms out of the technical, economic and social conditions in which he finds himself instead of imposing a learned formula on to the surroundings which may call for an entirely different solution.... What I do want is to make young people realize how inexhaustible the means of creation are if they make use of the innumerable modern products of our age and to encourage these young people in finding their own solutions."[5]

The contact between the faculty and the students at the GSD was unusually close at the time. Perhaps because the members of the faculty, most of whom were also practicing architects, had relatively little work during and immediately after the war, they were able to concentrate more on their teaching. Pei had an advantage over his classmates in his status as both a student and a teacher. He said later that he was surprised to find Gropius—who was known as "Grope" to his students—so open: "He was not at all as dogmatic as I had expected him to be." But while Pei admired Gropius, he considered Breuer a "confrère." Ulrich Franzen, a GSD student who would later go to work for Pei under William Zeckendorf before setting out on a major architectural career of his own, recalled that Gropius, however open he may have seemed to Pei, represented a rather "heavy-handed" approach to the curriculum and was "art-historically untutored," while Breuer approached architecture more as an artist. Pei, Franzen said, "seemed to fit best with the Breuer image."

Pei's friendship with Breuer extended to the families of both men. Pei and Eileen were frequent guests at the Breuers' house in Cambridge, where "Lajko," as Breuer was known to his friends (it was a Hungarian diminutive based on his middle name, Lajos), would inevitably serve goulash. On other occasions, Breuer and his wife, Constance, would dine at the Peis' on the Chinese peas they had grown in their wartime "victory" garden. So warm was the relationship between the architects that it would last until Breuer's death, in 1981. (In the late 1950s and early 60s, the families went sailing together in the Greek islands, and

Marcel Breuer, like Gropius, was a Bauhaus refugee. Gropius was the form-giver of the GSD program, but Pei found Breuer (above, center) more approachable.

although they had agreed not to talk shop, Pei and Breuer often found themselves staring off the rail as they passed coastal fishing villages, speculating on why the picturesque white buildings had been sited as they had and why the streets were laid out as they were. "It wasn't so much architecture that we talked about," Pei explained, "it was about how people lived. Of course, they are inseparable.")

The emphasis of the Gropius curriculum was on the development of the architectural plan, or layout, over the form a building might take. The plan was to flow from the purpose of the building and the human activities it was to contain, rather than from a preconception of how it might look as a piece of sculpture. And that plan was to be clear, logical, and readable. "The logic was carried to an extreme," said Pei. "Only later did I begin to understand that you had to develop a plan spatially to create architecture. But it was a wonderful discipline to have to focus on the essentials."

The design talent Pei had demonstrated at MIT was quickly recognized at Harvard, but Pei also made a name for himself as a teacher. According to Ulrich Franzen, he developed "a reputation among the students as an elegant designer who would make beautiful things—which was unusual for a teacher." Henry Cobb, who would later become a partner in Pei's firm, but was in 1945 also a student at the GSD, remembered Pei as "a brilliant critic." Students and faculty alike shared in the idealism of the Gropius mission. Chester Nagel, a close friend of Pei's and a fellow instructor, recalled the great expectations permeating the school at the time. "We were going to change the world," he said. "Architecture as Gropius saw it was no longer just decorative. He was after a renaissance of the imagination. We were looking for the essence—and we found it."

As Nagel remembered the pursuit of that essence, much of it took place not in the architecture studios of Robinson Hall, but in the watering holes around Harvard Square. (Pei recalled that what little money he and Eileen could spare was spent mostly on classical records, and on wine.) "We never drank very much," Nagel recalled, "but we drank happily. I never saw anyone intoxicated. We drank

The friendship Pei and his wife established with Marcel and Constance Breuer at Harvard in the 1940s was to last long past their student days. In 1958, they traveled to Greece together to sail the islands. From left: Eileen Pei, Constance and Marcel Breuer, Pei, and their friends the van der Wals.

out of reverence, reverence for art." Things were a bit more weighty in the master's presence. From time to time, Gropius would take a private room at the Faculty Club, where he would announce to his acolytes: "Let's talk about interpenetration, about tension, about counterpoint, about simultaneity—about how one could accomplish many purposes with a single stroke." After one such session, Nagel and Pei were walking across Harvard Yard. As Nagel reconstructed the moment, perhaps with some retrospective embellishment, he turned to his friend and said, "Gropius always concerns himself with universal truth." To which Pei, according to Nagel, replied, "Gropius *is* universal truth."

Years later, Pei had no memory of the exchange—uncomfortable, perhaps, with the degree to which Gropius had influenced so many of his students. Nagel, who insisted that his memory was accurate, was nonetheless indulgent about the spiritual excesses of those heady meetings, if no less committed to their intent. "We were trying to separate ourselves from the bombast of the old," he said. "If we had faults, it was because we were just starting."

Pei may have been impressed by Gropius, but he was not about to become a clone. During one discussion of the International Style, Pei called a number of its tenets into question. Gropius responded by inviting his student to select a design problem that would make his point. "I'm not disagreeing with you," Pei remembered Gropius saying to him, "but I want you to prove it." In a gesture that seemed prescient in light of several buildings he was to do later in life, Pei chose to design an art museum for the city of Shanghai.

Discussing the project in a letter to a friend in 1946, Pei spoke of his search for an architectural style appropriate to modern China. He told the friend, Frederick Roth, that for some time he had "been wondering about the process of searching for a regional or 'national' expression in architecture. To my surprise, Grope agrees with me that there is a definite reason for it and that though it will be very difficult, it will come as soon as modern architecture comes of age....My problem is to find an architectural expression that will be truly Chinese without any resort to Chinese architectural details and motives as we know them. So far I have read practically all the books on the subject but they have little to offer... I hope something will jell [*sic*] soon!"[6] It did. According to Henry Cobb, Gropius felt the Shanghai museum was "the best thing done in his master class."

Gropius was not so effusive in print, although he did not stint on praise for his student's project. In an article published in *Progressive Architecture*, in February of 1948, Gropius declared that Pei's building "clearly illustrates that an able designer can very well hold on to basic traditional features—which he has

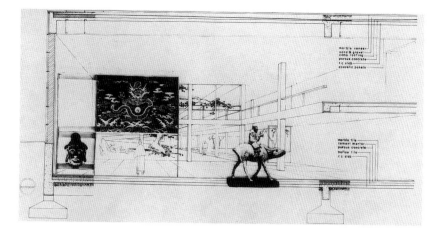

found are still alive—without sacrificing a progressive conception of design." Gropius went on to explain how the design had come about. "In our discussion," he wrote, "we tried then to find out how the character of Chinese architecture could be expressed without imitating such form motifs of former periods. We decided that the bare Chinese wall, so evident in various periods of Chinese architecture, and the small individual garden patio were two eternal features which are well understood by every Chinese living. Mr. Pei built up his scheme entirely on a variation of these two themes."[7]

Pei's project displayed a remarkable subtlety in the manipulation of forms to accommodate both Chinese tradition and post-Bauhaus modernity. The two-story building was to be sunk a half level below ground so that the walls enclosing the central tea garden would be low enough to permit a view into it from the outside. Smaller landscaped courtyards were scattered throughout the plan in such a way that a visitor contemplating the works of art on display in the galleries would never be far from a glimpse of nature. As the young architect explained his intention at the time: "All forms of Chinese art are directly or indirectly results of a sensitive observation of nature. Such objects, consequently, are best displayed in surroundings which are in tune with them, surroundings which incorporate as much as possible the controlling elements of natural beauty."[8]

For a teacher who had banished the study of architectural history from the core of his Harvard curriculum, Walter Gropius was giving a student considerable room to maneuver. In his seventies, Pei remained grateful for the opportunity. "Working with Gropius and Breuer," he said, "I was able to demystify architecture so that I could really learn."

When Pei obtained his master's degree in 1946, he still intended to put his learning to use in China. So confident were he and Eileen that they would soon be going home that they didn't bother to teach their son T'ing Chinese, secure in the knowledge that there would be ample time for the boy to learn it once they left the United States. Nevertheless, Pei decided that until the struggle between the Nationalists and the Communists in China was resolved, he would continue to teach at Harvard, which he did for two more years. At that point, however, while many of his GSD colleagues found themselves working on the additions and small residences that are the traditional tooth-cutting commissions of young architects, Pei was drawn to a very different, and professionally risky, course.

The student project Pei did under Gropius for an art museum for the city of Shanghai demonstrated an early concern for combining architecture and nature in a mutually supportive way and prefigured Pei's many later museum designs.

3. THE ZECKENDORF DAYS (1948–60): LEARNING TO THINK BIG

I. M. Pei's first meeting with William Zeckendorf was not auspicious. It was in the spring of 1948, and when the urbane assistant professor from the Harvard Graduate School of Design walked into the real estate tycoon's office at 383 Madison Avenue, Zeckendorf was, as usual, on the phone. The burly host gestured to Pei to wait, which he proceeded to do, surveying the room. Most of the pictures on the walls were of parking garages. The curtains on the office windows were stained by rainwater, and the couch needed reupholstering. To one side of the room stood an old Motorola radio, which had been converted to serve as a bar. "The whole environment was seedy," the fastidious Pei recalled. "It was clear that we were complete opposites."

William Zeckendorf was a big man in just about every way. His body—he stood six feet tall and weighed 235 pounds—was big, and made bigger outdoors by the Homburg hat he favored to protect his bald dome. Born in 1905 in Paris, Illinois, the son of a shoe manufacturer, he had dropped out of college, but his lack of formal education did nothing to restrain his ambition. In short order, Zeckendorf stormed New York, and in the 1950s was to become the biggest real estate developer in that or any other American city. Through Webb & Knapp, the unassuming property-management firm he took over and transformed into his development vehicle, Zeckendorf was to be involved in vast projects in New York, Washington, Denver, Philadelphia, and Montreal, among other cities. At its height, his empire would include, according to some estimates, roughly 20,000 apartments, ten million square feet of office space, 6,500 hotel rooms, and assorted other holdings worth some $300 million.

Zeckendorf liked big limousines (with "WZ" plates), big cigars, and big

William Zeckendorf, the most flamboyant real estate developer of his time, intrigued the young Pei with his grand ambitions. The developer did much of his deal-making on his car telephone, one of the few in private use at the time.

deals. The wine cellar on his seventy-acre estate in Greenwich, Connecticut, housed an estimated 24,000 bottles, making it one of the largest in the country. He loved telephones; there were six lines on his desk and—unusual for the time—one in his car. Gripping the car phone in his gray-gloved hand as he was driven through midtown traffic hectoring a reluctant banker or a balky politician, Zeckendorf was every inch the real estate mogul of comic book fantasy.

In one key respect, however, William Zeckendorf was different from the wheeler dealers among whom he did such ebullient battle: well into his career, he conceived a love for architecture. Buying, selling, and building were no longer enough for this renegade developer. So he set about looking for an architect who could give some formal respectability to the enterprises he was planning.

As Zeckendorf recounted it in his autobiography, he was at the time in touch with Nelson Rockefeller, a major benefactor of New York's Museum of Modern Art, about arranging some financing for a project he had in mind. During one of their conversations, Zeckendorf said with characteristic directness: "Nelson, don't you think it is about time that the modern Medicis began hiring the modern Michelangelos and Da Vincis? I plan to go into a great building program on a national scale, and I'd like to put together an architectural staff that could provide new thinking."[1] According to Zeckendorf's son, William, Jr., his father was looking for "the greatest unknown architect in the country."

Rockefeller said he would do what he could to help him, and selected a member of the Modern's staff named Richard Abbott to serve as a talent scout. After screening a dozen or so architects who had been suggested to him, Abbott recommended a young member of the Harvard architecture school faculty. It was I. M. Pei.

After the shock of his reception at the Zeckendorf offices had worn off, Pei quickly began to warm to Zeckendorf. From what the developer said as they spoke, it was clear that he was a risktaker and thought on the grand scale. Despite the bluster, there was obviously a powerful mind at work, and the bearish manner seemed to conceal a generous spirit. For his part, Zeckendorf found Ieoh Ming Pei to be "obviously intelligent and very imaginative"; it didn't hurt that the candidate also came across as "a bon vivant and a knowledgeable gourmet."[2] (They soon fell to discussing the relative merits of Burgundy, Zeckendorf's favorite wine, and Bordeaux, which was Pei's.) Zeckendorf was also fascinated that he, Pei, and Pei's father had all been born in the Chinese Year of the Snake (which recurs every twelve years and is supposed to confer wisdom, charm, and intuition). To the developer, it was "a case of instant recognition and liking."[3]

Pei, however, was not yet sure that he wanted to abandon his teaching or the prospect of a return to China. But Zeckendorf persisted, assuring Pei "that the kind of things we were going to do would be so different and so much better than anyone else in the country was doing that as an architect he would not resist the challenge."[4]

Zeckendorf's case was a compelling one. At the time, he was in the final stages of an extraordinary deal—the one he had been discussing with Rockefeller—to bring the fledgling United Nations to New York. Since the Civil War, the city's major slaughterhouses had been clustered in an area on the eastern edge of Manhattan. Late in 1945, a real estate broker had approached Zeckendorf about the possibility of his buying the land and using it for development. After considerable negotiating, Zeckendorf managed to assemble a parcel adjoining the slaughterhouses and ultimately acquired the slaughterhouses themselves, creating a site seven city blocks long and two blocks wide. What Zeckendorf had in mind was a new minicity—temporarily designated "X-city"—that would rise on a platform overlooking the East River. (The prototype for it was the deck that had been built over the old New York Central railroad tracks to create Park Avenue.) The East River scheme was to have surpassed Rockefeller Center in both size and ambition.

Just as Zeckendorf was securing the land, however, a bidding war was heating up among several cities for the permanent site of the United Nations headquarters. Alarmed that the new organization might be lost to San Francisco or Philadelphia, Zeckendorf offered to make his site—which then amounted to seventeen acres from 42nd Street to 49th Street—available to the U.N. "for anything they want to pay."[5] Although Zeckendorf's own hopes for the design of the complex were ultimately disappointed, the U.N. agreed to acquire the land (using Rockefeller money) for $8.5 million, a relatively small amount for the time. The deal went through on December 14, 1946. Zeckendorf promptly announced to his wife: "We have just moved the capital of the world."[6]

The prospect of working with someone who was capable of such swashbuckling was heady indeed for a young academic architect like Pei. But no matter how grand the scale, an alliance with Zeckendorf involved professional hazards. Here was a brash Jewish New Yorker of the sort the high-art architecture community shunned on principle. Pei worried over the offer and discussed it at length with his wife. Not the least of his concerns was that moving to New York for the kind of position Zeckendorf had in mind would mean even less of a chance for Eileen to pursue the career in landscape architecture she had put on hold to start a family. But she supported the move, and Pei told Zeckendorf that he would sign

Although hired as a designer, Pei (standing, right) proved so effective in dealing with Zeckendorf's business clients that the developer (extreme right) included him in virtually all of his important meetings.

49

on, becoming, in the fall of 1948, director of Webb & Knapp's nascent architectural division.

Relying on Eileen to close up their Cambridge apartment, Pei arrived for work to find himself in alien territory. He was assigned to share an office in the nether reaches of Zeckendorf's headquarters with the firm's public relations specialist, a former newspaperman named Jack Bell. In the course of his first days, Pei was introduced to legions of Zeckendorf's vice presidents—mostly financial types—who had no idea what the new man was doing there.

On Zeckendorf's recommendation, Pei rented a one-bedroom apartment for his family on the sixth floor of 30 Beekman Place, on Manhattan's East Side. Zeckendorf subsequently moved into the same building, having assigned Pei to renovate the penthouse for him. There was little time for the Peis to get settled. Zeckendorf would often call his young architect at six in the morning with some urgent question and growl into the phone, "How fast can you get dressed?" It was at this point that Pei began his lifelong habit of getting up in the middle of the night to sketch design solutions or make notes. "He needed eight hours of sleep," said Eileen, "but he often got only six. I would get up to go to the bathroom and find little pieces of paper all over the apartment reminding him to try this or that, or get in touch with someone."

Pei was frequently in and out of his boss's office a dozen times a day and often stayed well past business hours. Eileen fell to wishing that "Bill knew when the day ended." In hopes of getting the point across, she suggested to her husband that they invite Zeckendorf to dinner—at a civilized hour. He came, but had some difficulty settling his bulk at the dinner table, which, owing to the size of the apartment, had to be set up in the hall.

Pei and Zeckendorf were drawn together by more than fine wines or professional need. The younger man seemed to regard Zeckendorf almost as a surrogate father. According to Eileen, her highly educated husband was "like an empty vessel" eager to be filled with Zeckendorf's knowledge of the real world. For his part, the developer treated his architect very much like a son, perhaps finding in Pei's schooling and refinement some compensation for his own lack of both. Right from the start, Zeckendorf addressed his architect as Ieoh Ming and remained the only American who could pronounce the name properly. According to William Zeckendorf, Jr., Pei was "my father's dreamer."

The combination of Zeckendorf's entrepreneurial instincts and Pei's innovative design sense began to pay dividends almost immediately. At the time, there were great amounts of money available for housing through Title I of the

National Housing Act of 1949, the legislation that began the urban renewal era. Much of it was intended to help house the millions of servicemen returning from World War II. According to Pei, Zeckendorf saw in that federal program "an enormous pot of gold" waiting for an industrious developer willing to satisfy the need. But profit was not Zeckendorf's only motivation. "It was the blank page that attracted him," recalled the architect. "He was a visionary."

There were in those days relatively few one-bedroom apartments on the market in the country's major cities, but there were hundreds of old buildings with sprawling suites, particularly in New York. As Zeckendorf described the problem: "If you have a two-room apartment and your wife has a baby, you can't add another room. If you have a twelve-room apartment and business gets bad, you can't cut your apartment in half."[7] Pei thought the need for smaller apartments could be served without abandoning the inevitable return of demand for large apartments by designing a new, more flexible kind of residential building.

Pei's solution to the problem Zeckendorf posed was based on the shape of a helix, or spiral. The idea was classically simple. Pei proposed a circular tower organized in six concentric rings, the three inner rings containing circulation and utilities and the outer rings space for apartments. The apartments would be shaped like wedges, each a half floor higher than the last as they spiraled up around the core. Tenants could acquire one wedge and add adjoining ones as needed, or give them up if needs or resources shrank.

Once the design was finished, Pei was desperate for help in making a model of it and preparing presentation drawings. He contacted his former student Henry Cobb, who had recently finished up at Harvard and was willing to make a trip to New York to pitch in. When the model and the drawings were done, Zeckendorf was so pleased with them that he took out a patent on the design and went through a long negotiating process for a site overlooking the East River on which to put up the first version. But the problems of getting the unorthodox structure built proved too much even for a man of Zeckendorf's talents, and it remained no more than a grand plan. (Nevertheless, Zeckendorf continued to show it off. When he later met Le Corbusier, who had come to New York to work on an early design for the United Nations building, Zeckendorf made a point of displaying Pei's proposal. The renowned Swiss-French architect, whose *brise-soleils*, or sunbreak facades, had become something of a design signature, asked the developer and his associate how they planned to provide sufficient shade for the apartments on the sunny side of the helix. To which Pei declared with a burst of all-American gusto, "In this country,

Pei's unbuilt "Helix" tower was based on a spiral arrangement of wedge-shaped apartments. The photomontage of the model (top) shows the building as it would have appeared on the East River site where Zeckendorf hoped to erect it.

it doesn't matter; our buildings are all air conditioned!")

Pleased as he was by the apartment house proposal, Zeckendorf wasn't at first altogether sure that his "dreamer" was up to the urban scale the developer had in mind for his architecture department. Indeed, the architect said that he felt he still had to "prove" himself to his employer. He did it with a number of buildings that he described in later years as "terrible," but which did much to get him in condition for bigger things. The first of these early projects was a speculative office building in Atlanta, begun in early 1950 and leased to Gulf Oil. It was a 50,000-square-foot box that invoked the lean rectilinearity of Mies van der Rohe's precedents, but had no particular aesthetic distinction of its own. It did, however, show Pei again to be an innovative designer. Constrained by a small budget, yet eager to give the building some corporate presence, Pei chose a simple exterior curtain wall (a nonstructural skin attached to the building's frame), but instead of using the more common metal panels, employed slabs of marble. *Architectural Forum*, in its February 1952 issue, declared that "with one bold stroke, Architect Pei freed traditionally monumental marble from its use as a thin veneer on costly masonry walls and turned that veneer into the wall itself."[8]

After the Gulf Oil building, the pace of Webb & Knapp's one-man architecture division began to pick up fast. (Schedules moved so quickly that Pei's own office was for a time filled with uncrated urinals destined for a construction site that was not yet ready for them.) Zeckendorf's early fascination with parking garages and other mass facilities continued. At one point, he turned over the entire ground floor of his Madison Avenue building to prototypes of a huge device for raising and lowering automobiles, a move Pei considered a waste of prime real estate.

In the winter of 1950, work was coming into the office at such a rate that Pei, who had been carrying the design load by himself, finally went to Zeckendorf with an appeal for help. "Bill," he announced, "I can no longer handle all these things alone." Zeckendorf agreed to expand the team, and Pei turned again to Cobb, who had taken a job after graduation with the Boston architect Hugh Stubbins, Jr., where Pei had also worked. Cobb talked Pei's offer over with Stubbins, who was not encouraging about the prospect of working for a New York developer. He pointed out that time spent with Zeckendorf would not even count toward the three years of work required of young architects before taking their licensing examinations and told Cobb that he would be making "a terrible mistake." But Cobb, like Pei, thought the risk was worth it. "We had come out of school thinking we could remake the world," Cobb said of his days at the GSD

Although done on a tight budget, Pei's Gulf Oil building in Atlanta, begun in 1950, was made to appear almost luxurious by the use of thin marble slabs for the skin.

under Gropius and Breuer. "Zeckendorf wanted to remake the city. We had a shared passion for large-scale undertakings."

Cobb, who arrived at the Zeckendorf office on April 1, 1950, was a product of the Boston establishment, and his painfully shy manner made the early contact with Zeckendorf awkward. Cobb was, in the developer's words, a "most circumspect young man."[9] But working with Pei, he quickly proved his worth, stimulating Zeckendorf to write that "we came to the point that all I had to do . . . was lay down the basic guidelines of what I needed. The rest I could leave to them, because they had sat in on strategy and economic conferences and knew our needs. We had reached a point where we learned together and taught each other on every project we turned to."[10]

Cobb was followed less than a year later by Ulrich Franzen, who had been designing houses in Boston after finishing his degree at the GSD. Like Cobb, with whom he initially shared an office, Franzen was "drawn to Zeckendorf by the opportunity to influence the shape of the world in which we lived, rather than by merely shaping self-referential objects. There was lots of idealism in that office." Right from the start, Franzen was struck by how much Zeckendorf relied on the head of his three-man architecture team. "Bill would hang on Pei's every word," Franzen said. "He treated him with reverence."

The first major assignment the team handled was a 125-acre shopping center Zeckendorf was planning on the site of Roosevelt Field, outside New York, where Charles Lindbergh had taken off for Paris in 1927. The undertaking included a building for the Franklin National Bank, a sleek, five-story office structure clad in light gold anodized aluminum. It attracted considerable attention for its circular brick kiosks designed to provide drive-in banking, a relatively new service in those days. But the real energy went into the shopping complex. Eager to minimize the shoppers' fatigue and make the process more entertaining than was common in large shopping centers of the day, Pei and his collaborators concentrated the stores at the core of the site. They were organized on an asymmetrical grid that created "streets" of various widths, and the facades were given separate architectural treatments to make the normally tedious suburban ritual a bit more diverting. Trees and fountains further mitigated the inherent monotony of such a single-purpose setting, and a tunnel was provided to allow deliveries without interrupting the flow of shoppers above ground. Surrounding the buildings were parking lots linked by cloverleaf ramps to the nearby highways. If Roosevelt Field did not have the charm of a European market square, it was considerably less tiresome than the sprawling proto-malls that were already

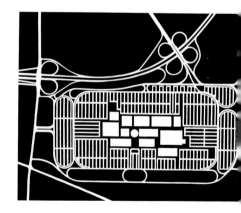

The aim of the asymmetrical grid of the Roosevelt Field shopping center was to integrate commercial and support facilities with parking in a combination that would be inviting to the shopper.

blighting so much of the American landscape. It was also an early example of Pei's sensitive integration of individual buildings into a framework of transportation and support services.

While the large-scale work progressed on Gulf and Roosevelt Field, a smaller-scale operation was proceeding on Madison Avenue. Sometime earlier, Zeckendorf had commissioned a renovation of his own headquarters. It was not going as he had hoped, and since he now had some first-class designers of his own, he turned the job over to them. Under Pei's direction, the entire building was air-conditioned, the office interiors and elevators were modernized, and the lobby was given a facelift. But the most remarkable part of the job was Zeckendorf's own quarters, a penthouse unlike anything seen before in New York. Eager to create an appropriately grand setting for the tycoon without compromising circulation, Pei designed an office-within-an-office by inserting a freestanding cylinder in what was basically a rectangular loft space on the top floor. This interior room was roughly twenty-five feet in diameter, its single circular wall made of teak with a clerestory of glass. To top it off—literally—the toilet, private dining room, and kitchen were assembled in a second cylinder, rather like a turret, located on the roof and reached by an elevator in a third cylinder at its core.

While Pei dealt with the design of the office itself, his new collaborators saw to the furnishings. Cobb concentrated on the elegant free-standing liquor cabinet, and Franzen did Zeckendorf's desk, which was equipped with a control panel that allowed the chief to change the lighting in the room at will. (He was known to end conversations that were not going his way by bathing the room in blue.) The terrace outside was embellished with a Lachaise sculpture, which Pei had bought for Zeckendorf for the then-princely sum of $5,000. Pei said the acquisition was as much for himself as it was for his boss, but at the time he was in no financial position to invest in such things. Construction of the office was completed in 1951 and ran considerably over budget. Zeckendorf was happy in spite of the cost. "We could not have afforded to spend any less," he said.

Even with the expanded staff, life at Webb & Knapp remained hectic. Pei already had two secretaries, one of whom dealt exclusively with his schedule. To keep abreast of all that was happening and still make room for the constant flurry of meetings and trips with Zeckendorf, Pei had to parcel his time with care. Watching him in action, Franzen was impressed by Pei's sense of what was important. Even then, said Franzen, Pei "could go into a meeting, listen to the problem under discussion, and come up with two sentences that distilled the essence."

Pei's renovation of Zeckendorf's Madison Avenue headquarters did away with the traditional concept of the corner office as the power position. The focus of the lower floor (above) was Zeckendorf's desk, designed by Pei's associate Ulrich Franzen. The upper floor (opposite) had panoramic views of New York, which are being enjoyed in this case by Henry Cobb.

Efficient as he was on the job, Pei was not always so on his own time. In 1951, he and Eileen were embarking on a four-month trip to Europe with the funds of a travel fellowship he had won at Harvard but delayed using when he accepted the Zeckendorf job. Among the guests at the farewell party on the *Rotterdam* were friends from the office, as well as Pei's father, who was visiting New York from Hong Kong, where he had settled after the Communist victory in China. As sailing time approached, the champagne flowed, but the guests of honor were nowhere to be found. It turned out that they had been confined to their stateroom because they didn't have their passports. They had mistakenly packed the documents in baggage they had planned to carry on board but which had instead been stowed in the hold—and they had not put their names on the bags. Eventually, porters managed to dig the bags out, and the Peis were allowed to surface, just in time for a glass before the well-wishers were hustled ashore. Pei remembered that his father couldn't stop laughing with delight about the whole incident, telling the others—to their surprise—that the mix-up was "absolutely typical" of his son.

Increasingly, the projects Zeckendorf was pursuing involved not just individual buildings and small-scale shopping centers, but whole sections of cities. He would have preferred work in New York, but had run afoul of Robert Moses, who as New York's Park Commissioner, City Construction Coordinator, and Chairman of the Triborough Bridge and Tunnel Authority, had become virtual czar of all the large-scale building in the city. Zeckendorf and Moses had clashed over aspects of the U.N. plan, and further conflicts seemed inevitable if Zeckendorf was to build on a large scale in his own city, so he began to look elsewhere for opportunities.[11]

As the developer later described the pattern of his nationwide operations, he and his team would first make a survey of potential development opportunities across the country. After reviewing maps and making informal visits, Zeckendorf would get on the phone to the appropriate city officials with a development proposal, explaining how "ripe" things looked for the future of their community. If the city fathers showed an interest, Zeckendorf would arrange a visit, load his team aboard the DC-3 he had bought for the company, and be on his way. Before landing, the team would circle the city to study the "target" much the way military reconnaissance pilots might before calling in the artillery.

Once they were on the ground, there was a rash of meetings and elaborate lunches, and boosterish briefings for the local press. The Zeckendorf team would then fly home to prepare a master plan for the area. That was followed by site plans and preliminary designs for specific buildings.

The earliest example of the success of this approach was a Zeckendorf project for Denver begun in 1952. The developer's relationship with the city would go on for fifteen years, but from the start, Pei's combination of design and planning talent, as well as his natural diplomatic grace, gave a purely commercial undertaking an intelligent dose of urban sensitivity. These qualities proved especially helpful in calming some prominent Denverites, who were at first not at all enthusiastic about the arrival of "this man from New York," as Pei remembered the locals' description of Zeckendorf. So skillfully did Pei handle the diplomacy in Denver that Zeckendorf thereafter made sure his chief architect was on hand for all the major client contacts.

The first of the Zeckendorf buildings for Denver was an office tower dubbed, in honor of Denver's elevation above sea level, Mile High Center. Pei, assisted by Cobb and Franzen, handled the overall design of the building, but for this project he further expanded the team to include Eason Leonard, a tall, amiable Oklahoman. Leonard had been working for the firm of William Lescaze, which did the first, unsuccessful, plan for the Webb & Knapp offices, and had been wooed into the Zeckendorf fold over lunch with Pei at New York's Harvard Club. Although trained as an architect, Leonard was given the job of managing the Mile High project, seeing to the administrative matters and maintaining the field office in Denver. "It would have been foolish to compete with I. M. or Harry as a designer," Leonard said. "There was no reason to think that I could outdo them." He flourished in the management role and went on to become the main administrative officer of the team.

By today's standards of megaskyscrapers wrapped in high-tech materials, Mile High Center was a thoroughly ordinary building. (It survives, but has been partially engulfed by One United Bank Center, a fifty-two-story office complex designed by Philip Johnson and John Burgee.) Located just across the street from the landmark Brown Palace Hotel, Mile High was a basic post-Miesian box. But for all its apparent plainness, the twenty-three-story building had considerable distinction for a commercial venture of the time. For one thing, it covered less than twenty-five percent of its two-acre site. The remaining area was devoted to an exhibition hall and to a plaza enlivened by fountains and pools, below which were shops and restaurants. (When Pei proposed the plaza, Zeckendorf responded, "Why waste all that space?" It went in because Zeckendorf was persuaded that it would mollify the balky Denverites and attract tenants.)

The facade of the office tower, instead of being a standard Modernist glass

What distinguished the design of Denver's Mile High Center from comparable office buildings of the period was the intricate interweaving of the vertical and horizontal facade elements to create an unusual visual texture.

wall, was organized into a delicately colored basketweave pattern that visually exploited different functional elements. The panels covering the columns and spandrel beams were made of dark gray cast aluminum, while the panels used to conceal the heating and cooling conduits were executed in off-white porcelain enamel. The vertical porcelain panels passed over the gray aluminum elements, while the horizontal ones were threaded behind them. The interlocking of these two grids with the "ground" of the window glass created a cagelike illusion of depth where there was in fact only a smooth plane. In this way, Pei was able to animate what was actually a predictably regular and otherwise banal surface.

Whatever its long-term design merits, Mile High, which was well received by the architectural press, established the credibility of the Pei team as more than run-of-the-mill commercial architects. "We were no longer just a bunch of university guys, a group of youngsters," Pei recalled.

Mile High Center was followed by Courthouse Square, a mixed-use project for Denver located just a block away from the office tower on a two-block site. By this time, the management side of the firm was under as much pressure as the designers, and Pei turned to a former colleague of Eason Leonard's at the Lescaze office, Leonard Jacobson, a short, perky New Yorker who had studied architecture at the University of Pennsylvania. After a year in the New York office, Jacobson relieved Leonard as the man in charge of the Denver field office.

Like Roosevelt Field, the Courthouse Square project was distinguished more by its organization of facilities, such as parking and pedestrian amenities, than by its architecture. Indeed, it was the first major project in a downtown area anywhere in the country to attempt to integrate retail services, hotel accommodations, office space, and parking. There was a three-level garage for 2,000 cars below ground. Above ground rose the May D&F department store, an unexceptional aluminum-clad box for which Cobb was primarily responsible. It was distinguished only by the novelty of the curved concrete shell that covered the main entrance and adjoining accessory shop. (At the time, it was the widest-spanning hyperbolic paraboloid in the country.) The ensemble also included a plaza and a skating rink facing 16th Street, Denver's main shopping thoroughfare. (Pei said Zeckendorf at first objected to the plaza and the rink, but, as in the case of Mile High, felt it was worth some additional "wasted" space to make allies of the Denverites wary of his out-of-town ways.)

The fourth element of the composition was the 884-room Hilton Hotel. Franzen was to have done the design, but had decided to leave the firm to try his hand as an independent architect. To replace him, Pei brought in Araldo

After Mile High came the nearby Courthouse Square project, which made full use of Pei's expanding team. Araldo Cossutta was responsible for the Corbusian hotel (rear, left), while Henry Cobb oversaw the May D&F department store, which had as its entrance what was then the largest hyperbolic paraboloid in the country.

Cossutta—like Cobb and Franzen, an alumnus of the Harvard architecture program—who was only thirty at the time and somewhat taken aback by the amount of responsibility Pei turned over to him. "It was a wonderful opportunity," he said, "and a credit to his flexibility. Frankly, I was surprised that Pei accepted what I did."

His building was a twenty-one-story slab of buff-colored precast concrete linked to the May D&F store by a pedestrian bridge. The structure was a direct stylistic descendant of Le Corbusier's muscular concrete apartment block in Marseilles (1952) and, with its sunbreaking grid made of red granite aggregate and its ornamental screen along the lower floors, certainly the most attractive of the three Zeckendorf buildings. But, for the moment, aesthetics was less an issue than the assembling of diverse commercial facilities in an efficient and coherent fashion. While all the buildings of the group look dated today, the massing remains a success, and the concern for providing recreational open space as part of a commercial development set a much-imitated precedent for other architects.

From the firm's point of view, however, the most significant achievement of the Denver buildings was the pattern Pei began to establish for distributing his own efforts and those of his people to maximum effect in carrying out a complex commission that involved a great deal more than design. To a degree, the process was forced upon him by the scope and pace of Zeckendorf's operations, but Pei did it well, and the results, if they did not yet qualify as high design, were far better than what any other major developer was producing.

Webb & Knapp's planning activities increased considerably in 1953, when Zeckendorf embarked on a massive redevelopment scheme for a downtrodden section of Washington, D.C. In his autobiography, the developer declared that Southwest Washington, as the complex came to be known, "was the most long, drawn-out and frustrating of all our projects. Had we had a true idea of what it is really like to get a great, innovating project under way in Washington, we would never have tackled the job."[12]

One reason he did tackle it was the persistence of Philip Graham, the publisher of the *Washington Post*, who had heard Zeckendorf lecture on urban redevelopment at Harvard. Not the least of the deterrents was the social climate of Washington at the time. As Pei recalled later, the prospect of "a Chinese and a Jew" remaking a black ghetto in what was still a very southern city did not strike the collective fancy.

After several attempts, Graham succeeded in arousing Zeckendorf's interest in trying to rehabilitate a 500-acre tract of the city that had become

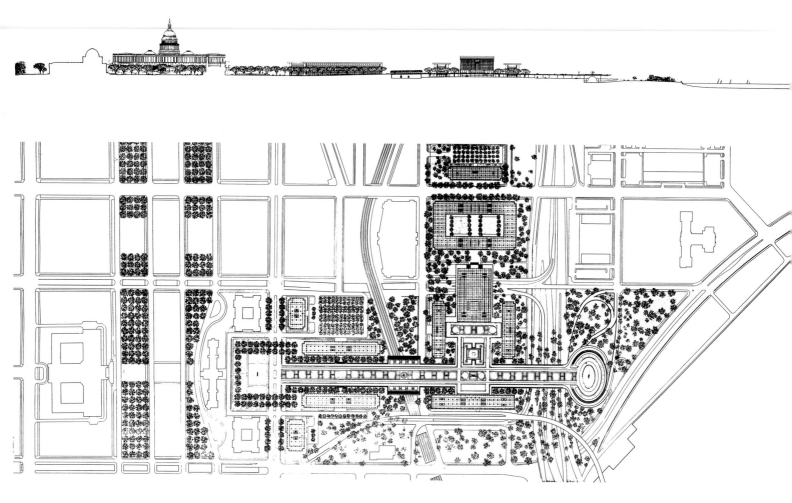

isolated behind the elevated tracks of the Pennsylvania Railroad. The developer set Pei to work analyzing the site and then invited the head of Washington's Redevelopment Land Agency to New York to review the result. According to Zeckendorf, the RLA man was treated to "a couple of dry martinis and a good lunch"[13] in the Webb & Knapp penthouse, at which point he was presented with a master plan for the entire area.

The plan—which would have been the biggest in the country if completed as originally designed—centered on a 300-foot-wide mall running along Tenth Street from the Smithsonian Institution across the triangle formed by the railroad and the Potomac and Anacostia rivers. The mall was carried over the railroad tracks by means of an esplanade, linking the thriving center of the city to its declining quarter and, it was hoped, reviving it. There was to be a complex of office and cultural facilities named L'Enfant Plaza (in recognition of Pierre-Charles L'Enfant, who laid out the city in 1791), as well as government buildings, townhouses, high rises, and a marina on the Potomac. So enthusiastic was the local response that, for one of the few times in their competitive history, the editorial writers of the *Post* and the *Washington Star* agreed on an issue in print.

The enterprise was as bold as it was big, and it demonstrated perhaps more than anything else yet done by Pei and the rest of the Zeckendorf team their

The plan for Southwest Washington involved a bold reordering of a downtrodden portion of the city. The core was a 300-foot-long mall that was to have linked the Smithsonian Institution and the Potomac.

talent for taking on cities as integrated units, rather than piecemeal. James Freed, who was hired well into the project as a design architect by Pei, had an initial experience not unlike Cossutta's on the Denver Hilton. "Almost as soon as I arrived I was told to design some buildings," he said. "It was the postgraduate course I never took. Here I was doing things architects are not supposed to do until much later in their careers." Also like his more senior colleagues, Freed was seduced by Zeckendorf's ambitions. "We were all running around doing things for Bill— plugging things in, sweeping the floors. But *he* thought big, so *we* thought big."

While the plan for Washington enjoyed considerable success—roughly eighty percent of it was eventually built—it fell prey to bureaucratic competition and assorted delays. By 1959, Webb & Knapp, after agreeing to numerous alterations, was having trouble finding the mortgage money to go forward with construction. At that point, the General Services Administration inserted into the plan a building designed to bridge the mall, breaking its clear path to the Potomac. Zeckendorf fought the change, but by this time political backers as well as financial supporters were fading from the field and Zeckendorf had to relinquish control. A reporter asked Zeckendorf how he felt about having the undertaking go forward under other hands. The developer's reply: "I'm the guy who got the girl pregnant. Those fellows you see around here are merely the obstetricians."[14]

Pei's judgment was characteristically more restrained. In a retrospective analysis written for the *AIA Journal*, he concluded: "Despite the most enlightened administrative intentions throughout the history of this project, it would appear that the highest goal of the art of urban design—that of a new urban organism, each part functionally and visually related to the others and to the whole—was not attained. Perhaps this was not possible in those early years of the redevelopment process but it remains a goal for the future."[15]

The next project of comparable scale taken on by the Webb & Knapp office was Place Ville Marie, a seven-acre redevelopment in the heart of Montreal. More even than during the work on Mile High, Pei's time and talents were being stretched thin by Zeckendorf's ambitions in Washington. At the same time, Cobb, although only twenty-eight, was emerging as a major talent in his own right. Making a virtue of necessity, Pei proposed to Zeckendorf that he turn over responsibility for the Montreal job to his young colleague, to which Zeckendorf immediately agreed. Thirty years later, Cobb was still impressed with the decision. "Bill was amazingly ready to take the risk of having very young people do big things," he said.

Cobb on the Webb & Knapp plane (top) presenting his original proposal to Zeckendorf for a pair of towers for Place Ville Marie in Montreal. The developer dismissed the scheme as "melee." Cobb's final design included a forty-eight-story cruciform tower (above) and an office complex that was at the time the largest in the world.

Begun in 1955, Cobb's plan was centered on a forty-eight-story, cruciform office tower. (An early design had included two smaller buildings, but Zeckendorf, who wanted nothing less than a monument, told Cobb: "Harry, you don't make melee out of a blue-white diamond." Cobb thought he had got the point, but had to ask around for the meaning of "melee." It turned out to be jewelers' jargon for small diamonds.) When it was finished, Place Ville Marie encompassed 3,071,097 square feet, more than any other office building complex in the world.

Meanwhile, Webb & Knapp's architecture department kept growing. In addition to Pei, Cobb, and Cossutta on the design side, there were Eason Leonard and Leonard Jacobson doing management. Below them was a steadily expanding support staff. The office payroll now listed approximately seventy people, who were working on various aspects of a dozen projects. Pei realized that he could not deprive his collaborators of the same design identity he himself was increasingly eager to have. "These people were growing up," he said with no condescension. "They wanted to stake their own claims. It was only natural, and the time came when I had to give them a sense of belonging." Accordingly, the team took its first step toward shedding its public image as Webb & Knapp's in-house design team. Although it still continued to work exclusively for Webb & Knapp, it was christened, in 1955, I. M. Pei & Associates, a partnership of Pei, Cobb, and Leonard.

Shortly after Place Ville Marie got under way, Zeckendorf had what Pei described as a "brief rapprochement" with Robert Moses in New York. Two major Title I housing projects had run into serious financial trouble. One, known as Manhattantown, had been taken over by the city for nonpayment of taxes, and the other, known as NYU-Bellevue, was about to go the same route. Moses turned to Zeckendorf as someone who could bring the developments back to life.

The Manhattantown project had a design in place, but NYU-Bellevue, while a master plan had been done for it by the firm of Skidmore, Owings & Merrill, was not yet fully formed. Gordon Bunshaft, an SOM partner and the designer of Lever House, the Modernist classic on New York's Park Avenue, advised Pei against getting involved, declaring that "housing is lawyers' work." Pei in turn advised Zeckendorf against taking on the development, telling him it was "just another housing project." But Zeckendorf was interested, told Moses he would do it, renamed the area Kips Bay, and asked Pei how he would handle the site, which was bounded by 30th and 33rd streets and First and Second avenues on Manhattan's East Side.

Pei's first move was to reduce the six buildings called for in the master plan to two large slabs, leaving the remainder of the site open for parks and gardens. This, he felt, would "help take the project-itis out of it." Next, he decided against the obvious course of lining the slabs up symmetrically and slid each toward opposite ends of the site. This simple move created a more dynamic composition and reduced the sense of uniformity that would have been reinforced by having the slabs face each other directly. Pei had hoped to embellish the open space by adding a large sculpture, and he had a thirty-foot-high Picasso piece in mind. He presented the idea to Zeckendorf, who was sympathetic but firm. "I can give you fifty saplings or this piece of sculpture," he said. Pei's response: "I'll take the trees." (Pei did not give up on the sculpture, which was later purchased for his residential towers at New York University.)

Because the buildings were to be subsidized by Title I and had to conform to the regulations of the Federal Housing Authority, Pei faced some major design constraints. The main one was that the FHA would provide mortgage insurance only for rooms that satisfied its own space requirements. The agency also considered balconies eligible for subsidies, but Pei felt balconies were of no use in city buildings. Passing them up, however, would mean passing up FHA money.

The struggle with the agency was made easier by the fact that Pei, despite his youth, had been made a member of its advisory board. But it was still not easy and, as in the case of the Picasso, brought out one of Pei's emerging characteristics in such situations—his ability to wait out people who gave him an answer he disagreed with. "You can't win with bureaucrats in one meeting," he said. "They see right through you. You have to be patient." As he would demonstrate innumerable times later in his career, the patience he exhibited with the FHA was to pay off handsomely.

With a deft massaging of the rules, Pei designed his slabs with poured-in-place concrete walls in the shape of honeycombs. The unorthodox shape made the walls part of the structure of the buildings, but the recesses within the walls were crafted in such a way that they would qualify as balcony space under the FHA regulations. Those recesses, into which the window glass was inserted behind the surface plane, also meant that tenants would enjoy a measure of privacy as well as shade from the sun. Carefully detailed, with rounded upper corners to suggest arches, they gave the facades a visual texture unprecedented in low-income apartment construction. If the aesthetic sources for Kips Bay lay, like those of the Denver Hilton, in Le Corbusier's ruggedly textured concrete facades, the structural and spatial logic derived entirely from Pei's success

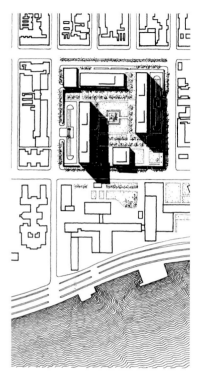

The Kips Bay apartment complex on Manhattan's East Side demonstrated the Pei firm's skill at the creative use of poured-in-place concrete, which was used to produce an innovative facade treatment (top). Pei's decision to align the two apartment blocks asymmetrically (above) animated what might otherwise have been an overwhelmingly static composition.

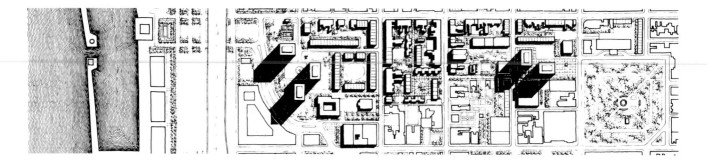

at beating the government at its own housing rules.

The disadvantage of the solution was that it created rooms that were slightly longer and narrower than tenants found comfortable. It also proved costly. As he would in virtually every job from then on, Pei gave special attention to the material. James Polshek, a young architect who had joined the firm right out of the Yale School of Architecture, remembered Pei prowling the construction site checking each bag of concrete to make sure the color was consistent. When the question of the rising cost came up, he said, with a sentiment that was to bedevil many of his later clients, "If you do it right, even if it's over budget, history will remember you well."

There were some compromises. The cost of the elaborate poured-in-place technique meant that there was not enough money left to finish the surface as well as Pei had hoped. William Zeckendorf, Jr., who worked with his father and Pei on the project, said later that his father approved the other expenses only because he believed in the importance of the architecture. (In the end, the buildings were on budget.) As the elder Zeckendorf put it, Pei's slabs were proof that "housing need not be monstrous." Pei, who had been growing increasingly frustrated in his role as a team manager rather than as a designer, felt that Kips Bay was for him the "beginning of doing, instead of just planning."

As their operations were refined, the members of I. M. Pei & Associates found that one of the most powerful tools in their possession was the site model, which showed the local officials who were to be involved in a given development what it would look like when finished.

These models, which were usually far more detailed than those of other firms, proved especially effective in winning competitions held by various cities to select developers for municipal projects. One of the biggest victories was the so-called Society Hill project in Philadelphia. There, the city was eager to rehabilitate a declining area on its Delaware riverfront. The site had been the earliest residential area to be settled in Philadelphia, and it rapidly became an elegant neighborhood. But as the city grew, the area gradually declined, deteriorating into little more than a slum by the early part of the twentieth century. A key to its revival was the removal of a wholesale food market, which had dominated the area, to South Philadelphia. All the surviving eighteenth-century buildings were surveyed, and the best were acquired by the city and sold to buyers who agreed to restore them. The site of the food market was designated for new residential construction. With the support of Edmund Bacon, who was then executive director of the Philadelphia City Planning Commission, a national competition

An irregular composition was also important to the Society Hill development in Philadelphia, where Pei brought his three towers (left) into a dynamic relationship with his cluster of small townhouses. (The two towers to the right, which were part of the original plan, were never built.)

was organized for developer-architect teams to come up with a comprehensive plan.[16]

The major planning challenge in this case was to insert a modern housing complex into an area that, although it had fallen into disrepair, still contained the largest concentration of eighteenth-century architecture anywhere in the United States. The Webb & Knapp entry, which was accepted in 1957 and completed in 1964, called for five high-rise towers and thirty-seven townhouses (the towers were later reduced to three, and a subsequent phase of the project added twenty-seven more houses). The genius of the solution was that it managed to make the mix better than the sum of its parts by creating a smooth transition in scale and form from the colonial to the modern.

The key to the plan, which was conceived by Pei and worked out by his team, was the positioning of the towers and the relationship between them and the low-rise buildings. The three thirty-one-story structures were set in such a way that they would terminate vistas along several local streets and frame views of such local attractions as the old Christ Church. The buildings shared the same rectangular plan, but because they were placed asymmetrically, they created a visually varied ensemble. Two presented their long facades to the city, while one faced it end-on. And each was arranged off-axis with the others, creating a variety of irregular compositions when they were viewed as a group.

The towers used the same cast-in-place, load-bearing concrete screen wall found in Kips Bay, providing floor-to-ceiling windows. As in the New York buildings, the windows were set deep into the concrete screen. The shadows formed by the recessing of the windows created a sense of depth that mitigated the monolithic impact of similar buildings with flat facades. The towers' weakest points were where they met the ground: the arcades formed by the slender columns at the bases were unrelieved by any windows or other inviting detail and as a result were rather chilly spaces.

But the towers met each other and the nearby townhouses gracefully. A fountain at the center of their common court animated the automobile turn-around, and a spacious lawn that was neither barrier nor no-man's-land made a gentle transition to the three-story buildings, which were organized around smaller courts that provided parking for the residents (residents of the towers parked in garages underground). The rear facades were appropriately more inviting than those on the street, which had miniforecourts protected by walls to create a simultaneous sense of transition and privacy.

The combination of the large elements with the small was a delicate one,

The Society Hill towers rise thirty-one stories, but because of their unorthodox siting, they make a minimal intrusion on the historic fabric of the nearby eighteenth-century buildings.

The Green Earth Sciences Building at MIT allowed Pei to ease away from his executive role with Zeckendorf, but he was still not able to see the details of the design through as he had hoped.

and it was achieved through the materials as well as the massing. The towers were of concrete, the townhouses of brick that invoked the older buildings. The details of the townhouses—small windows, arched doorways, and wrought-iron balconies—further asserted their link to the older buildings. But the new buildings were allowed their modernity through the abstraction of their form. So often the problem with high rises is that they overpower what surrounds them. At Society Hill, they were arranged rather like parents sheltering a community of offspring. Here was rational and sensitive use of the contemporary urban vocabulary to create an unusually inviting mixture of residential experiences.

Despite his architectural and planning successes, Pei was beginning to feel that he would at some point have to strike out on his own from the Zeckendorf camp. The relationship had enormous advantages in providing Pei and his people a scale of operations that was the envy of many other architects of their age, but it limited the firm to a finite range of commissions, and the prospect of other clients was both alluring and essential if the group was ever to have a truly independent identity. The establishment of I. M. Pei & Associates had been a step in that direction, and the management side of the team was further strengthened by the addition of James Freed, who had arrived in 1956, and, in 1957, of Werner Wandelmaier, who had come aboard to finish up the Denver Hilton. Pei now considered that he and his team were a "serious" architecture firm, and, as he put it, he was growing weary "explaining to Zeckendorf's vice presidents why whatever his people were working on was the right thing to do, and that we weren't just dreamers from another world."

The opportunity to open the door slightly came in 1959 with a personal invitation to Pei from the Massachusetts Institute of Technology to design a building for its Earth Sciences Center. Zeckendorf agreed to let Pei do the freelance work on the condition that it didn't cut into his Webb & Knapp responsibilities. To do it at all while maintaining his schedule for Zeckendorf meant turning over more than half of the design work on the MIT building to Araldo Cossutta.

Perhaps the main achievement of the MIT building, which was funded by Cecil Green, an MIT alumnus and founder of Texas Instruments, was its organizing role on the campus. The site was to the east of the center of the campus, which was dominated by the dome of the old main building, and set among a collection of low structures of no special character. Pei decided to make his building tall, so that it would seem to gather the lesser buildings to it.

The form of the tower, which went through a number of versions, finally evolved as a sculpturally straightforward monolith in concrete. The building rose twenty-one stories overlooking the Charles River, its narrow ends framing a grid of windows very much in the emerging tradition of Kips Bay and the Society Hill towers.

Like the Philadelphia towers, though, the Green building was more effective as a point of emphasis in a larger composition than it was when it touched the ground. In this case, the central space between the end walls was left open and divided into three bays, which continued the pedestrian flow of the campus through the bottom of the building, but they were uninvitingly void of any detail. They also proved somewhat hazardous when the wind blew. Cecil Green later recalled MIT professors complaining about having their papers blown from their hands because of the wind-tunnel effect created by the design of the entrance. Pei was deeply embarrassed. "Here I was from MIT," he said, "and I didn't know about wind-tunnel effects."

Pei was concerned by more than the effect of wind on the Green building. Although he had been heavily involved in the design, the pressures of his executive role in the office had left him little time to see it through. And he was not entirely happy with the work Cossutta had done on it. Cossutta's original version had oval windows, which Pei found unacceptable. When a shortage of money forced a simpler solution, Pei was relieved, but he nevertheless realized that the building was still not precisely as he had wanted it.

Despite his reservations about the Green building, Pei's architectural relationship with his alma mater would continue into the 1980s with the Dreyfus Chemistry Building (1964–70), the Landau Chemical Engineering Building (1972–76), and the Wiesner Arts and Media Building (1978–84). But the most immediate effect was that Pei, through Green, met Erik Jonsson, another Texas Instruments executive, and, as mayor of Dallas, the man who later hired Pei to design the Dallas City Hall.

In spite of the demands on his executive abilities, Pei had been able to do two other buildings on his own. There was the house he had built for himself and his family in Katonah in 1952, and the Luce Memorial Chapel (1954–63) on Taiwan, a soaring, frankly expressionistic structure Zeckendorf had allowed Pei to pursue for the parent organization of the school he had attended in Shanghai. One was a rigorous Bauhaus box, the other an essay in Expressionist form. Together, they suggested both a stylistic flexibility and an understandable uncertainty about his own aesthetic direction.

The oversight of the firm's fortunes ruled out more than an occasional

Pei's design for his family's weekend house in Katonah drew on classic Modernist precedents in its strict geometry, but was inflected with an Oriental sensibility, particularly in the use of wood.

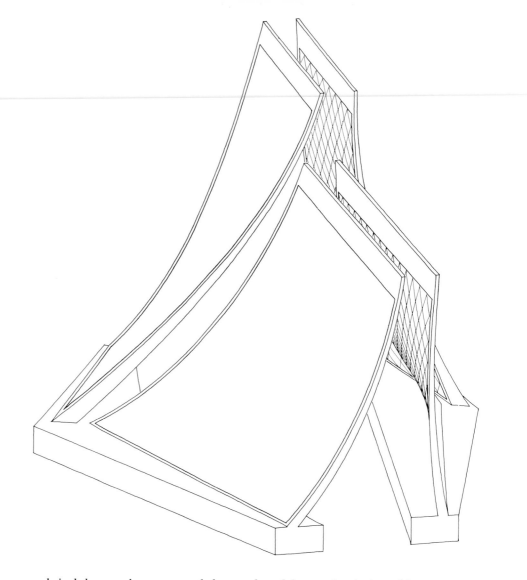

such indulgence, however, and the need to delegate the design of larger projects persisted. One of the more successful ones of this period was University Plaza, a group of residential towers for New York University, on which Pei worked closely with James Freed. Begun in early 1960, it used the concrete-waffle facades that were becoming something of a Pei signature, but here they got a further refinement. Located just off Washington Square Park in the heart of the low-scale Greenwich Village section of the city, this trio of thirty-story towers was positioned, like the ones in Philadelphia, according to a pinwheel plan. The deep grids of the window walls were offset against slim, sheer walls that formed the frame for the adjoining set of windows. The arrangement of the towers and the "spinning" of the facades created, even more effectively than in Philadelphia, a sense of variety amid uniformity. (The progeny of these towers would include some similar complexes at Bushnell Plaza, finished in 1970, in Hartford, Connecticut, and at Harbor Towers, completed in 1971, in Boston.)

By the late 1950s, the Zeckendorf empire had begun to show serious signs of financial instability. There were many theories about what actually brought it down, but it was clear that the great tycoon had simply overextended himself. His hotels were being hurt by air travel, which allowed executives to fly in and out of a city in a day without putting up for the night. The company's debt was growing, and creditors were proving more insistent than they had been. Zeckendorf's charm and energy were simply no longer sufficient to maintain the high-wire act. When the money crunch began, Zeckendorf's advisers told him to let his architects go. He insisted on keeping the entire team, which then numbered about seventy people.

While grateful for Zeckendorf's immediate support, Pei was worried about the impact the long-term fortunes of the parent company might have on his satellite organization. And he had other reasons for feeling uncomfortable. The large-scale planning jobs in Washington, Montreal, Philadelphia, and elsewhere had provided invaluable experience, so much so that even thirty years later Pei would give Zeckendorf credit for "teaching me everything about evaluating a piece of land; I never looked at one the same way again." But it had its artistic limitations, as did the steady diet of low-income housing, like Kips Bay, and commercial development work of the Courthouse Square sort. "I knew that if I stayed within the envelope of the company, I would never get the kinds of jobs I really wanted," he said. "I didn't qualify for them because I was part of Webb & Knapp." The image about which Stubbins had warned Cobb was still plaguing the firm. Indeed, Pei was excluded from the American Institute of Architects, the profession's governing body, for a number of years for being what some members of the group described privately as a "house architect." As a result the firm was simply not considered for the more artistically challenging and high-visibility projects Pei was seeking. He always felt, for example, that the Zeckendorf connection had cost him the chance to design a portion of New York's Lincoln Center for the Performing Arts, one of the most sought-after opportunities of the day.

Pei also felt frustration at having to leave so much of the architecture to others. Indeed, while he was primarily responsible for the design of Mile High Center and took part in all the subsequent Webb & Knapp work to varying degrees, the only designing he did entirely on his own for the firm during those years was Zeckendorf's office. And for all the benefits of working with the country's most flamboyant developer, the relationship was not always easy. "Design is something you have to put your hand to," Pei said. "But I worked for the man, and he needed me for other things. I had to take the bad with the good. I felt trapped in the role of looking for jobs, being a procurer of commissions. While my people had the luxury of doing one job at a time, I had to keep track of the whole enterprise. My growth as a designer was stunted; I should have reached my maturity much earlier. In a way, Zeckendorf's financial problems were the beginning of my opportunity as an architect."

Picasso's *Bust of Sylvette,* shown peeking from the shadows of Pei's University Plaza apartment complex in New York, is the same sculpture the architect had failed to persuade Zeckendorf to install at Kips Bay.

The combined pressures of Zeckendorf's finances and Pei's impatience led in 1960 to what had by then become inevitable: the formal separation from Webb & Knapp. It was an amicable one; Pei and his people were allowed to stay on in their space at 383–385 Madison, paying only token rent. (They didn't move to 600 Madison, their current address, until 1966.) But whatever professional opportunities the separation promised, it meant considerable personal pain. The break was especially hard because, as William Zeckendorf, Jr., said later, "the relationship between I. M. and my father was so intense. They pushed each other." And it had come to include both families. After Zeckendorf's son had come home from the Korean War, Pei gave him the only surprise party he had ever had.

In a farewell letter to Pei and his people dated August 1, 1960, Zeckendorf wrote: "It is more than twelve years since Ieoh Ming Pei became associated with Webb & Knapp, Inc. and more particularly with me personally . . . in this relatively short but yet long time we witnessed outstanding accomplishments which were brought about by sympathetic, intelligent cooperation and mutual effort betwixt the art of design and engineering and the related economic aspects that confront the self-financed private capital entrepreneur in real estate. Together we have made history and have passed many milestones that will be looked upon by future writers of the contemporary scene as having perhaps had a profound effect upon American construction and the way of life that emanates from good design. . . . The advent of I. M. Pei & Associates becoming an autonomous firm is hardly different from all things in nature in that when maturity is achieved the new entity must find its own way and its own place in the orbit of human life."[17] Pei said that rereading the letter nearly thirty years later "brought tears to my eyes."

The architects who followed Pei out of Webb & Knapp represented a powerful entity. The team system had been refined and was working well. Pei—however much it frustrated him—was a uniquely effective salesman, locating and maintaining clients, while at the same time overseeing the conceptual phases of the design process. Cobb, Cossutta, and now Freed stood ready to take the designs of the projects from there. Normally, while Leonard, Wandelmaier, and Jacobson would see to the management end, each senior designer would assemble a team of junior architects who would remain with the job from the earliest design stages through construction. (Most firms passed the project on to a separate team to do working drawings once the design was done.) One of the virtues of the Pei system was that it allowed the younger members to get a broad range of experience in all phases of the architectural process. So closely did the teams work together with Pei, who would critique individual designs at regular intervals, that,

while the younger architects enjoyed unusual freedom, they began to develop a common design "language." While a practiced eye might detect in a given building traces of Cobb's more abstract touch or Cossutta's fondness for Beaux-Arts symmetry, the fundamental Pei concerns for rigorous geometry, innovative technology, quality materials, and crisply executed details were becoming widely recognizable, and, to judge by the enthusiastic coverage in the architectural press, highly regarded. As Cobb described it, the firm had combined "the strength of a group practice with the strength of an atelier."

While the Pei system was in place, so was the leadership. Cossutta, who became a partner of the firm in 1963, would leave in 1973 to establish his own practice, but Pei, Cobb, Freed, Leonard, Jacobson, and Wandelmaier would remain together into the 1990s, creating one of the most stable architectural organizations in the history of the profession. It was to serve as a model for many smaller firms to follow, some of them founded by Pei alumni. Indeed, the firm itself may one day be regarded as one of Pei's most formidable constructions. But in 1960, its members, and especially its founder, were primarily concerned about getting enough work to keep their newly independent venture afloat.

While the prospect of operating as a fully fledged architecture firm out from under the Zeckendorf wing was exhilarating for Pei and his people, the idea of finding new commissions on their own was daunting. "At last I was free," Pei said, "but I was very aware that I could no longer rely on Webb & Knapp for work." The need to find it was particularly pressing, since Pei was now responsible for a staff that numbered seventy-five, and the only job still on their drawing boards was the final phase of the Green Earth Sciences building at MIT. The quest was made no easier by the discovery that, whatever the Zeckendorf experience may have contributed to Pei's knowledge of planning, urban renewal, and low-cost housing, the developer's financial reputation lingered as a deterrent to the very clients the architect was hoping to attract as a free agent. People who knew of Zeckendorf's money troubles were understandably wary of a firm that had served as his resident architects. Moreover, as Pei learned to his disappointment, the high-design world still looked down its collective nose at him for his association with Webb & Knapp.

To Pei's great relief, he soon discovered a client willing to set aside whatever negative image the Pei team retained and to gamble on its talent. He was Walter Orr Roberts, a renegade astronomer who was making a name for himself in the foothills of the Colorado Rockies as head of an organization called the National Center for Atmospheric Research.

Pei in the late 1950s reviewing design documents in the Zeckendorf office. With him are Leonard Jacobson (far left) and Eason Leonard (to Pei's right), who were to become partners in the firm. The combination of Pei's architectural ambitions and Zeckendorf's financial troubles led, in 1960, to a formal separation from Webb & Knapp, but the personal relationships with the embattled developer remained close.

4. THE NATIONAL CENTER FOR ATMOSPHERIC RESEARCH (1961–67): THE JOURNEY FROM PLANNING TO FORM

The National Center for Atmospheric Research, known as NCAR, is not on the way to many places, and its name does not slide easily across the tongue. It sits atop a 535-acre mesa at an altitude of some 6,000 feet just outside the city of Boulder, Colorado. Apart from scientists, most of those who know anything about it have seen it only in architecture books, or as a setting for Woody Allen's wacky futuristic film, *Sleeper*.

Approaching NCAR from Boulder, the visitor is likely to have a series of conflicting impressions. The complex of pinkish buildings that reveal themselves gradually over the slopes of pale earth and waving grasses may look at one moment like a family of brooding dolmens and at the next like a cohort of Greek warriors in battle helmets. At the same time, the buildings could be a cluster of gigantic space-age periscopes poking up from some alien vessel that had burrowed beneath the rocky ground.

If the shapes of NCAR evoke ancient and futuristic images simultaneously, they should. The institution is dedicated to some of the most advanced science, but the inspiration for its forms is drawn from the most primitive of architectural precedents. Bringing the science and the architecture together proved to be an awakening for Pei. In a newspaper interview given in 1978, he described the importance of NCAR to his aesthetic development this way: "It was not really until the early 1960s that I began to design again. Oh, I had always looked over the shoulders of the architects working with me, and I would participate in the concept and occasionally draw a line to test out an idea or to help someone consolidate his own direction in a design. But it really wasn't until I was asked in the early 1960s to do the National Center for Atmospheric Research in

Pei at the National Center for Atmospheric Research with Walter Orr Roberts in 1985. Like many of the clients for whom the architect has done his best work, the unorthodox scientist was to become a lasting friend.

Boulder, Colorado, that I was thrown fully into the process once again. . . . I realized, all over again, how intensely personal the process of design is—not personal in the sense that you insistently look for a way to assert your own identity, but in the sense that you have to find the way for circumstances to assert themselves."[1]

The discovery was a crucial one. As the scope and pace of the work at Webb & Knapp had increased, Pei had been drawn steadily away from the hands-on aspects of architecture. Skilled as he had become at sizing up vast chunks of urban space like those for Courthouse Square, Society Hill, or Kips Bay, he had all too often been obliged to leave the more intimate problem-solving to Cobb, Cossutta, Freed, and others. And it showed. The weakest aspects of Pei's high rises in Philadelphia and New York were not the composition of the buildings on the skyline, but the chilly colonnades at ground level, and it was no surprise that MIT professors had their notes blown from their hands by winds whipping the entrance of the Earth Sciences building. Pei had been too occupied by other matters—organizing the office, attending to Zeckendorf's clients, overseeing a variety of projects simultaneously—to see many of his buildings through. Handling only the conceptual phase of a work of architecture clearly had its limits, and Pei was lucky that, at NCAR, he was given a chance to break the habit.

Pei was by no means a clear choice for the NCAR job. For all the variety of the projects he and his colleagues had done for Webb & Knapp, he had never worked on a major building that was not surrounded by other structures, whether those of a city, a suburb, or an academic campus. And while his own house in Katonah occupied a bucolic setting, that setting was as nothing compared to the majestic wildness of the Rocky Mountains.

In what was to become a typical pattern for Pei, the NCAR commission turned to a large degree on a close personal relationship with a forceful and unorthodox client. Indeed, if there has been a single strand linking Pei's best buildings, it has been the intensely creative relationships between Pei and the clients who commissioned them. The best of those clients have been what Pei described as "cultivated" people. By that he did not necessarily mean only people devoted to the arts, although that would often be the case. It was more that they were both interesting as individuals and interested in the process of making architecture. If one sets aside the very large figure of William Zeckendorf, who was more employer than client, Walter Orr Roberts was the first of these remarkable people.

Even for a scientist, Roberts, who died in March 1990 at seventy-four, was a rare visionary. He had earned a Ph.D. in astronomy at Harvard, working with faculty members he later described as "radicals in scientific philosophy," and in the late 1950s had left the conventional scientific track to settle in Boulder, where he ran the University of Colorado's High Altitude Observatory. For years, he had been looking longingly at the mesa that rose above the city at the foot of the rugged sandstone outcroppings known as the Flatirons. He had been brooding privately that he might one day create there "the Caltech of Colorado," so that a select group of scientists, working as close to the elements as possible, could devote themselves to scientific inquiry without the intrusions of city life.

In 1959, Roberts was suddenly offered the post of director of the University Committee for Atmospheric Research, a leading scientific institution made up of representatives of several universities. The problem was that the committee was located in Delaware. Roberts declined the invitation, not wanting to leave the work he was doing in Boulder or the rugged country that surrounded it. To his surprise, he was offered the position again a year later, and this time he accepted, but only on the condition that the committee establish a laboratory in Boulder under his direction. Roberts got his way, and planning was set in motion for a new research center.

Nearly thirty years later, Roberts could look back with ample satisfaction on his resolute behavior. His organization had grown to represent fifty-five universities in the United States and Canada and, with a staff of 750 scientists, was doing pioneering studies of such subjects as the depletion of the Earth's ozone layer, the effects of acid rain, and the causes of wind shear. It also owned an architectural classic.

Roberts in his early seventies had not changed much from the days when, in his mid-forties, he outlined his vision for NCAR to Pei. Even as a retiree, Roberts looked remarkably like an unreconstructed hippie. A rumpled man with a boyish smile, he was given to intermittent bursts of giggling laughter. His dress—denim sunhat, well-worn shirt, sandals, unpressed trousers held up by both suspenders and a belt—seemed quirky even for someone his age. He still walked the mountains to get a feel for his research, having never been content to conduct his science from the comfort of a laboratory. "How he would talk about the weather!" Pei exclaimed when recalling Roberts as a young client. "It was absolutely fascinating. He would look up at a clear blue sky and say that it was going to rain, and when—and then it did!"

When he began to work with Pei on the center, atmospheric science was, according to Roberts, "in a rather sorry state." Among his goals for NCAR was to

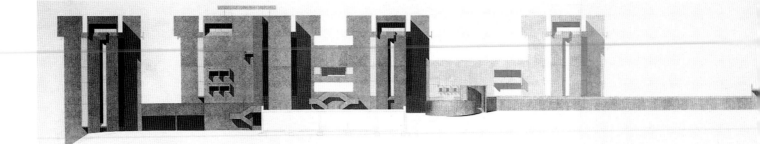

create a center that would stand as "a symbol of the new thrust of the atmospheric sciences, of the reality of atmospheric science as an exact science." But he also felt it vital that the architecture of the center reflect his vision of the process of scientific discovery. It was, in Roberts's view, an accidental process, full of "surprise meetings" among data, people, and ideas.

Roberts envisioned a facility that would accommodate and encourage such exchanges. "I wanted a building with no long corridors," he said, "one that was complex and had tight, isolated spaces where small groups could gather and talk. I wanted chance encounters to be stimulated by the structure. Chaos is an integral part of creativity, and I wanted a building that would be somewhat chaotic, that would encourage random interaction, a place where if you wanted to go from point A to point B, there were five different choices, and no way to tell which was the best without a guide."

Another concern was that the building be as flexible as possible. In research of the kind the scientists practiced, equipment and techniques were changing constantly. Accordingly, they wanted movable walls so that offices and laboratories could be expanded and contracted as needed (scarcely a room at NCAR has not been rearranged since it opened). And there was to be maximum wall space for bookcases and blackboards. That meant a minimum of windows.

But Roberts, who had a fondness for the hill towns of Tuscany, also insisted that the building allow the dramatic natural setting to penetrate to the interior. "Nature," as he put it, "was to come up to the door."

Getting permission to build such a facility at all on the site Roberts had selected was a significant achievement. To discourage commercial development of the mesa, the city of Boulder had established what was called the "blue line," an altitude limit above which city water and other services would not be supplied. To change that, an amendment to the blue line was put to a public vote. NCAR promised that the area surrounding the building would become a nature preserve and that the building itself would be designed to be sympathetic with the existing landscape. To the delight of the scientists, the amendment passed, by a margin of nearly four to one.

But there was a further obstacle. The land comprising Table Mesa, as the natural acropolis was known, was owned by several different people and promised to be a difficult site to assemble for a single purpose. That problem was solved by the state of Colorado, which acquired the land and turned it over to the National Science Foundation for use by NCAR.

The next problem was to find an architect who could combine the

Pei's decision not to "compete" with nature in the NCAR design produced a complex of forms that instead echoed the powerful outcroppings of the mountainous site. Because of insufficient funds, the cluster of towers at the extreme left of this drawing was never built.

scientific requirements of the program with the community mandate for an environmentally appropriate building. Sounding almost like William Zeckendorf at the time he hired Pei for Webb & Knapp, Roberts said years later that he had wanted someone "young and unknown" with "a lot of promise for the future." To find that person, he turned for advice to his friend Tician Papachristou, a Boulder architect, and to Wallace Harrison, a partner in the New York architecture firm of Harrison & Abramovitz. A committee was then assembled made up of the deans of seven architecture schools associated with NCAR's member universities. The chairman of the search committee was Pietro Belluschi, then head of architecture at Pei's alma mater, MIT.

In addition to Pei, the committee considered Edward Larrabee Barnes, Harry Weese, and Skidmore, Owings & Merrill, among others. All of the final candidates were brought to the wilderness site so that they could develop a sense of what might be done there. As the selection process went forward, the committee issued a memo on Pei, concluding that "the project would be for him a quite new challenge and would provide personal and professional advantages and satisfactions that could lead him to be tremendously involved."[2] He was chosen, in the fall of 1961, by unanimous vote.

Following his selection, Pei returned to Boulder to consult with Roberts about his intentions for the building. The meeting rapidly went far beyond the predictable questions of budget and square footage. The two men hiked the length and breadth of the site and spent several hours sitting on the lip of the mesa discussing the nature of creativity and scientific research. As it turned out, they agreed on almost everything. "We're kindred spirits in a way," Roberts said years after NCAR was finished. "Pei was always interested in the subtle nature of interactions among people. To me, the most important thing about science is how people work together, and conflict is part of it. Pei cared about that, too."

Seeing such abstractions into built form was a new experience for the architect. After years of executive architecture and planning under Zeckendorf, he had assembled a unique portfolio, but it did not include anything like what Roberts was asking him to do. "It wasn't something I could jump right into," he said. "I had to start from scratch." In doing so, Pei turned to examples of how others had handled comparable settings. Primary among the architects whose work provided a starting point for Pei at NCAR was Le Corbusier. In his pilgrimage church of Notre-Dame-du-Haut, completed in 1955 in the foothills of the Vosges mountains, the Swiss-French architect had exploited a dramatic site by revealing his building to visitors in stages, leading them up a circuitous path from

below. For his High Court building in Chandigarh (1956), Le Corbusier had used massive concrete hoods to shelter the building from the Indian sun. And at La Tourette, a monastery near Lyons completed in 1960, he had used muscular concrete forms to subdue the side of a steep hill. But neither Le Corbusier nor any other of the modern masters had dealt with a site so much at the mercy of nature as was Table Mesa.

The nearest example of modern architecture in a comparable setting was the United States Air Force Academy, designed by Skidmore, Owings & Merrill and then under construction in Colorado Springs. There, SOM had chosen to create a deliberate contrast with the nearby mountains. The main complex of buildings was long and low, the geometry strictly rectilinear and defiant of the irregular landscape behind it. The focus of the composition, the Cadet Chapel, sprang up as a file of triangular forms, as crisp and regular as the columns of airmen who would parade before it. Pei went to see the Academy and instantly concluded that it was not the right approach for NCAR. While SOM's design may have been appropriate to a military institution, its rigid formality was not, Pei felt, what Roberts was after for a "chaotic" scientific enterprise.

For that, something other than modern architecture was needed as a source. On a trip he had taken in 1960, a year before meeting Roberts, Pei had visited Ollantaytambo, an ancient Inca settlement in the Andes mountains dominated by six enormous ceremonial stones. The memory of these brooding masses returned to Pei while he pondered the NCAR site. Stonehenge, too, emerged as a point of reference, although its flat site separated it fundamentally from the Table Mesa problem. The strongest inspiration, Pei said, was much closer to Boulder. During the development of the NCAR scheme, Pei and Eileen took an automobile trip through much of the American Southwest. Just east of Cortez, Colorado, they came to Mesa Verde National Park. There they saw the mud-and-stone buildings that had been set into recesses in the enormous sandstone cliffs by Pueblo Indians in the thirteenth and fourteenth centuries. Even as ruins, the irregular Pueblo towers with their dark, staring windows were powerful to behold. When Pei saw them, he exclaimed, "Here it is, a work of architecture that is at peace with nature!"

How to adapt what he had seen to the needs of NCAR was a problem Pei attacked as perhaps only an architect of forty-four eager to make up for lost time could. He walked the site repeatedly and even spent a damp night on it in a sleeping bag. As he remembered his on-site investigation in a conversation with an NCAR researcher years later, he and Roberts also downed a considerable

amount of wine on the mesa while they refined their ideas of what should rise on it. Perhaps recalling the visits he had made as a boy in China with his mother to mountaintop Buddhist retreats, Pei described his investigation of the NCAR site as "an almost religious experience." Never before had he learned to know so intimately the ground on which he was to build.

Nevertheless, Pei's first design fell well short of what Walter Roberts was looking for. It was a tight cluster of vertical forms, which the director rejected as "just a bunch of towers." He instructed the architect to try something "more spread out." According to Roberts, Pei took the judgment hard. Eileen recalled that her husband often stayed up late into the night struggling with different versions of the building. But Roberts had meant no harm by calling for another solution. "In science," he said, "nothing ever comes out right the first time: everything evolves. I didn't see the rejection as criticism."

At the dedication of the laboratory complex in 1967, Pei reflected on the problems he had had in finding what Roberts was seeking: "The site is, indeed, the most beautiful we've ever had to deal with. You would think that, blessed with this kind of beauty, architecture would come easy. But it was not easy. We tried many buildings here, many, many designs, but they all fell apart. We didn't know why they fell apart until much later, when we discovered something we should have known all along, and that is that when you're confronted with nature—such power and beauty—you just don't try to compete with it. You try to join with it, and this is exactly what we tried to do."[3]

The change in Pei's approach paid off. When Roberts saw what turned

The full force of the architecture becomes apparent only gradually as one negotiates the deliberately indirect approach road.

The concrete for NCAR was mixed with crushed stone from the adjacent peaks to further the impression that the building was part of the landscape. Bush-hammering was used to create the corduroy-like texture. Here, Pei examines test slabs of the finished material before making the final selection.

out to be the final version, he "fell in love with it." The project that so merited his affection was an unusual one. There were two clusters of six-story towers that rose roughly 100 feet above the ground. Joining the clusters was a lower, two-story element. One set of towers contained laboratories, the other office space. The section between included the lobby, meeting rooms, a lounge, a cafeteria, and the library. Stretching out beneath the aboveground portion of the building were two underground levels. A third cluster of towers for additional labs and offices rose at the southern rim of the mesa.

NCAR as it finally emerged was, above all, about indirection. To minimize its impact on the city of Boulder below it, Pei sited his building well back on the top of the mesa. Intense study was given to the approach road. "How should one assault high ground?" Pei asked himself, betraying his vision of NCAR as something of a fortress. The answer he came up with: "Quietly, by night." He interpreted his conclusion by deliberately making the route up the mesa as long as possible, prolonging the journey in order to impress upon the visitor the monastic character of the destination and to heighten the impact of the ultimate arrival. Thus instead of a grand boulevard, he settled on a gently curving two-lane road that snaked about the flanks of the mesa, revealing only glimpses of the building among the lichen-spotted rocks and purple-topped thistle until it presented itself as a whole at the summit.

Even then, Pei disturbed the existing conditions as little as possible, choosing for the final approach a gap between existing rocks and trees. The deference to what was there, and the deliberate prolongation of the journey, extended to the path from the parking lot to the front door. Where the path might have skirted a wizened pine, it approached it directly, then made a half-circle detour around it before continuing. The technique had its origins in the design of the Suzhou gardens where Pei had played as a child, and it was one he would refine when he returned to China to work on the Fragrant Hill Hotel.

The forms of the NCAR buildings are harsh and occasionally self-conscious. Recalling Le Corbusier's buildings at Chandigarh, the towers rise unembellished to hoods that cover deep-set windows, creating the anthropomorphic impression that is so striking to visitors. The insistent verticality and rough concrete surfaces invoke Paul Rudolph's overtly brutalist Art and Architecture Building at Yale, begun in 1961. A somewhat gratuitous sculptural canopy at NCAR's main entrance suggests an oversize sentry on duty. But the overall effect of an armored retreat is appropriate to a setting that is alternately battered by snow and seared by alpine sun. This is not a building for the plains of India or even, as

Never before had Pei designed for a natural setting as dramatic as the one Walter Roberts secured for NCAR in the foothills of the Colorado Rocky Mountains. When Modernist precedents failed him, Pei turned to ancient sources for inspiration.

At once a fortress and a monastery, the building combines bulwarks against the elements (above) and towers from which to contemplate them in isolation (opposite).

Although the massing of the complex appears to be haphazard, it is in fact a highly ordered arrangement of sculptural shapes.

The dominant rectilinearity of the major forms is relieved at key points by the judicious use of curves (opposite).

As he would in many subsequent
buildings, Pei provided spaces to
encourage casual encounters
(above). Many of those spaces
(opposite) were designed to reinforce an appreciation of how
architecture interacts with its
natural surroundings.

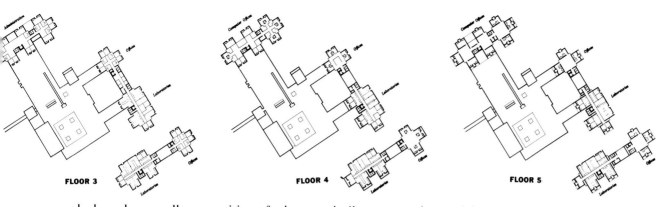

FLOOR 3   FLOOR 4   FLOOR 5

look at the overall composition of what was built suggests the need for the extra mass, which would have extended down the south side of the site, anchoring the structure more firmly. "I wanted the buildings to hug the mesa," Pei said, "so that they would appear to be tapping the soil. Now we just perch there."

There were fairly common shakedown problems after the building was finished, but some were serious. The roof leaked, and the problem led to a lawsuit, which was settled out of court. A more fundamental problem involved the expanding and contracting of the clay soil beneath the building—an unforeseen development that produced large cracks in the building. The repairs cost a good fraction of the total price of the building. Despite these problems, the director pronounced himself well satisfied by the final product, finding it "fabulously successful and extremely satisfactory functionally." It was also on budget.

It was no less successful for Pei as a stage in his development as a design architect. He had put his hand to virtually every important decision about NCAR's form and organization. And unlike the powerful but ultimately rather bland mass of the tower at MIT, which he had been obliged to share with Cossutta, NCAR showed the personal inflections of the architect who conceived it. Nevertheless, it was very much the work of a career in progress. Skillful as the siting of the building is, and masterful as the design of the approach road and the attention to the quality of the concrete may be, it is a structure that tries a bit too hard. It conveys an overall sense of youthfulness, from which it suffers as well as profits. The forms are the right ones, but in places are overwrought. Eagerness clearly threatened to overcome insight.

Pei himself confirmed this impression. Although he later described NCAR as his "breakout building," the one that allowed him to follow through on the details of a design as he had not been able to on so many of the projects he had initiated at Webb & Knapp, he also judged it "an almost sophomoric" work. "As form, it remains striking, but it is not brilliant," he said. "There are no important spaces. But for me as a conceptual designer, it was seminal. More and more as I look back, I realize how important NCAR was. I have always been drawn to elemental forms, and it was the first chance I had to express that."

It was also the beginning of an enduring friendship, one of many Pei was to establish with his best clients. Indeed, during the coming years, when Roberts came to New York, he would often visit the Peis at their Beekman Place apartment. Eileen Pei remembered going into the kitchen during one of the visits to find Roberts conducting a scientific experiment for her children in the sink.

5.

THE JOHN F. KENNEDY LIBRARY (1964–79): GATEWAY TO FAME

John F. Kennedy's assassination became, for an entire generation of Americans, what the bombing of Pearl Harbor had been for an earlier one. In Dallas on November 22, 1963, the closest the United States had ever had to a prince was murdered while still a political youth. Whatever Kennedy might have become, for good or ill, as a president was instantly and forever irrelevant. What remained was a unique and pervasive grief, and a feeling that the United States would never be quite the same—and certainly never as hopeful—again.

All over the country, planning began for memorials to the slain president, but none was to be as ambitious or as keenly followed by the public as the John F. Kennedy Library. Although there had been some plans for such a library before Kennedy's death, the assassination instantly gave it a new and tragic significance. The design of the building would clearly be an opportunity of enormous potential for the chosen architect. The selection of I. M. Pei took just about everybody— including Pei himself—by surprise, especially in light of the competition, which included most of the leading architectural talents in the world at the time.

When the saga of the Kennedy Library began, Pei was well on his way as an architect, but still considerably below the summit of his profession. To be sure, increasingly important commissions had been coming into his office—so many, in fact, that Pei again had to give up much of the direct involvement in design he had so relished during work on the National Center for Atmospheric Research. Confronted by the responsibilities of an expanding firm, he had to revert to something like the executive role he had played under Zeckendorf: locating clients, coming up with the initial design ideas, and then passing on the execution

For the John F. Kennedy Library, Pei was selected from a field of competitors that included some of the most experienced architects in the world. He is shown here with the president's widow, Jacqueline, and his brother Robert at the 1964 press conference announcing the decision.

Since leaving the Zeckendorf organization, Pei had amassed a portfolio as an architect that had grown to include a wide range of work, reflecting an equally wide range of influences. The Newhouse Communication Center (top) revealed a debt to Frank Lloyd Wright's use of ornament, while the National Airlines (TWA) terminal (above) showed strong traces of Mies van der Rohe's lean geometry.

of the actual buildings in varying degrees to his colleagues. In recognition of the expanding role of his collaborators, Pei in 1966 would change the name of the firm from I. M. Pei & Associates to I. M. Pei & Partners.

Nevertheless, Pei was still able to remain the principal design partner on a wide range of projects. In those, he showed remarkable stylistic eclecticism, working his way through most of the strongest architectural influences of the period. If NCAR and the Luce Chapel in Taiwan had owed something to Le Corbusier in their romantic anthropomorphism, the Newhouse Communication Center at Syracuse University (1961–64) tipped a hat to Frank Lloyd Wright with its weighty roof, strong horizontals, and ornamental masonry. The design for the block-long National Airlines (now TWA) terminal at Idlewild (now Kennedy) Airport (1962–70) in New York City evoked Mies van der Rohe's crisp exercises in enormous spans wrapped in glass. And in the series of airport control towers for the Federal Aviation Administration (1962–72), the Dreyfus Chemistry Building at MIT (1964–70), the Wilmington Tower in Delaware (1963–71), the campus for New College in Sarasota, Florida (1963–67), and the Cleo Rogers Memorial County Library in Columbus, Indiana (1963–69), strong traces could be found of Marcel Breuer. Altogether, there was much trying on of styles and approaches, a testing of the past and the present in search of a future.

Urban planning also remained a mainstay of Pei's work. The most notable example was a sweeping renovation of downtown Boston. As early as 1954, Boston officials had been searching for a way to replace the downtrodden area around Scollay Square with a government center. Pei, working closely with Cobb, developed a plan that transformed what had become known as a "sinkhole of depravity."[1] demolishing roughly eighty-five percent of the buildings in a sixty-acre area of central Boston and relocating 859 businesses. The warren of narrow streets that had laced the neighborhood was replaced by a network of major thoroughfares and a host of new buildings, including a massive city hall designed by the young firm of Kallmann, McKinnell & Knowles.

These and other undertakings had gone far to establish Pei as a national presence, but the Kennedy Library was to have a unique impact on him personally and on the firm generally. It was to be the longest job the Pei office had ever been involved with, and—except for the travails that were to overtake the John Hancock Tower in Boston—it was to be the most painful for the senior partner. Although intended as a memorial to a president, it became no less a symbol of the deep unhappiness the country itself was to experience in the decade following his death. Pei remembered that at the time the project for the library

began, Kennedy was regarded as "a god." By the time it was dedicated, fifteen years later, America was hard put to find a mere hero. Pei himself went through a parallel course from elation to disappointment. "The years we spent on the Kennedy Library were very wasteful ones," he said. "As far as architecture is concerned, they did nothing for me, nothing for my growth."

Whatever suffering Pei endured on the way to its completion, the library proved to be a turning point in his career. If NCAR had finally allowed him to test himself (however briefly) as a hands-on architect, his very selection for the library commission did nothing less than pave the way to superstardom. The reputation among potential clients that had dogged Pei ever since leaving Zeckendorf—that he had been the "house architect" to a man with money trouble—vanished. The Kennedy Library, recalled Pei years later, "brought us back. It removed that stigma, and it opened the future."

The American tradition of building presidential libraries had been established well before John Kennedy arrived at the White House. Franklin Roosevelt formalized the practice by donating his papers to the nation and housing them near his family home at Hyde Park, New York. Kennedy began the planning for his own library early in his administration. As a product of Boston and Harvard, he had not surprisingly discussed the possibility of retiring to Cambridge after leaving office. Apart from his own ties to the area, Kennedy wanted his library to be an active resource used by scholars and a place that would encourage young people to go into politics. Accordingly, he had considered a different sort of presidential library, one that would include a museum for his personal effects, a repository for his archives, and an institute for the study of government. The selection of Cambridge, with its multiplicity of educational institutions, made eminent sense. Moreover, since he would have been only fifty-one if he left the White House at the end of a second term, in 1969, he hoped to teach at Harvard.

Having decided that the library should be located in Cambridge, Kennedy had little trouble selecting a site. It was on the Charles River, just across Boylston Street from Harvard's mock-Georgian "river houses," the most sought after of the undergraduate dormitories. The trouble with the site was that it was occupied by marshaling yards used to store the rolling stock of the Massachusetts Bay Transportation Authority.

From the outset, it became clear that the so-called car barns were going to be extremely difficult, if not impossible, to acquire for the library. Removing them meant finding an alternate storage area for the trains and rerouting a goodly amount of subway track. So Harvard's president, Nathan Pusey, who was eager to

The architect's fondness for simple, sculptural forms had grown stronger with his series of fifty control towers for the Federal Aviation Administration (top) and the Wilmington Tower (above) in Delaware.

have Kennedy's papers at the university, proposed instead a 2.2-acre site in Brighton, diagonally across the Charles from the car barns and next to the campus of the Harvard Business School. The university would donate the land. The offer was accepted. In October of 1963, Kennedy was in Cambridge with friends to see a Harvard-Columbia football game. At half time, with the score tied at 3–3, he and two aides left, and as they passed the Business School, Kennedy proceeded to tell them about the library that was to rise nearby. A month later, he was dead.

Within months of the assassination, the Kennedy family went into action to make the library a reality.

The formal process of finding an architect was put in the hands of a Kennedy family friend named William Walton, who had served as the president's campaign manager in New York and later was appointed chairman of the Commission of Fine Arts, which had responsibility for the architecture of all federal buildings. Walton was a colorful man by any measure and perfectly suited to the Kennedys' combination of buccaneering and taste. As a journalist with Time-Life, Walton had jumped into Normandy with the 82nd Airborne division (from General James Gavin's own plane) in the early hours of the D-day invasion. He was also an accomplished painter. It fell to Walton to frame the requirements and screen the possible architects for the Kennedy project. The job was, as he later described it, "the plum all of them wanted."

Early in 1964, a building committee was established, and an extraordinary meeting was convened at the Washington home of Senator Edward Kennedy, the late president's brother. Among those present were Jacqueline Kennedy, Attorney General Robert Kennedy, Sargent Shriver, and Arthur Schlesinger. Also present were members of the Advisory Committee on Arts and Architecture, a widely representative body assembled by the Kennedys to help guide the selection process. Its members included Pietro Belluschi, dean of MIT's architecture school; Louis Kahn; Mies van der Rohe; I. M. Pei; Hideo Sasaki, a landscape architect from Cambridge, Massachusetts; Benjamin Thompson, a Cambridge architect; John Carl Warnecke (a friend of the Kennedy family who was to design the Kennedy Memorial in Arlington, Virginia); and John Kenneth Galbraith, a former United States ambassador to India who was then a professor at Harvard.

At the start of the meeting, the late president's own hopes for the project were reviewed. Discussion then turned to the nature of the building itself, which Mrs. Kennedy said "must express the beliefs that Jack gave his life for." Warnecke summed up the change in the scope of the project since the president's death by saying, "What was originally planned was a building. Now the total structure must be a fitting memorial."

If there were as yet no firm concepts in mind about the architecture of that memorial, a clue was dropped at this meeting about the direction of the family's thinking. Robert Kennedy told the group, "If the President stood for anything, it was innovation. It was the ability of young people to do things that had formerly been done only by older people. To him the appeal of any competition was that someone young and relatively unknown might be the best man and might come up with something absolutely brilliant."[2]

The next step was a meeting at the Ritz-Carlton Hotel in Boston in April of 1964, to which a stellar group of architects had been invited. In addition to the architect members of the advisory committee, the group included Alvar Aalto from Finland, Franco Albini from Italy, Lucio Costa from Brazil, Sven Markelius from Sweden, Sir Basil Spense from England, Kenzo Tange from Japan, and Paul Thiry and Hugh Stubbins, Jr., from the United States. For two days the group pondered the assignment and discussed ways of advising Mrs. Kennedy—who was to have the final say—on selecting an architect. The possibility of holding a competition was raised and almost immediately dismissed because, as Walton put it, "the architect must, first and foremost, be compatible with Mrs. Kennedy and other members of the family," something a competition could not guarantee. ("You would have to surrender to the judges," explained Walton.) Finally, all agreed that each of the architects should recommend the names of three others they thought would be qualified for the assignment, place them in a sealed envelope, and deliver them to Walton.

The following morning, as the group was boarding the Kennedy plane *Caroline* at Boston's Logan Airport for a luncheon visit to the family compound at Hyannisport on Cape Cod, Walton collected the envelopes and repaired to a nearby hangar to count the ballots. The seven names that appeared most often were Gordon Bunshaft of Skidmore, Owings & Merrill, Philip Johnson, Kahn, Mies, Pei, Paul Rudolph, and Warnecke. Walton recorded the results and destroyed the ballots in order to preserve the secrecy on which the architects had insisted.

The gathering at Hyannisport was more than a social nicety. It was intended at least in part to give the Kennedys a sense of what sort of men they were dealing with. Tange, according to Walton, was "charming," as was Aalto. Mrs. Kennedy was immediately drawn to Kahn. "How I loved that man," she said, remembering the occasion years later. "He had that light." But he virtually

Pei was far less established as an architect than the other guests, but he made an indelible personal impression on Mrs. Kennedy, who had ultimate responsibility for selecting an architect.

disqualified himself in the eyes of some others. "He kept going off into left field," said Walton, describing the architect's frequent flights into poetic abstraction. "Bobby would look at me and just roll his eyes." The seventy-eight-year-old Mies, puffing on his signature cigar, reminded Mrs. Kennedy of "an Egyptian potentate" and, she said, conveyed "a sense that he didn't really want the job."

After the Hyannisport gathering, the Kennedy team assembled folders on the work of the leading candidates, and over a period of weeks Walton and others of the advisers traveled to half a dozen cities looking at examples of the architects' work. Each man was then interviewed in his office. In anticipation of Mrs. Kennedy's visit to New York, the Pei headquarters had been given a lightning face-lift, and Leonard Jacobson had been assigned to dust off the model of the Idlewild terminal project, which had been stalled for some time, so that there would be something tangible to look at. A young draftsman who was working for Pei at the time remembered that the occasion was treated like a royal event and that he and a number of his colleagues were standing like children on tiptoes to get a glimpse over the partitions as the famous visitor swept through.

When Pei greeted Mrs. Kennedy, he began by apologizing that he had so little to show her and confessed with elaborate self-effacement that "the big commissions of the monumental sort—they don't usually come my way." He then proceeded to screen a selection of slides of the firm's work. According to Mrs. Kennedy, who had not actually visited any of Pei's buildings, what impressed her most about his presentation was his description of how he had tried to make each design respond to its location, choosing shapes and materials he thought were most appropriate to the purpose of the building and the specific conditions of the site. "He didn't seem to have just one way to solve a problem," she said. "He seemed to approach each commission thinking only of it and then develop a way to make something beautiful."

The occasion was in marked contrast to some of Mrs. Kennedy's meetings with the other contenders, who seemed to her already to have made up their minds about what kind of library they would do. "This building was going to be complicated," she said. "I thought I. M.'s temperament was right. He was like a wonderful hunting dog when you slip the leash."

Pei's presentation also pleased the other members of the delegation. One of them was Stephen Smith, husband of the president's sister Jean, who was also present. Smith had been appointed president of the Kennedy Library Corporation, the body that was to oversee the project. As Smith remembered the meeting at Pei's office, the architect's limited portfolio made an immediate impression.

Pei was vacationing in Italy with his family when Eason Leonard cabled him. The subsequent call to Walton revealed that Pei's dark-horse campaign had succeeded.

The group was especially struck by the Society Hill buildings in Philadelphia. Walton recalled that they were also interested in the Luce Chapel, NCAR, and Pei's design for the Everson Museum of Art, which was about to go into construction in Syracuse, New York. "When we saw Pei's work," said Jean Smith, "there was no question he was it. His work is like he is—the poetry comes through." Pei was careful to expand the discussion beyond architecture and at one point began talking about Kennedy's love of the sea.

During the visit to Pei's office, Walton remarked to the architect in Mrs. Kennedy's presence that his most recent buildings seemed to represent a major step forward in his career as a designer. Pei agreed and conceded gracefully that the job should probably go to Mies as the most prominent of the contenders. But then he added, according to Walton: "I feel that I am on the verge of my best work." Walton recalled that Mrs. Kennedy "almost gave him the job right then and there." She might as well have. In the elevator after leaving Pei's office, she whispered to her sister-in-law, "I don't care if he *hasn't* done much, I just knew he was the one."

Mrs. Kennedy later conveyed her feelings to André Meyer, a prominent financier and close friend, who thought she should look at a Pei building in the flesh before making a final decision. Having been involved through his firm, Lazard Frères, in the financing of Kips Bay, Meyer said, "Let me show you what he has done for us." As Mrs. Kennedy recalled it, they went, on "a wonderful, misty evening," for a leisurely stroll through the Kips Bay complex. In the course of it, Meyer cautioned her, "This Pei, he is very expensive." She was undeterred. "I marshaled all these rational reasons to pick I. M.," she said, "but it was really an emotional decision. He was so full of promise, like Jack; they were born in the same year. I decided it would be fun to take a great leap with him."

The chosen architect, meanwhile, had left for a vacation in Italy with his family and was staying at a house near Pisa. While there, on July 22, 1964, he received a telegram from his partner Eason Leonard. It read: "Please telephone Mr. William Walton at ADams 2-0017 in Washington immediately." Pei went to a cafe in the town square to call the United States. "It took forever to get through," he said. His wife brought all four of the children to the square to wait with him while the trans-Atlantic operator struggled for a connection. When Pei finally got Walton on the phone, he heard the incredible news.

The official announcement of Pei's selection was made at a press conference on December 14, 1964, at New York's Hotel Pierre. Robert Kennedy was there, as were President Pusey of Harvard and Eugene Black, the president of the

Facing the Harvard College "river houses" across the Charles River from the business school and the athletic fields, the library was to occupy the site of the car barns of the Massachusetts Bay Transportation Authority (foreground).

World Bank, who reported that fund-raising for the project (which included collections of nickels and dimes contributed by schoolchildren across the country) was going well.

Pei's better-known colleagues might have been forgiven for resenting the choice of such a relatively green talent, but there was widespread support for the decision in the architecture world. Pei's former teacher Marcel Breuer was quoted in the *New York Times* as saying, "Pei is a person of complete honesty, and his personality and his architecture have a total identity. There is no fakery or facade. He was a wonderful choice for the Kennedy Library."[3]

Pei's original timetable for the library was reasonable, if not generous: six months for the acquisition of the site, six months for design, a year for working drawings, and two and a half years for construction. Quoting Robert Kennedy's remarks at the press conference, *Progressive Architecture* headlined its brief piece on the selection in its January 1965 issue, "Good Luck, Mr. Pei!"[4] Little did anyone know just how much luck he was going to need.

The first problem was the location. As Warnecke had pointed out at the first planning session in Washington, it would now have to accommodate a memorial as well as the original museum, archives, and institute for government. The Brighton site was rapidly becoming too small. Furthermore, no one was happy about the highway traffic in the immediate area or the view of the local power station. Once Pei was selected, he reinforced the objections and set about persuading the backers that the car-barn site originally picked by the president was worth fighting for after all.

Theodore Musho, an associate in Pei's firm who had joined the office in 1961 and was to become his main collaborator on the design, said he thought the negotiations over the site brought out a central characteristic of Pei's personality. "I. M. sees architecture as politics," Musho said. "He proved it by getting Rose Kennedy to go to the Massachusetts State House and say, 'This is what my son would have wanted.'"

Pei credited his years with Zeckendorf for preparing him for the political struggle that so quickly enveloped the project. ("The training finally paid off," he said.) But he also had help from Mrs. Kennedy. "Jackie supported the reopening

The original scheme for the Kennedy Library included a truncated glass pyramid intended to flood the main space with light.

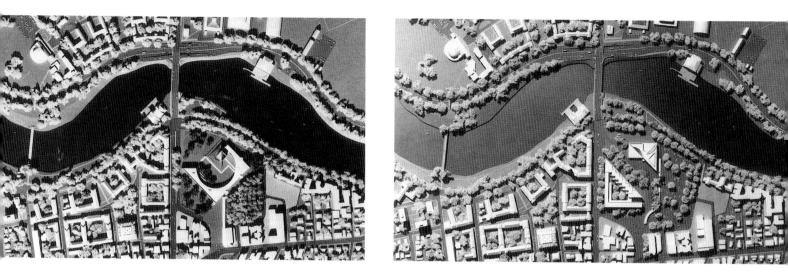

of the car-barn site," he said. "Without her, Harvard would not have gone along."

Even though moving the car barns meant delaying the entire project, the development actually pleased Harvard enormously. The university had long wanted to rid itself of the unsightly tracks and sheds, and it saw the relocated library as a unique vehicle for expansion in a tightening Cambridge real estate market. For Harvard, said Walton, the powerful intervention of the Kennedys turned out to be "a dream come true."

In October of 1965, the Commonwealth of Massachusetts appropriated $7 million to buy the MBTA site, and the following March the agency accepted $6,098,400 for slightly over twelve acres. The MBTA agreed to be out by 1970 and began looking for storage space for its equipment in South Boston.

Pei's first proposal for the building included an eighty-five-foot-high truncated glass pyramid that was to serve as the centerpiece of the museum portion. It was embraced by a five-story semicircular building intended for the archives, the Institute of Politics, and the Kennedy School of Government, a reorganized and renamed Harvard graduate school which was to be operated by the university. The pyramid, as well as the plan, which was based on a series of superimposed geometric shapes, marked the first appearance of a vocabulary that was to evolve in Pei's work over the next twenty years, reaching its purest articulation in the design for the Louvre in Paris and the Meyerson Symphony Center in Dallas. But it had a special appropriateness to this early undertaking in the name of a martyred president. "The man died young—in his beauty, not his wisdom," Musho said. Accordingly, the main space was to be flooded with daylight to express "a sense of optimism and hope."

When the tentative design was ready and a model had been made, Pei and Musho packed it up for a private presentation to Mrs. Kennedy at her New York apartment. When they arrived, as Musho recalled it, Mrs. Kennedy was busy speaking with the conductor Leonard Bernstein about the commission for a Mass to be played at the opening of the Kennedy Center for the Performing Arts in Washington. Pei and Musho were asked to wait. (Musho described Pei as "nervous as a kite" while they cooled their heels.) When Mrs. Kennedy finally came in to greet them and see the model, the architects fell to explaining the

The model of the first proposal (left) shows a semicircular composition tethered by the pyramid. In the second version (right), the pyramid has disappeared and the building has been reduced in size and split into two distinct masses.

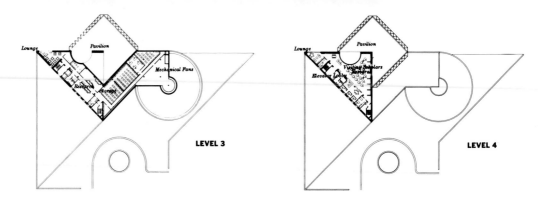

LEVEL 3

LEVEL 4

organization of the spaces and the inspiration for the glass-enclosed atrium. They gave her some time to ponder it and then asked, fully expecting suggestions for changes, "What do we do?" To their shock and delight, the president's widow replied, "Don't do anything. I like it the way it is." Watching her study the model, Musho concluded, "She understood the philosophy of the building."

So it seemed. As Mrs. Kennedy remembered the event, she found that the design fulfilled her hope that the building "would inspire young people. A presidential library is by nature static, but the way I. M. described this one involved you so in his excitement. It sounded wonderful."

Nevertheless, the refinement of the design required time, and delays over clearing and preparing the site—which proved to be unexpectedly swampy— slowed the process for what turned out to be years. "The desire to grasp at the uniqueness of something like this leads to constant redefinition, and recurrent analysis," Musho told a reporter with massive understatement some years later.[5] The design was not unveiled to the public until May of 1973.

Pleasing as the original design may have been to its client, it did not strike the residents of Cambridge, including some Harvard academics, with the same force. A number of faculty members felt the centralization of existing departments of the university into a single complex to create the Kennedy School of Government was not appropriate and preferred their scattered locations around the campus. More telling was the feeling that the planned reorganization was an artificial effort intended to support the building, rather than an academic mission. "There is no educational or philosophical framework," said one miffed professor. "It's a confluence of parts of the Faculty of Arts and Sciences and the Kennedy School of Government—some economics, government and political science with an international flavor."[6]

Other citizens of Cambridge, meanwhile, began to fear that, whatever the aesthetic merits (or academic demerits) of the architecture, the institution itself would pose a threat to the community. Opponents argued that the complex would in fact be more of a tourist attraction than a scholarly enterprise, and while many welcomed the idea of a library, many more feared the impact a museum might have on the surroundings. The main complaint was that it would draw such crowds—estimated at two million people a year by some—that the added automobile traffic would make the already congested Harvard Square area impassable and that the small-scale character of the neighborhood would be ruined by the monumental presence of the buildings.

Pei lost count of the meetings that were called to calm the community. But

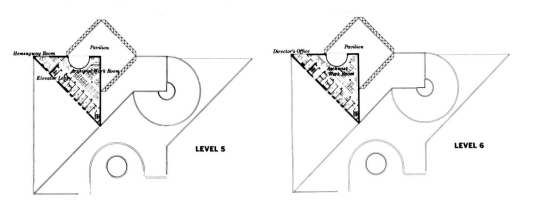

LEVEL 5

LEVEL 6

LEVEL 7

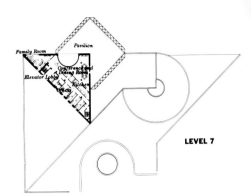

LEVEL 8

LEVEL 9

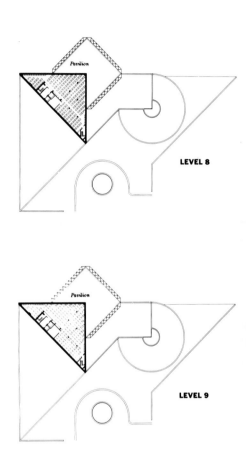

he rarely missed the important ones, eagerly manning the lectern to explain the design. Mrs. Kennedy was impressed by his patience. He was, she said, "as faithful to those meetings as you'd be to your children's school play."

Nevertheless, the nine years that had passed since the announcement of the project had been ample time for opponents to marshal their forces. The naysaying over the project itself was fueled by what was happening to the country at large. Inflation was worse than at any time since the Korean War. As early as 1970, Pei had estimated that the funds originally set aside for the library—roughly seventeen million dollars—would by then cover only sixty percent of the cost. But most important, perhaps, was the radically changed social and political climate of the nation. Robert Kennedy had been assassinated in 1968. The war in Vietnam was consuming thousands of lives and billions of dollars with no prospect of ending. The romantic image of the Green Berets (President Kennedy's elite force which had been promoted as socially conscious commandos) had been replaced by that of Lieutenant Calley, the murderer of women and children at My Lai. Reflecting on the period in a 1980 article in *Architectural Record*, Pei concluded that "much of the country and its intellectual community had become blinded to, or otherwise despairing of, the integrity and meaning and value of the Presidency."[7] The library proved a ready target for those soured on the promise of Camelot.

By then, too, Pusey had left the presidency of Harvard. For Pei, that meant that his "champion" was gone. And the architect was beset by problems of his own elsewhere. Having landed the commission for the John Hancock Tower in Boston at least partly as a result of the fame that came to him with the Kennedy job, he was now dealing with the growing disaster created by the cracking of its windows, which began in November 1972, when the building was still under construction.

In the face of the mounting opposition in Cambridge, and the rising inflation nationwide, Pei and his team embarked on a revised design. Unveiled in June of 1974, it was to cost the same seventeen million dollars estimated for the original, but was one-third smaller in bulk and roughly half the height of the first structure. Instead of a single large building, there were two smaller ones separated from each other by an open-air corridor. One of the structures was to house the museum and archives, the other the Institute of Politics, the Kennedy School of Government, and the remaining facilities. The eighty-five-foot-high glass pyramid was gone; instead, there was a forty-nine-foot-high triangular mass done in brick in an attempt to blend with the nearby Harvard dormitories. To accommo-

As it was finally built on Columbia Point, the library was a single mass, but the plan was based on what was becoming a familiar Pei pattern of interlocking geometric shapes.

date the changes, masses of documents originally intended for the archives were to be transferred to the Boston suburb of Waltham.

From the start, the local resistance to the library had had far less to do with architecture than with feelings that the undertaking was a high-handed assault on the shabby-genteel character of the Harvard Square area. The new design did little to alleviate that feeling; if anything, it intensified it. Father Richard J. Shmaruk, an associate pastor of St. Paul's Church in Cambridge and a member of the Harvard Square Task Force, a civic group opposed to the library, saw the scaling-down as proof of the Kennedys' underlying priorities: "In order to salvage the museum, which we now see as the big thing, the Kennedys will be leaving sixteen million documents in Waltham and bringing in only six million documents which the scholars will presumably use. This has opened our eyes. The Kennedys want people, droves of people to come to a new kind of Disneyland. The scholars can go to Waltham. This emasculates the President's dream—it has become a mockery, a farce, a facade."[8]

By this time, Walton and many of the other backers of the library were near the end of their collective tether. Walton conceded that there were some legitimate community concerns, but he was growing increasingly bitter about what he called the "Brattle Street elite." Most of the community problems were solvable, he insisted, "but the upper-class hippies didn't want to solve them, they just wanted to show their political power." Smith, who was watching the costs soar with the delays, took a similar view. He accused the Cambridge upper crust of exploiting fears that the library would bring in "shorts-wearing, gum-chewing" mobs. "There are a lot of under-used psyches in an academic community," he said.

Mrs. Kennedy, who had become Mrs. Aristotle Onassis on October 20, 1968, was growing steadily more removed from the library saga, but was nevertheless concerned about the deepening quagmire in Cambridge. Looking back on the events, she said she realized the opponents "could have kept it in the courts for twenty years." Musho, who was by then carrying the day-to-day design burden while the senior partner saw to the Hancock crisis and the other commissions that had come to the firm, said that the sniping drove the team to consider leaving the archives building at Harvard and taking the museum somewhere else. That way, Musho said, Harvard could "let the people in Hawaiian shirts go there. It was terrible what some of those mature people in Cambridge said." But that option was not attractive either. When a proposal was made during one meeting that the museum be put in the unused space below the Kennedy Center in

The excitement that followed Pei's selection to design the Kennedy Library was soon replaced by frustration over the resistance raised by the Cambridge community. When the building was relocated to a point of land in Boston Harbor, it gained a dramatic setting, but it had already lost much of its architectural inspiration.

Located on a site with no real natural or architectural context (opposite), the library was conceived as an isolated piece of sculpture, allowing Pei to indulge his taste for intricate combinations of pure geometric forms (above).

The most impressive aspect of
the design is the 110-foot-high
atrium. Using a technique he
would refine in the East Building
of the National Gallery, Pei
provided only a glimpse of the
enormous space (above) from the
main entrance, delaying the full
impact. The unembellished volume focuses the visitor's attention on the enormous flag and the
decorative effect of the spaceframe (opposite).

Pei's design makes full use of the seaward view (opposite), which is in a constant state of flux as the weather changes. The overwhelming scale of the atrium (above) tends to humble the visitor, an appropriate effect for a building that was intended to be as much a memorial as a museum and research center.

111

Washington, Mrs. Onassis exploded, "Are you proposing that we put the Kennedy Library in a *basement?*" That, said Musho, "was the end of that."

So persistent was the opposition that some members of the Kennedy team began brooding about pulling Pei off the project altogether and starting over with someone new. Only when some insiders threatened to quit and go public with the scheming was the idea abandoned.

The architecture critic Mildred Schmertz, writing in the December 1974 issue of *Architectural Record*, got to the heart of the matter: "The problem of the Kennedy Library is not primarily one of architectural design in the limited sense of the word, it is one of context. If the Library is built, the City of Cambridge must change to accommodate it. Many of the Library's opponents don't like what they foresee."[9] Their fears were fueled by an environmental impact study, which was released in 1975 and concluded that the project would subject the community to an additional one million visitors a year. (Curiously, it also concluded that the impact would not be serious, a view that further inflamed the opponents.)

The attacks were especially wounding to a man who had such ties to Harvard. This, after all, was the place where Pei had got his first glimpse of what architecture as an art could be. His wife had studied there, he had served on the faculty, and in the years since then he had sent all three of his sons there. Sandi was at the architecture school at the height of the controversy and had to watch his father's work battered on a regular basis by the *Harvard Crimson*, the undergraduate newspaper. Although Pei saw his son frequently during the period, he did not discuss the controversy that was boiling around the library. Nor did he tell Mrs. Onassis about his mounting frustration. "Do you think I. M. would ever let me see the pain he was in?" she asked rhetorically. "*Never.*" He did let his wife see it, and she became increasingly aware of the toll the struggle was taking on him. "I could tell how tired he was by the way he opened the door at the end of the day," she said. "His footsteps were dragging. It was very hard for I. M. to see that so many people didn't want the building."

The criticism often turned personal. Smith felt that some people were being deliberately cruel to Pei. Musho was later quoted as saying that "the question was not program, not cost, not even the physical reality of the building. The question was: How can you cope?"[10]

As the community resistance mounted, Harvard began to distance itself from the project. "The university was willing to have it at that point," Mrs. Onassis recalled, "but only if it was so small that it wouldn't attract the throngs. By then I was annoyed by them; we had given them so much. I think some

Although powerful in its use of grand architectural gestures, the library in its final form lacked the attention to detail that would come to characterize Pei's later buildings.

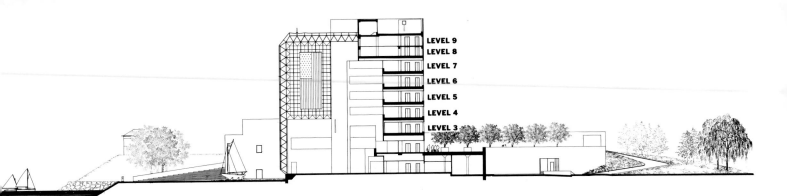

LEVEL 9
LEVEL 8
LEVEL 7
LEVEL 6
LEVEL 5
LEVEL 4
LEVEL 3

members of the Kennedy family were a bit too reverent about Harvard."

In the face of the environmental impact study and the prospect of extended litigation if the project went forward, the library forces finally capitulated, announcing in February of 1975 that they would no longer try to build the museum and the archives in Cambridge.

Almost immediately, invitations began to pour in from other institutions eager to house either or both of the facilities. There were well over a hundred in all. One possible site was the University of Massachusetts at Amherst; another was offered near Hyannisport. Yet another possibility was the Massachusetts town of Fall River, where the destroyer *Joseph P. Kennedy, Jr.* was moored. One of the more attractive sites was the disused Boston Navy Yard in Charlestown. But none was quite right.

Neither was Columbia Point, a spit of largely artificial land protruding into Boston Harbor eight miles from the original site and adjacent to the Harbor Campus of the University of Massachusetts. But Robert Wood, who was then president of the university and a friend of Edward Kennedy's, was eager to have the library, which would offer his comparatively humble institution some glory by association. What was more attractive to the Kennedy team was that Wood was offering enough land—9.5 acres—to keep the museum and the archives in one place, while providing sufficient space for the parking that had been such an obstacle to the Cambridge solution. Under his proposal, the School of Government and the Institute of Politics would be left behind at Harvard.

A meeting of the Kennedy Library Committee was called for November 24, 1975, in Pei's office to consider the various alternative sites, and the decision was put to a secret ballot. Columbia Point passed by one vote. Mrs. Onassis was among those who voted for it, and after the decision was announced, she turned to her sister-in-law Eunice Shriver and said, "I'm so glad. It has gone on long enough. The death agony can't last forever." Reflecting on the decision in 1989, she cited something Joseph Kennedy had said to her not long after her marriage to his son, "You do the best you can, and then the hell with it."

The supporters of the new site went to some lengths to put the best face on it. President Kennedy had been an enthusiastic sailor, they pointed out, and here was the sea at the front door. He had come up through Boston politics, and there was the Boston skyline spread out on the horizon. He had tended toward the intellectual, and if UMASS wasn't Harvard, it was at least a university. "Ironically," said Smith with some effort, "Columbia Point turned out to be a better setting than Cambridge."

Sections through the library and its site (above and opposite) show the relationship between the research and public areas of the building.

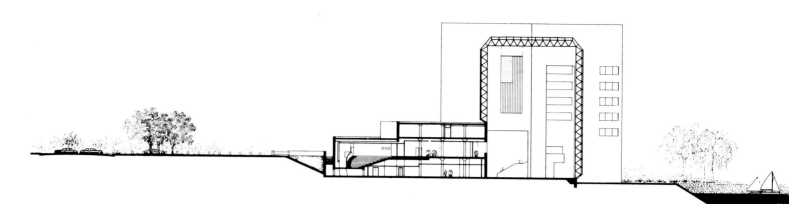

But for all its allure on paper, the proposed site had problems. For one thing, it lay close to the UMASS buildings. Pei felt it was too close, that the location "was not commensurate with the importance of the building" and that the library would be perceived as "a parasite on the university." Furthermore, at low tide, the view from the building would have included a broad expanse of rich-smelling mud.

By this time, some members of the library group were desperate to avoid further delays. Having already considered and rejected the idea of dropping Pei earlier in the process, they quietly consulted with Hugh Stubbins, Jr., who had been among the original candidates for the commission, on an alternate design for the site Pei so disliked. To most architects, such a no-confidence vote would have been a stunning humiliation. Pei took it in stride. "I thought Stubbins was being opportunistic," he said. "But I kept it to myself." Pei remained confident that he would prevail. And he did.

But it took some doing. The site Pei wanted was one just to the north of the one that had been selected. And it was not perfect, either. Indeed, it had been created out of landfill dumped there during the excavations for the UMASS campus, and it was crossed by a huge sewer pipe that pumped millions of gallons of Boston's waste into the harbor just off the point. But at least this bit of land was farther from the university buildings, and it provided a better view of the water. As Musho put it, "If you were going to be here, you ought to be here for a reason, which was the water."

To persuade the Kennedy people that they should move once again, Pei's team arranged for the hire of a large flatbed truck, which was driven to the site the family had selected. The main participants, including Mrs. Onassis and Edward Kennedy, were brought aboard and shown the view. They then clambered down while the truck was moved to the northeast tip of the point, where they reembarked. Confronted with the clearly superior panorama of sea, islands, and ships, they quickly decided to move. Pei, for one, had a brief burst of reinspiration. As he said later, "Here, for a public-spirited President we needed to create a public-spirited building—a place where the impetus to serve, to educate, and to lead, could be sheltered, informed, and symbolized by the building and its contents."[11]

Work on the third and final design began in March 1976. And there was much work to be done. Because the site was located on fill, pilings had to be sunk 150 feet down to reach rock. And since much of the fill was made up of sewage and garbage, a complicated drainage and venting system had to be designed to prevent contamination of the building's interior by methane gas. "It wasn't very poetic," said Wandelmaier, who handled the management of the job, "but it was a

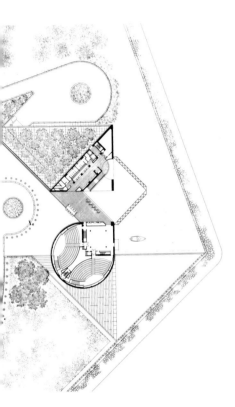

fact. We went back and forth on all sorts of options to find one that was compatible with the design." But the designers were able to exploit some of the hazards to their profit. By adding more fill to cover the exposed sewer pipe, they could "bury" the lower portion of the building, allowing visitors to enter at "ground" level and find themselves overlooking the lower portion of the main public space, which measured 80 feet on each side and soared skyward to a height of 110 feet.

That public space was the offspring of the truncated pyramid in the first Cambridge design and was intended to have the same inspirational effect. While it could be glimpsed immediately upon entering the building, its full impact was deliberately withheld. The most striking characteristic of Pei's final design for the Kennedy Library was just this—gratification delayed through a manipulation of the approach. (It was a technique he was to use to much better effect, however, for the East Building of the National Gallery.)

In plan, the Columbia Point building recalls the intersecting forms of the original Cambridge design: a circle, a square, and a triangle. But the intersections are considerably more complex. The visitor approaching the 113,000-square-foot building is met by a two-story mass in the form of a parallelogram. Rising to the left is a wedge-shaped nine-story tower clad in chalk-white concrete. The upper portion of the tower contains the building's archival, educational, and administrative functions. ("We put the archives in the tower, because that's where the brains ought to be," quipped Musho.) One wall of the tower is perforated by small windows, the other is blank and intersects the dark-glass prism housing the atrium. To the right is a white cylinder that falls off toward the water and is bordered by a curving stairway.

At the entrance, there is a view through to the water beyond the atrium, but the "procession" leads off to the right and into the cylinder, which houses two auditoriums for the showing of films on the president's life and career. From the auditoriums, visitors descend to the darkened galleries that contain the exhibits (designed by the firm of Chermayeff & Geismar). Only after passing through these is the visitor routed out onto the atrium floor to confront the full height of the glassed-in space and the spectacle of Dorchester Bay beyond. The atrium itself is unembellished except for an enormous American flag suspended from the space-frame ceiling.

Outside, facing the water, is President Kennedy's sailboat, *Victura*. The grounds are planted with dune grass and wild white roses, an idea proposed by Mrs. Paul Mellon, a friend of the Kennedys' and an avid landscape designer who, at Mrs. Onassis's request, had redone the White House gardens. (She explained the idea for the dune grass to Musho by saying, "I think the president was a wind man.")

One element of the landscape plan, this one proposed by another collaborator, did not survive. The idea was to place a cluster of ornamental rocks at the edge of the site, and a young member of the staff had been assigned to scour the Massachusetts coast for appropriate samples. When they had been located, some distance north of Boston, Pei and Mrs. Onassis dutifully journeyed to the spot to take a look. But the travel schedule had not been coordinated with the tide, and by the time they arrived, the rocks were all but covered by water, looking, Mrs. Onassis recalled, "like little hippopotamus ears." The rocks were quietly abandoned.

The library was dedicated on October 20, 1979. The ceremony included a reading of the inscription on the wall of the atrium, a quotation from President Kennedy's inaugural address: "All this will not be finished in the first one hundred days. Nor will it be finished in the first one thousand days, nor in the life of this Administration, nor even perhaps in our lifetime on this planet. But let us begin." Although fraught with meaning for the president's own unfulfilled hopes, the words seemed bizarrely appropriate to the saga of the building itself.

The critical reaction to the completed Kennedy Library was oddly muted. Pei loyalists praised it for all the predictable reasons, saying how appropriate the bold forms were to the memory of a bold president. But even some more independent voices seemed hesitant to depart from the expected text. Perhaps it was the shadow of the murdered president and the fading glow of the Kennedy family that held them back. Perhaps, too, it was the growing prominence of the architect, who, having been anointed by the original commission and having survived the calamity of the Hancock windows, was now enjoying an outpouring of adulation for the East Building of the National Gallery of Art, which had opened to the public in June of 1978. In any case, there seemed to be a general feeling of sympathy for the pain that had been suffered in delivering the library and no wish to compound it with a lack of kindness.

An exception was John Morris Dixon, writing in the January 1980 *Progressive Architecture*, who said in a brief review of dead-center accuracy: "The building's forms lack the underlying formal order one expects of a Pei work; and the blank surfaces fail, at close range, to exhibit the refined, eternal-looking qualities for which the firm is noted.... The whole architectural experience is of incomplete gestures, thwarted satisfactions." [12]

Indeed, as a monument, the Kennedy Library makes all the right moves:

The site for the library (above and opposite) offers vistas of downtown Boston and the city's harbor.

soaring, gleaming, thrusting. But there is clearly something lacking. The exterior geometry is too obvious, as if the parts had been ordered from a Pei catalogue and assembled according to an instruction book. At the same time, the interior organization is too complex, leading visitors through a programmatically logical, but ultimately confusing and uninspiring maze. The payoff is supposed to be the arrival in the atrium, but here, too, the proportions seem off. The space itself is, for all its apparent grandeur, pinched; the volume is too tall. The enormous flag has unquestioned power, but, consistent with the rest of the building, scant grace. The Kennedy Library *looks* like an I. M. Pei building, but it doesn't *feel* like one.

Pei survived the trials of the Kennedy Library, but the architecture did not. It had been left behind in the wake of less maddening commissions that allowed him to develop his taste for sculptural forms, elegant spaces, and the precise assembly of fine materials. By the time the library opened, Pei had refined the ideas on which it had been based, but the loss of his personal commitment to seeing it through with the passion in which it had been conceived was all too evident.

There was no lack of reasons for the absence of spirit to animate this architectural flesh. After all, from the beginning, just about everything that could have gone wrong with the project did. The fifteen-year saga had drained the architect himself of his enthusiasm for the building. The money had shrunk, and the original staff working on the building had turned over many times. According to Pei, it was largely through the efforts of Musho that the building retained any distinction at all. "Ted slugged it through," said the senior man. "He shouldered the heaviest burden, trying to make something of it, trying to keep the project engaged." To make matters worse, the magic had all but gone out of the Kennedy myth to which the library was devoted.

Pei might have been expected to resent the treatment he had received. He had been shunted from a university he loved. He had been exposed to public scorn at a level that would have driven many men from the job. And, on at least two occasions, he was on the point of being abandoned by his backers. Characteristically, Pei was neither bitter nor particularly forthcoming on his feelings about his patrons, putting the experience behind him with a steely capacity to concentrate on the present and the future. Reflecting on the library in 1988, he said with only a brief downward glance: "Circumstances made it impossible for the Kennedys to be a great client. By the time the building was finished, I was seeking my satisfaction elsewhere."

Walton thought he saw more hurt than Pei was willing to reveal. "We had

taken him through the worst," he said. "Three designs, three sites. That's not the way to get first-rate architecture. Pei's heart had been broken along the way."

In a twist of architectural irony, the very fact that Pei was able to "seek his satisfaction elsewhere" was almost entirely due to the original Kennedy commission. The publicity following his selection to do the library put the stamp of approval on Pei among the country's arbiters of architecture. Neither the public pain of the Kennedy Library process nor the shortcomings of the result could overshadow the fact that his mere selection from a field that had included the world's best architectural talent had elevated him at a stroke to international credibility. At least as important, however, was the personal association with the Kennedys and their entourage, which gave Pei access to the highest levels of social and artistic patronage. As he put it years later, "It gave me a mystique; I could go into the community as others could not."

Another very real benefit was a lasting friendship with Mrs. Onassis. After so much time and distress, she might have been forgiven for turning away from the architect in whom she had put so much instinctive trust so many years before. Indeed, she was well aware by the time the library was finished that it had become, as she put it, a "two-bit commission" for Pei. But as the years passed, she and the architect remained close, visiting each other regularly and occasionally going out to dinner at Pei's favorite Chinese restaurants, where he would have arranged in advance for a selection of house specialties. When a magazine did a cover story in the summer of 1989 to celebrate Mrs. Onassis's sixtieth birthday, Pei abandoned his customary restraint in talking to reporters on personal matters and allowed himself to be quoted, saying of their relationship, "We have that chemistry, we understand each other." [13]

By then, Pei's library had become an unexceptional fixture on the Boston landscape looking out across the harbor to the Hancock Tower, which itself had survived a siege of misfortune. But well before that elegant spire became a Boston icon, Pei would be involved in yet another project occasioned, at least in part, by Kennedy's death.

Kennedy loyalists made much of the fact that the president had loved the sea and that the wind-swept Columbia Point site was therefore more appropriate for the building than Cambridge.

6.

THE DALLAS MUNICIPAL ADMINISTRATION CENTER (1966–77): SYMBOL FOR A CITY

The conclusion of the Kennedy Library saga was years off when the city of Dallas began a journey of its own that was, although far distant from what was then happening to Pei in Massachusetts, nonetheless related to it.

If John F. Kennedy's death had made him a martyr, it had made of the place where he died an international symbol of all that seemed wrong with the United States. According to J. Erik Jonsson, who was then president of two of the three organizations that served as official hosts of the Kennedy visit to Dallas, "We were painted worldwide as a city of hate." Among Jonsson's goals when he soon afterwards became mayor of Dallas was to change that image, and I. M. Pei's architecture became one of the tools with which he intended to do it.

Born in 1901, Jonsson was a tall, genial man who had grown up as an only child on the fringes of poverty in Brooklyn, New York, and Montclair, New Jersey. He had earned enough money working after school to attend Rensselaer Polytechnic Institute, in Troy, New York, where he paid his way by working in a variety of jobs. "It did me good," he said. "I came out of there completely unafraid of the future. How could you be afraid? I'd always been able to make out somehow. So had my parents. We weren't rich, but we enjoyed our lives."

By 1930, Jonsson, a mechanical engineer, was working for the Aluminum Company of America. Through a family connection he moved on to Geophysical Service, Inc., which was to become Texas Instruments. In 1934, the company headquarters was transferred from New Jersey to Dallas, and Jonsson was asked to go along. He did, and when he got to Dallas, he liked what he saw. "It was the people," he said. "In the early 1930s in the East, many people had given up because of the Depression. I can't blame some of them. In Dallas, what I saw was

The monolithic force of the Dallas Municipal Center is made clear in this early drawing by Pei's associate on the project, Theodore Musho. By angling the facade of the building toward the downtown commercial core, Pei hoped to create a symbolic public-private dialogue.

Like Walter Roberts at NCAR, Erik Jonsson was to become a friend as well as a client. Here Jonsson is shown with Pei at the dedication ceremony for the finished building.

people who hadn't begun to give up. They just dug in and worked a few hours longer each day. I thought they were completely devoid of gloom or fear of consequences." Jonsson was so taken by the positive spirit of Dallas that he decided to stay permanently.

The company prospered, and so did Jonsson, who eventually became its president. But he had not forgotten what life was like before he had made his fortune, and he retained a Yankee's belief in the value of hard work and community service. He was particularly involved in efforts to promote higher education in science and engineering in Dallas, and in the late 1950s, while he was president of the local chamber of commerce, he helped found the Graduate Research Center of the Southwest, which eventually became the Dallas branch of the University of Texas. President Kennedy had been eager to visit Texas, and because Jonsson was such a prominent citizen, he was made a member of the delegation that extended the invitation to the president to come to Dallas.

As Jonsson spoke about the events of November 22, 1963, nearly twenty-five years later, the burden of that fateful invitation was clear in his voice. The cheerful people who had attracted him from the chillier society of the East Coast were, he said, suddenly portrayed as the gunslingers of cheap Western lore. "After the assassination, they were walking around in the style of Anne Boleyn with their heads under their arms," Jonsson recalled.

In mid-January of 1964, Jonsson was asked to fill out the fifteen months of the unexpired term of the city's mayor, Earl Cabell, who had decided to run for Congress. The city fathers, as Jonsson remembered it, turned to the Texas Instruments executive as "someone skilled at handling hot potatoes," the hottest of which was the city's shattered reputation, something for which no one wanted to take responsibility, but which everyone wanted fixed. One proposal was that the city simply hire a public relations firm. Jonsson rejected the idea. As he remembered his reaction, he declared to his fellow citizens, "Hell no, what we have to do is to earn our way out of this and show that we are decent people—God-fearing people who have a job to do and are going to do it." He was confident that it was possible, but he felt that the effort needed a focus. "People were grieving," he said, "and I thought that if I could get them busy and working with a common bond, we could do almost anything."

To find that common bond, Jonsson proposed a program he called "Goals for Dallas," which led to an extended series of public deliberations about the city's future and a book based on them.[1] "We wanted to find out what we needed to do to be a great city," Jonsson said.

The deliberations gave added impetus to planning Jonsson had already set in motion for a new city hall. The old one wasn't much of a building. Jonsson described it as having "a couple of hen-house and dog-house additions." Lee Harvey Oswald had been confined in a jail in the building when he was captured following the assassination, and the entire nation came to know a fragment of the place when, with television cameras whirring, Jack Ruby lurched from a crowd to shoot Oswald as he was being transferred from the city hall to the county jail.

With Jonsson's prodding, the idea of a new city hall took hold. "It was to be in itself a symbol of the people here," he said. The next problem was establishing a site for the building. A five-acre parcel on the southern edge of town had been set aside years before, during an earlier campaign for a new city hall, but the momentum had been lost, and the funding had failed. After much research, the "goals" committee agreed that the location was still a good one and that the new building should rise on it. Having settled on the place, the committee began a search for an architect. "The assignment was to build the best city hall in the world for a city that proposed to be one of the best cities in the world," said the mayor. "It didn't matter if the architect was from Timbuktu."

Through his Texas Instruments connection, Jonsson turned to John Burchard, who was then dean of the architecture school at MIT, as a consultant. With Burchard's help, a list of possible contenders was compiled, and letters went out to roughly twenty-five architects. The three finalists were Philip Johnson, the New York office of Skidmore, Owings & Merrill, and I. M. Pei & Partners. The fact that no Texas architects made the list caused something of a stir locally; the fact that one of the architects who did was Chinese-born made some people in Dallas feel that the search was vaguely un-American. But Jonsson felt that this was a time when the goal had to take precedence over local pride.

Pei had built nothing in Dallas, and apart from the work for Zeckendorf, he and his firm didn't have much to show elsewhere at the kind of scale and character Dallas was interested in. His selection in December of 1964 as the architect of the Kennedy Library may have catapulted him to prominence in Eastern architectural circles, but that didn't necessarily mean much in the Southwest. For the people who were making the decisions about a city hall for Dallas, the Pei building that counted the most turned out to be the twenty-story Earth Sciences building at MIT, which he had done while phasing out of the association with Zeckendorf. No less important than the architecture was the fact that the MIT tower had been paid for by Cecil Green, who had been a longtime colleague of Jonsson's at Texas Instruments. Jonsson had gone to the dedication and had been impressed by both Pei and his building. He liked its direct, four-square form, and he casually suggested to the architect that he should think about doing a building in Dallas someday.

The other buildings that offered the Dallas group a sense of what Pei could do on his own were the Luce Chapel and the National Center for Atmospheric Research in Boulder. But the chapel was an inspirational form that had little to offer as a model for a municipal headquarters building of the sort Jonsson had in mind. And NCAR occupied a site so dramatically different from the one in Dallas that it provided no clue to the committee about what the architect might do in their urban setting. Although the Kennedy Library design might have helped in that regard, it had not yet been made public.

George Schrader, who became the Dallas city manager during the early phase of the city hall project, recalled that while Pei's portfolio of completed buildings may have been relatively thin, the way he addressed himself to the city's architectural needs during the interview for the commission was compelling. Like Jacqueline Kennedy before them, the committee members were immediately struck by Pei's concern about the specific needs of the client and the opportunities for the site. "Pei had a reputation for a thorough, unique kind of preparation," said Schrader, "and he made it clear that he wanted to get an understanding of the local people and find a way to stitch the city hall into the rest of the community."

Pei made an equally strong impression on Jonsson. "He had an open and inquiring mind," said the former mayor. "It was his imaginative approach that appealed to us." One of the examples that remained with Jonsson was Pei's concern that the building be constructed of a material that related to the city's natural setting. "He said that whatever the building might be made of, the material 'should seem to come out of the ground around it,'" remembered Jonsson. Pei was awarded the commission in February of 1966.

Jonsson was to become one of those special clients with whom Pei developed a close personal relationship (over the years, Pei and Jonsson would make a point of visiting each other when passing through their respective cities). They shared a commitment to hard work, and both approached problems with no doubts that they could eventually be solved. But they also shared a deep reserve about their personal feelings. Characteristically, Jonsson kept his own feelings about rehabilitating his city's reputation as a "city of hate" to himself in his early talks with Pei, and it apparently was not part of the architect's thinking on the project. So circumspect was Jonsson about the assassination issue that, nearly twenty-five years later, Pei was surprised to learn that it had even played a role; the architect was not even certain whether the building had been started before or after Kennedy was shot.

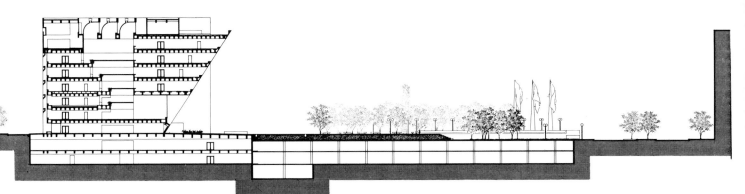

For Pei, the city hall, or the Municipal Administration Center, as it was to be called officially, was an unfamiliar and formidable challenge. Unlike the Luce Chapel, the academic tower for MIT, the scientific monastery of NCAR, or the Kennedy Library, this was to be a working building for the public at large. And the barren urban site was no mesa at the foothills of a great mountain range.

Nevertheless, Pei took it on with his usual enthusiasm. In assessing the project, he relied heavily on the experience gained during the Zeckendorf days of making grand plans for great stretches of urban America. "I had been to so many cities and talked to so many mayors and city leaders," Pei said, "that to get a profile of a city was almost second nature to me, almost easy. I just hadn't had a chance to apply the results to a single building until this one came along."

The physical planning was only part of the undertaking as Pei saw it. "It was the first time I had had to look into the personality of a city," he recalled. "When you do a city hall, it has to convey an image of the people, and this had to represent the people of Dallas." To get a feeling for those people, Pei talked to as many residents as he could and made a point of sitting in as an observer on meetings of the city council. He also joined Jonsson and a group of eighty-seven prominent citizens on a three-and-a-half-day retreat to a remote town in central Texas as part of the continuing "Goals for Dallas" program. "The people I met—rich and poor, powerful and not so powerful—were all very proud of their city," he said. "They felt that Dallas was the greatest city there was, and I could not disappoint them. They were entitled to have something that represented their pride."

There was another dimension to Pei's feeling about the constituency for the city hall. As Dallas had grown in the 1950s and early 60s, its downtown had sprouted a cluster of high-rise buildings owned by assorted banks and private corporations. That trend was bound to continue (it eventually produced the skyscrapers that were to become world-famous as a backdrop for the *Dallas* television series), and Pei sensed that the public sector needed some symbolic strengthening in the face of such commercial concentration. Moreover, for all the construction that had gone on, there was little of architectural quality in the city. Pei argued that the new building should face the business district, in order, he said, "to create a dialogue with the downtown, a public-private dialogue with the commercial high rises."

The argument was persuasive, but there was an obstacle. Some of the city's worst buildings lay between the growing downtown core and the site for the proposed city hall. "The middle of nowhere" is how the architect described

Lest later construction compromise the powerful gesture of his building toward downtown Dallas, Pei persuaded Jonsson to acquire the land in front for a civic plaza. Income from the parking garage below it, the architect explained, would help defray the cost of the overall project.

125

his first reaction to the collection of rundown stores and warehouses. Surveying the area with Jonsson, Pei announced that to establish the dialogue he was after, the dilapidated structures would have to go and that they should be replaced by a "buffer zone" and a plaza. But that meant adding roughly seven acres to the parcel of land Jonsson had to work with.

Pei's approach was strongly reminiscent of the way he had pressed the patrons of the Kennedy Library to pursue the car-barn site in Cambridge, rather than settle for the original piece of ground that had been offered to them on the opposite side of the Charles River. As in that case, Pei set about convincing his client that a building alone would be incomplete without an appropriate setting, and he did it by focusing not only on what the city hall would look like, but on what would be seen from it. "What do you want outside the door?" he asked Jonsson. "What is there now is not acceptable. And if you don't control it, you never know what will happen across the street. I can't design a building like this and have no control over what is on the other side of the street." As Jonsson remembers Pei's view, the architect argued that "you can't afford to spend the money and have it ruined by the environment." If the bid for the no-man's-land seemed to Jonsson as high-handed as it did imaginative, Pei knew what he was about. "It was a bit of the Webb & Knapp approach," the architect conceded, "and it shocked them."

Pei's insistence on considering issues larger than the building at hand may indeed have been something he learned from Zeckendorf, but it was to remain a fundamental characteristic of his approach to architecture wherever he practiced it. Time and again, he would gracefully extract agreement from his client on what the client thought was the entire undertaking, and then—well past the point of no return—explain, equally gracefully, how much better the project would be with the addition of a plaza, or a sculpture, or a better grade of stone. Zeckendorf had blocked Pei's appeal for a Picasso at Kips Bay, but in those days, Pei was still learning. For some subsequent clients, who felt that they were being manipulated, the strategy proved hard to take. "Ieoh Ming can put a guy to the test," said Theodore Musho, whom Pei assigned to help him with the city hall while he was still working on the early phases of the Kennedy Library. "In this case, he forced the mayor to define the role of his building for the city." Whatever Jonsson had originally intended the building to accomplish for the city's self-image, he now was faced with an additional mission for it, one that had to do with the entire urban fabric.

To press his case for the additional land, Pei invoked Rockefeller Center in New York, using it as an example of the effect he hoped to create. Without private patrons of the Rockefellers' stature, however, Jonsson, who quickly came to appreciate Pei's intentions, had to find another way to come up with the money. He fixed on the idea of creating a series of buildings to be built in the buffer zone after completion of the city hall. The main one would be a library, which would be located on the site of the "eyesores." Since this, too, would be a municipal project, a decision to go forward with it, even at some future date, allowed the city to condemn the existing buildings and annex the property. (The library, designed by a local firm, was finished in 1982 and later named for Jonsson.)

Pei was not unsympathetic to the financial burden he was adding to the project, and in an effort to ease it he proposed that a garage be inserted beneath the plaza. That, he pointed out, would handle the anticipated automobile traffic, but also help pay the cost of the increasingly pricey undertaking. (Not long afterwards, when land values had already begun to climb, a small portion of the newly purchased land was sold to the Federal Reserve Bank for a sum that did much to cover the purchase price of the entire parcel.)

Having decided that the city hall must face downtown and having talked the city into securing the land in between, Pei set about developing a physical form for the new building. What emerged from the basic concept of a horizontal counterpoint to the downtown high rises was a building that, when seen from the side, was wider at the top than at the bottom and appeared to lean toward the center of the city. One source for the form was Pei's perception of what he felt would be the ideal relationship between the city bureaucracy and the people of Dallas. He hoped, rather romantically, that if most of the civil servants could be concentrated high in his building, the average citizen could come in off the street and meet with a minimum number of officials, rather than be confronted with the usual maze of offices and clerks.

Whatever the merits of the lay sociology behind the roughly triangular form, it was also a powerful example of Pei's continuing interest in sculptural shapes. The pronounced canopy inevitably evoked Le Corbusier's High Court building at Chandigarh, a building that had already been echoed in Pei's research center in Boulder. In Le Corbusier's muscular concrete structure, the body of the building is sheltered under a massive hood that is supported by enormous piers arranged asymmetrically on the facade. The Dallas building is more clearly directional, its hood thrusting dramatically outward above the plaza. The idea, the architect said, was to "lay claim" to the plaza in front and "make it part of the entire composition."

In this case, the entire composition included the city of Dallas itself. Indeed, the shape of the building derives much of its meaning not just from the political and social relationship Pei attempted to establish with the tall buildings to the north, but from the formal relationship between its weighty mass and the lean verticals of the skyscrapers. In explaining the evolution of the shape years later, Pei made it clear just how simple the connection was meant to be. Grasping a red felt-tipped pen as he bent over his office desk, he quickly sketched a cross section of the site on a scrap of notepaper. The mass of the city hall and the spires of downtown made a perfectly balanced whole. The relationship between them was not unlike the one between the building and the Henry Moore sculpture *The Dallas Piece*, which Pei later secured for the plaza: the role of the sculpture was to balance the building at the scale of the plaza, just as the role of the building was to balance the spires of downtown at the greater urban scale. The massiveness of the building, said Pei, was a way to "assert" its presence in relation to the downtown cluster. "If it had been a ballet dancer," Pei said of his heavyset design, "nobody would have noticed it."

Pei and Musho worked on a number of versions of the tilted form. Ultimately, three towers containing stairs and utilities were added to the facade, two framing the main entrance and one at the extreme left. Although they did not actually support the protruding roof, they gave that impression, visually stabilizing a mass that might otherwise have appeared about to topple onto the plaza. Nevertheless, opponents of the building—and there were many—had great sport with the form, attacking it as overblown and sure to collapse. One local paper, the *Dallas Times Herald*, ran a cartoon showing Mayor Jonsson crouched under the roof, his arms forming the two towers at the entrance as if to hold the building up. [2]

The cartoon had been inspired as much by the building's cost as by the architectural form. The original estimate for the city hall had been twenty-five million dollars. With the addition of the plaza and the underground garage, the city decided to revise the number upward to about thirty-seven million dollars; the schedule called for completion in 1972. Bonds were voted in August of 1967, but hopes of a speedy and economical conclusion were dashed almost immediately. Construction bids came back about twenty million dollars over the estimate.

A major reason for the high bids was Pei's earlier commitment to Jonsson to make the building "seem to come out of the ground." The material Pei had selected to create that effect was a warm, buff-colored concrete that would both blend with the pale palette of the arid Dallas region and create the monumental effect for which Pei was striving. At the time, concrete was as economical as it was aesthetically appropriate. But the carpenters who were needed to build the

The controversy over both the shape and the cost of the city hall led local cartoonist Bob Taylor to satirize Jonsson as the main force holding the building up.

wooden forms for pouring the concrete were scarce because of a local building boom, which included work on the new Dallas–Fort Worth airport. Determined not to abandon the material, Pei and his local associated firm, Harper & Kemp, began to trim back on other aspects of the building. But inflation was high at the time, and the cut-back design turned out to be even more expensive than the original.

In the face of the mounting costs, Jonsson asked Pei to rework the design a second time. One approach the mayor and the architect considered was to erect only the shell of the building, leaving some of the facilities to be filled in later when more money had been raised. After discussing the options with the three major local banks, Jonsson decided instead to cut down the parking proposed for the area beneath the plaza and eliminate a new jail that was to be part of the complex.

By then, Jonsson had been mayor for nearly seven years, and he decided not to run for another term. He left office in 1971, with progress on the building virtually stalled. But George Schrader was determined to get it done, as was Jonsson's successor, Wes Wise. They felt that by further trimming and restructuring of the financing, it could still be built. Among the economy measures they proposed was postponing the partitioning of the nearly 800,000 square feet of office space until additional funds could be raised. But the key turned out to be the garage after all. The anticipated revenues from the municipal parking would, they concluded, be enough to get a new bond issue off the ground. So, in a move that would have made Zeckendorf smile, the garage was restored to the plan, and construction began. When it was finished, the project had taken eleven years, five more than expected. A project that was to have covered five acres now embraced seventeen, and the cost had gone from twenty-five million dollars to nearly seventy million.

The result was impressive by any measure. The six-acre plaza in front of the building extended 425 feet out from the facade, creating a space roughly twice the size of St. Mark's Square in Venice. The garage beneath the plaza could hold 1,325 cars. The plaza itself was punctuated by three eight-story-high flagpoles and a large ornamental pool, as well as Moore's sculpture. (After the three-part work arrived, Pei and the sculptor spent the better part of a day fine-tuning its location to find just the right relationship with the building.)

The city hall itself rose eight stories from the plaza and extended two stories below it. Its dramatic roof was supported by a cast-in-place, post-tensioned concrete system that included fourteen bearing walls and roof-level box beams. It was 600 feet long, reaching out over the plaza at an angle of thirty-four degrees.

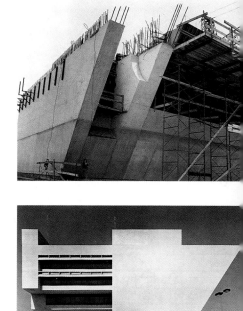

Top: The Pei firm's skill at the creative use of concrete was put to the test by the Dallas building, which required the development of some entirely new techniques to preserve its seamless appearance. Above: For all its weight and visual power, the building can look unstable from certain angles, leading diehard critics to predict well past its completion that it would eventually collapse.

A major achievement of the building was its elegant concrete surfaces. Beginning with his work on Kips Bay, and continuing through that on NCAR, Pei had steadily refined his technique in the use of concrete, and Dallas was yet a further step. Normally, the wooden forms used to enclose poured concrete would have left seams exposed on the surface. Since the aim of the Dallas design was to create an even more monolithic effect than the one Pei had achieved in Boulder, neoprene gaskets were recessed into the Dallas formwork, allowing the concrete to bond without apparent joints, creating virtually unbroken planes. To avoid surface cracks after the material was poured, Pei used a shrinkage-compensating concrete developed especially for the job.

That technological effort contributed greatly to the heroic impact the building makes on the visitor. Approaching it across the plaza, one is drawn powerfully in by the outward reach of the sloping form. This is clearly a serious building, one that almost seems to frown under the load of municipal responsibility it contains. Its outward-reaching gesture to the towers of downtown can be clearly understood from the plaza, and one indeed feels that a symbolic link has been forged between the separate monuments raised to the public and private sectors. The asymmetrical spacing of the stair towers relieves what might, without them, have been a sense of authoritarian predictability, and the paired towers to the right of the facade announce the main entrance with clarity. This is a major success in urban space-making, and if the plaza remains uninviting on a gray day, it perks up well when the sun is out and a food festival or political rally adds some human activity.

Closer up, though, the monumentality of the overall form of the city hall begins to falter. From certain angles, the inverted-step profile of the building's east and west facades creates the illusion that the entire mass is V-shaped in section and that it might well be more unstable than the main facade suggests. As one circles the building, this illusion is relieved, because the rear is after all a vertical plane. But it is a plane of no special allure, largely because the original plan accommodated a possible addition to the rear of the building. Clearly, a back side as expressive as the front would not have made an appropriate surface on which to attach such an addition. In its absence, however, the rear of the building tends to weaken the mighty thrust of the main facade.

Whatever the effect may be of the slanted front from afar, it is less than magnetic at close range. The banded windows do not reach to the ground, but are separated from it by a fifteen-foot-high blank wall of concrete. The only opening in that wall is the main entrance, but until one has come within the shelter of its flanking stair towers, the overwhelming impression is of hard, impenetrable

Pei's approach to the Dallas Municipal Center had as much to do with his perception of the proud spirit of the local citizenry as it did with questions of architectural form.

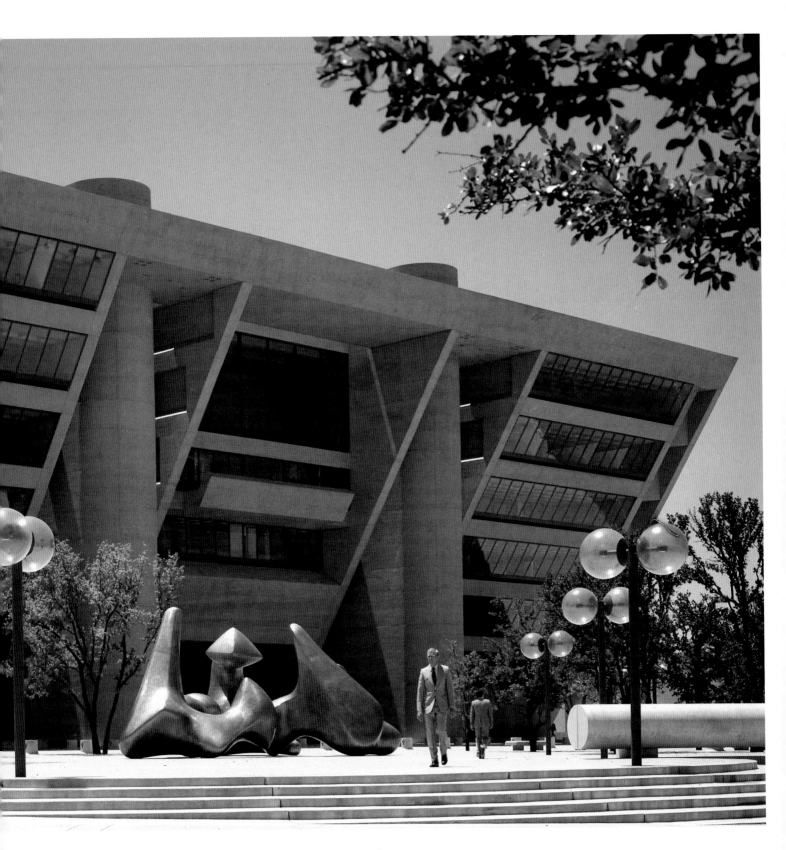

The domineering effect of the city hall's exterior (above) is mitigated on the interior (opposite) by the generous amounts of natural light and the stepping back of the upper balconies.

surfaces and unfriendly, even threatening, geometry. There is a sense here that, for all the care Pei had been able to devote to making NCAR as inviting as it is monumental, the abstraction of Dallas was allowed to overtake its humanity. This standoffish impression is particularly striking in light of the efforts Pei had made to come to know the local citizenry before embarking on the design. Caught up as he was in the Kennedy Library at the time, it is perhaps understandable that in Dallas he fell back on broad gestures that failed to adequately address the experience of his building at ground level. It was, nevertheless, a shortcoming that was to plague a number of his later works and continued to point up the human cost of Pei's dedication to abstract form.

As in most of those other buildings, however, the Dallas chill vanishes once one is through the door. The main lobby reveals a striking view upward and to the left toward a central atrium. The open space rises a hundred feet from the second floor to quarter-round vaulted skylights above the eighth floor. These give the interior a steady flood of northern light, warming the space despite the coolness of its concrete enclosure. The horizontal thrust of the atrium is punctuated by fourteen-foot concrete beams supporting the skylight hoods and by lesser beams supporting tiers of balconies.

The space is at once grand and intimate, and the coming and going of staff in the upstairs offices that give onto it creates a welcoming sense of bustle. (Pei had already begun to appreciate the decorative potential of people moving through his space, and its success in Dallas would be exploited with steadily increasing effect in his later buildings.) To the front of the building, the offices are closed off from the atrium by windows that form a sheer plane; to the rear, however, they are organized along the balconies, which step forward for two levels, and then back as they rise, effectively varying a volume that could have been oppressive if allowed to become a symmetrical shaft.

Even as the building was being completed, the architect was busying himself with revisions. While he may have shortchanged some details on the exterior, he paid close attention to those on the inside. When the form work for the concrete on part of the basement interior proved unsatisfactory, Pei had it changed and decreed a different one for the upper stories. He was even involved in picking the color of the telephones for the offices.

After so much time and expense, one might have expected the original public resistance to the project to evolve into outright hostility over the result. And complaints did persist, particularly about the bleakness of the plaza.[3] But most of them were overtaken by the impact of the completed architecture. The local media took on-the-street polls at the time of the official opening and couldn't find

Opposite: A form that can be forbidding on a gray day can create a welcoming sense of shelter when the weather and the people are right.
Above: While the overall mass of the city hall fulfilled Pei's intention of establishing the public sector as a powerful presence in Dallas, the street-level aspects are hardly inviting to the individual citizen.

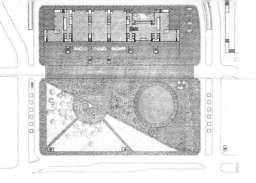

anyone who didn't like it. "Public ambition had caught up with the idea," Schrader said.

Not the least of the building's attributes for officials like Schrader was that Dallas finally had a fitting place to receive dignitaries. "Once," he said, "we had the Lord Mayor of Copenhagen here, and the mayor was ashamed to take him to his office. Not anymore. Now there's a place to take him to dinner and eat off china."

The acceptance of the building grew steadily, but so, said Schrader, did the public appreciation of what a major monument had done for the town. "Anything unusual in this community is viewed as extravagant," he recalled. "One of the things the building did was to create a consciousness of architecture in Dallas." As Schrader remembered Jonsson's contribution to the process, it was "galvanizing this community into thinking about the future; he inspired the citizens to loftier ambitions than they would otherwise have come up with and shifted the community into a consideration of quality, instead of price. From then on, everybody wanted to upstage what had been done before." The architecture that has followed the city hall has not always been of its caliber, but there is no question that the municipal sights had been raised. Not the least of the testaments to the impact of Pei's design was the fact that his firm was hired to do five more buildings in Dallas, including the Morton H. Meyerson Symphony Center, which was completed in 1989 and did much to confirm the city's faith in high design.

Surprisingly, perhaps, Pei was one of the city hall's severest critics. "By and large, it succeeded," he said. "The urban design is almost faultless in terms of volumes and open space—the relationship of one part of the city to another part of the city. The form of the building I am happy with. The only part that has not succeeded to my satisfaction is the architecture itself. The spaces are there, the concept is fine, the space inside is wonderful. It is a good building, but it could have been more refined. It's perhaps stronger than I would have liked; it has more strength than finesse. It's very hard to explain, but finesse can be strength; I only learned that afterwards. There's a lot of brute force in this building. It's not wrong, but that same force could have been conveyed in a different way. And I am sure I would find a different way now. It's a difficult question, and a bit of a contradiction. But, let's face it, to develop finesse, you have to have designed many buildings. At that time, I hadn't done enough."

The unmistakable strength that it did have, however, was as much the result of the relationship between Pei and his client as it was a result of the demands of the site and the building. That relationship may not have been as intense as the one between Pei and Walter Orr Roberts at NCAR; there were no

The formal layout of the plaza in front of the city hall created what was a bleak expanse for much of the year, serving more as a setting for the architecture than a place for promenading.

long sessions sitting out on a mountainside discussing the abstract nature of scientific inquiry. But Jonsson and the people he represented became for Pei almost a single personality. The architect said years later, "The client was not one person, but 'the burghers of Dallas,' who collectively were a great client."

Increasingly, the success of Pei's relationship with his clients would determine the success of his architecture. Indeed, a review of his best buildings turns up that special relationship again and again, even if it does not involve a single individual. It was present with Zeckendorf and, at least in the early stages, with the Kennedys. It continued with Paul Mellon, for whom Pei was to do some of his best work in the East Building of the National Gallery. And it extended to the government of China (via his own childhood) in the design of the Fragrant Hill Hotel and to the government of France in the addition to the Louvre.

As an early member of that select group, Jonsson found the architectural result of his special relationship with I. M. Pei to be just about everything he had wanted. His aim for the building had been to represent the people of Dallas. "And it does," he said. "It's made of one material. It's strong, and the people of Dallas are strong people. Concrete is simple, and they are simple people—in the best sense of the word, plain people. So the monolithic structure was entirely appropriate."

If this vigorous structure did not immediately redefine the image of Dallas in the wake of the Kennedy assassination, it certainly improved things, if only by attracting national attention to the fact that Dallas was willing to take risks in a quest for artistic excellence—and stay the course when that quest was threatened by delays. Not long before the building opened, the architecture critic for the *New York Times*, Ada Louise Huxtable, traveled to Dallas to inspect it, which she did in detail. (George Schrader remembered her turning up the corner of some carpeting to examine a joint in the floor.) When her review appeared in the paper, in November of 1976, it was headlined "One of Our Most Important Buildings." While she dwelt on the city's former reputation for "nondescript" architecture, she gave the city hall a rave, describing it as a building for which "Dallas should feel nothing but pride." +

According to Jonsson, one of the most vigorous opponents of the city hall persisted, even after it was dedicated, in referring to it as the "tilt-front building" and predicted to all who would listen that it would eventually fall over. "He got his just deserts," said the former mayor with evident satisfaction. "Well after the building was finished, he took his son in and was overheard to say to the boy, 'What a magnificent building!' He didn't know he was being overheard, but it got around."

Time and use, as well as the construction of other buildings near it, have softened what Pei called the "brute force" of the city hall, while confirming his hopes for it as a work of urban design.

7.

THE JOHN HANCOCK TOWER (1966–76): A NEAR FATAL BEAUTY

Just across the Charles River from the Earth Sciences Center at MIT stands the prismatic office tower the Pei firm built for the John Hancock Mutual Life Insurance Company. From the riverbank in front of the MIT building, Hancock has an almost unearthly presence. Rising behind the brick townhouses that line the Boston side of the river, it seems impossibly slim, dominating its surroundings with the icy elegance of a beautiful woman who enters a crowded room and instantly renders everyone around her silent. Seen closer up from among the proper mansions of Back Bay, the building seems no less exotic, its shiny skin shimmering with the reflections of passing clouds as if it had slid up through the floor of the city from an oiled silo. Few would argue nowadays that Hancock is not one of the most arresting skyscrapers of the modern era.

Hancock as it was built was not designed by I. M. Pei himself. Although Pei took part in an initial site-development study, the final building was the product of a design team headed by his partner Henry Cobb. But no story of Pei's career would be complete without a consideration of the Hancock saga. Among the reasons is that it was one of the most dramatic examples of Pei's willingness to turn over such an important commission to a partner. In so doing, he allowed Cobb to assert himself as never before in the public consciousness as an autonomous designer. He also speeded the evolution of the firm toward a true association of separate, if related, architectural sensibilities. Most of all, however, the Hancock job showed the durability of Pei's unique partnership under pressure, pressure that in the case of Hancock put the future of the entire firm in doubt.

Robert Slater, who was chairman of Hancock in the mid-1960s, was an aggressive man. He wanted big things for his company, and, like many corporate

Despite the trials it—and the Pei firm—suffered during its construction, Henry Cobb's Hancock Tower has become an iconic presence on the Boston skyline and a classic of Late Modernist skyscraper design.

139

executives of the day, he saw a new headquarters as one of those things. Hancock had long had its headquarters building in Boston, just off Copley Square, but it was a squat tower topped by a stunted pyramid, and certainly not the sort of architectural statement appropriate to an increasingly competitive business enterprise of the 1960s. Slater's ambitions were fueled by the construction, in 1963, of a massive tower by Hancock's rival, the Prudential Insurance Company. The building, which was designed by Charles Luckman, stood only a few blocks from Hancock's headquarters. It was by far the tallest in the city, and, to Slater's profound irritation, it had been built by a company that had its headquarters not in Boston, but in Newark, New Jersey. No matter that it drew instant public derision for its graceless bulk and stimulated Robert Campbell, the architecture critic of the *Boston Globe*, to christen his annual slate of worst Boston buildings the "Pru Awards." This was an affront perpetrated in Slater's backyard.

So he set about planning for a new and bigger statement of Hancock's rightful presence. Only a short time earlier, I. M. Pei & Partners would not have been an obvious choice to remake Hancock's architectural image. After all, the firm's portfolio of high rises was limited to the Mile High Center in Denver, Montreal's Place Ville Marie complex, and the apartment buildings for Kips Bay, University Plaza, and Society Hill. But the Kennedy Library commission had established Pei in the public eye far more forcefully in Boston, the Kennedys' home turf, than it had in Dallas, and the local opposition to the library had not yet surfaced with anything like its full force.

Nevertheless, Cobb said years later, "It was a relatively bold choice for Hancock to pick us for their building. The company saw the project initially not so much as the design of a skyscraper, but as a master plan for their entire property. And for that kind of work we had a solid reputation through Zeckendorf. After it became a question of a very tall building, it became much more iffy for Hancock to ask us—and iffy for us to accept."

The Pei candidacy got a major boost from Edward J. Logue, who as head of the Boston Redevelopment Authority had picked the Pei firm to redevelop the downtown core into a government center and had been impressed not only by its planning prowess, but also by its sensitivity to good design. Without Logue's backing, Pei himself concluded later, "a company of Hancock's stature would not have vested this kind of responsibility in such a relatively young, untested firm." According to Cobb, Logue used his powerful combination of Irish charm and political savvy to such effect that the first round of meetings with the Hancock people was a virtual "love-in."

The Hancock site was something of an aesthetic minefield. It occupied

The sleek form and elegant proportions of the John Hancock Tower
have overcome the notoriety of its early troubles, making it a powerful
contribution to its urban context.

142

By carving off-center grooves in Hancock's narrow facades (opposite), Cobb added visual intrigue to what might have been an oppressive mass. The use of reflective glass served to dematerialize the tower's bulk (above), while providing a Minimalist mirror for the amplification of H. H. Richardson's ornate Trinity Church.

four acres of land immediately adjacent to Copley Square, one of Boston's most beloved public spaces. At Hancock's end of the square was, in addition to its own 1922 headquarters building, Trinity Church, a major work by the renowned nineteenth-century architect H. H. Richardson and a shrine of the Boston establishment. Along the south side of the square was the Copley Plaza Hotel, designed by Clarence H. Blackall and Henry Hardenbergh and a landmark of shabby-genteel hospitality; and at the far end was the Boston Public Library, a vintage Renaissance Revival masterwork by McKim, Mead & White. Although by the mid-1960s the square had lost much of its former elegance, it remained a semisacred space in the Boston public mind. Putting up a skyscraper next to it would be a touchy undertaking at best. "We knew we were treading on very sensitive ground," said Pei, "and we had to consider whether that was good for Boston." Such considerations were especially important to Cobb, who was born and grew up in Boston and had an intense affection for his home city. He remembered that he and Pei "debated long and hard about whether it was right" to do what they had been asked to do.

As they saw the situation, there were not many alternatives. Robert Slater made it clear at the first signs of hesitation that he was prepared to move his company out of Boston if he didn't get his building. Pei and Cobb, whatever their sensitivity to Boston's urban fabric, had been lured since their Zeckendorf days by high-risk undertakings and were clearly eager to take on such a conspicuous challenge. After some additional agonizing, they concluded, according to Pei, that "we could shape Copley Square for the future, and the future was not a nineteenth-century drawing room, as some of our critics claimed. We convinced ourselves that a tall building could play a part. And if we didn't do it, the possibility existed that someone else would."

The first design was completed in the summer of 1966. It was to provide 1.5 million square feet of office space on Hancock's four acres. (The original Hancock building was to have been demolished.) A collaboration among Pei, Cobb, and other members of the firm, the proposed building was to be a cylindrical masonry shaft. A portion of the cylinder was sliced away, leaving a flat surface that was separated from the cylinder by narrow vertical slots and faced in glass. Two low-rise buildings embraced the tower rather like arms, leaving a roughly triangular plaza facing out toward Trinity Church. The design was presented privately to Hancock and to Boston officialdom. Just about everyone endorsed it, including Logue (who had disliked the Prudential tower from the start but had backed it because Boston needed the construction during a period of slack development). To critics who caviled about the size of the Pei proposal,

Opposite: When it was completed, Hancock was, at 790 feet, the tallest building in New England and could be seen on a clear day from as far away as southern New Hampshire. Above: Pei's original design for Hancock—a complex of buildings centered on a sliced cylinder—was shelved after the company increased its demands for floor space.

145

Logue blustered, "If you don't understand a company wanting to go taller, you don't understand life."

Everything seemed set to move, but Hancock was undergoing some internal changes and delayed action on the design for an entire year. In the summer of 1967, after consulting with various outside advisers on the organization of the building and its appropriateness to the company's now-altered priorities, Hancock decided to go forward, but with a substantially different set of requirements. The company had concluded that, instead of the 1.5 million square feet it had originally called for, it now needed two million. And instead of distributing the square footage over the entire two-block site, Hancock wanted to retain its original building and put all the additional space in the new tower, which would occupy only half the original acreage. The office floors, Hancock said, now had to be 30,000 square feet apiece, rather than the 22,000 square feet provided for in the Pei design.

Stunned by this massive midcourse correction, Pei and Cobb considered expanding their original masonry tower, but concluded that they couldn't make it big enough to accommodate Hancock's needs without compromising the design. Logue said Pei told him that he briefly considered giving up the job. Suddenly, recalled Cobb, they were playing "a much tougher ball game."

The change in Hancock's demands was bad enough, but the year's wait had totally upset scheduling in the Pei office. Another major Boston project, the Christian Science Center, had been in motion since 1965 under the direction of Cossutta. That project was going smoothly, but the Dallas City Hall was encountering the first of its troubles with labor and funding. Meanwhile, Pei was caught up in the early phases of the Kennedy Library and in plans initiated by Senator Robert Kennedy to rehabilitate a section of New York City's Bedford-Stuyvesant ghetto. In addition, the firm was working on the design for a commercial complex in Toronto for the Canadian Imperial Bank of Commerce.

Pei felt he had to make a choice of which projects then under way he would involve himself in most heavily. Cobb had been in on the early stages of the Toronto project, but as the partner who had been most responsible for Place Ville Marie, the biggest building the partnership had yet done, and as a well-connected Bostonian, he was the obvious selection to follow through on Hancock. So it was decided that Pei would take over the Toronto job, that the first Hancock design would be scrapped, and that Cobb would start in on a new one. As Cobb put it later, "It was the prudent thing to do under the time pressure."

For Cobb, the chance to build a tall building in Boston was a mixed

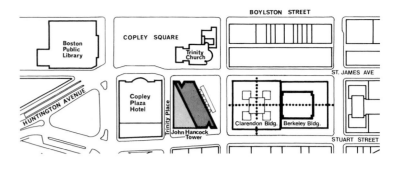

opportunity. If the Kennedy Library was to be perceived as a threat to the small scale of Cambridge, a skyscraper in Back Bay was, well, something Cobb's class of people just didn't do. And when the new dimensions of the undertaking became known to the public, a host of critics in the Boston architecture community drew themselves up to declare that "it was immoral to accept such a commission." As Pei himself later observed, "Very few Boston architects would have dared touch the site."

Despite the opprobrium, Cobb plunged in. He began work on September 15, 1967, having been told by Hancock that he would have to present a revised scheme to the board of directors and have it approved by November 15. The increased size of the building was not entirely the result of Hancock's need for additional office space. "We were never directed to make it taller than Prudential, but we understood in a fairly clear way that it should be," said Cobb. He proposed a building of 790 feet, or sixty stories, making it the tallest in New England; on a clear day, it would be visible from southern New Hampshire.

However, height was less important to Cobb than the proportions of the building. His first move was to confront the problem of how to minimize the impact of a building as big as Hancock on Copley Square. Although the building he had worked on with Pei was basically cylindrical, Cobb decided to make his new one a parallelogram, skewing the mass so that it would present its slimmest facade to the square. To further "dematerialize" that mass, he chose to clad it in reflective glass rather than masonry. That way, he argued, the building would pick up the images of the surrounding buildings rather than impose itself on them. Instead of looming over the square and its nineteenth-century landmarks, it would, insisted its architect, serve as "background and foil" to them. He then carved V-shaped slices into both of the short facades, positioning them slightly off the center line.

From the earliest stages of the new design, Cobb was confident that it was the right solution to the problem he had been given. "The Hancock building restored to Copley Square the dignity it had lost through the construction of the Prudential tower," he said defiantly years later. "When you stood in Copley Square and looked out from Trinity Church, what you saw was a great civic space that had been made into a mockery by Prudential, a project which asserted in the most blatant way that it had nothing to do with the public realm of Boston, and least of all with Copley Square."

Whatever the locals may have thought of Prudential, they didn't yet see Hancock as the improvement Cobb did. The new design was vigorously opposed

One of the keys to the tower's ultimate success was the decision to set it at an angle to Copley Square, thus minimizing its profile and the impact on the historic space as well as on its landmark neighbors, Trinity Church and the Public Library.

by the Back Bay Association, a civic group with considerable influence in the community. The proposal also ran afoul of those members of the Boston architecture community still smarting over the selection of Pei for the Kennedy Library and his other Boston commissions. The Boston Society of Architects mounted a spirited campaign to block the building, taking their case all the way to the national headquarters of the American Institute of Architects. John Burchard, the former dean of the architecture school at MIT (and the man who had advised Erik Jonsson on the selection of Pei for the Dallas City Hall), pronounced Cobb's tower "a monster."[1] Even Logue, who had done so much to land the Hancock job for the firm in the first place, turned on the project, calling it "the wrong building in the wrong place—an outrage."[2] Logue had left the Boston Redevelopment Authority, so he no longer had any real power over the building, but the combined outcry, said Cobb, "made us look like carpetbaggers and destroyers."

The critics did not prevail in their attempts to stop the building, but other problems surfaced soon after construction began, in August of 1968. Trinity Church and the Copley Plaza Hotel had both been built on wooden pilings driven into landfill. While digging proceeded for the Hancock foundations, retaining walls used to hold back the surrounding earth gave way, causing the ground under the church and the hotel to shift. Windows broke, and cracks appeared in the walls. The church transept began to tilt away from the central tower, and timbers in the tower were pulled out of their seats; some steam and water lines broke. Additional shoring halted the problems, and work continued.

As the building began to rise, however, what had seemed an outrage in the abstract to so many began to gain some followers. Cobb's emphasis on proportion was paying off. The slab was indeed enormous, but its slim profile had incontestible grace, and because of its unconventional siting at an angle to the street, its impact on Copley Square was not nearly as oppressive as many had feared. In fact, some of the building's most vocal critics began to see it as a positive addition. And that impression gained support as the taut glass skin was applied, giving Hancock a crystalline delicacy few people outside the Pei office could have appreciated when the design was first presented.

The skin was double-layer mirror glass. The building was to be wrapped in 10,334 sheets of it, each measuring four-and-a-half by eleven-and-a-half feet (and weighing 500 pounds). Although the glass had already been used widely elsewhere, this was the first time it had been applied in such large units. Cobb felt the large panels were essential to get the sleek effect he wanted.

In January of 1973, while the building was still under construction, a particularly violent windstorm hit Boston. After it had passed, dozens of Han-

Although Hancock temporarily threatened the firm's fortunes, it eventually gave Cobb the public recognition he had been lacking while designing in Pei's shadow.

cock's window units had cracked. Some had shattered and fallen to the ground. (No one was injured.) There had been occasional breakage in the months before, but it had been accepted as normal during construction. After the January storm, however, it was clear that something was fundamentally wrong. Approximately one-third of the windows were temporarily replaced with sheets of plywood, leading to a rash of grim jokes about the world's tallest wooden building. The jokes escalated to anger as other windows continued to crack. To rule out the possibility of further breakage, the Pei firm eventually ordered that the entire building be reglazed with conventional single-thickness tempered glass.

The aesthetic effect of the new glass was to create a marginally less smooth surface than the one Cobb had hoped for. But he was lucky to get what he got. The Hancock people, desperate to reassure doubters, had proposed solving the problem by using panes one-third the size of the original ones. They argued that people looking at the building would assume that small windows were less likely to break than big ones. There was a certain logic to the psychology of such a proposal, but it would have meant losing the proportions and the sheer surface that were basic to Cobb's abstract design.

Well aware that he was on thin ice arguing aesthetics in the face of all that had happened, Cobb appealed to Gerhardt Bleicken, who had succeeded Slater as Hancock's chairman. Cobb's argument, as he reconstructed it later, was that if the smaller panes were used, "the integrity of the building as a work of architecture would be destroyed, and that the building, instead of being a credit to the company, would have brought it further into disrepute. I wanted to convince him that I had Hancock's interests in mind, as opposed to protecting myself." Bleicken, in what Cobb has understandably called "an enormous vote of confidence," agreed. "He performed with great courage and great intelligence in a situation that was not of his own making," said Cobb. "Had the decision gone the other way, it would have been a really awful building. Like all minimalist things, every move counts; when you make the wrong move, and you have very few moves to make, that move is even more destructive." Cobb said Bleicken's decision marked "the most important day of my professional life." The reglazing was completed in May of 1975.

Despite the happy architectural outcome, the failure of the glass led to a flurry of lawsuits. In September of 1975, despite Bleicken's personal vote of confidence, Hancock filed a complaint against the firms involved with the design and construction of the tower. Named in the suit were Libbey-Owens-Ford, manufacturers of the glass; the H. H. Robertson Company, subcontractor for the curtain wall; Gilbane Building Company, a general contractor; Aetna Casualty

As the original windows broke, they were replaced with sheets of plywood; a spate of grim jokes followed about "the world's tallest wooden building." Unknown to the public were additional worries about the structure's very stability.

and Surety Company and Federal Insurance Company, performance bonding companies; and the Pei office. The damages were to cover the cost of labor and material for replacing the windows, as well as additional design and engineering work, and the lost use of the building suffered during its repair. The architect was charged with providing designs that were "not good and workmanlike" and did not represent "an adequate determination of the forces and conditions to which the curtain wall would be subjected."[3]

Libbey-Owens-Ford promptly sued Hancock for damaging the manufacturer's reputation in claiming that it was negligent in providing the original glass. The company further attacked the Pei firm, saying the problems were the result of an "error in the architect's windload specifications for the tower and underdesign of the building."[4] Pei's response was to countersue Libbey-Owens-Ford for fraud and misrepresentation, arguing that LOF had withheld information on defects in the seal of its thermopane glass and on other cases in which the material had failed. The architects insisted that the performance specifications the firm had drawn up for the glass had been correct and that the problem lay in the manufacture of the material itself. The litigation continued until 1981, when a settlement was reached that included an agreement by all parties not to discuss the matter publicly "in perpetuity."[5]

It was not until 1988 that the public learned that there had been problems with the building even more disturbing than those of the glass. Robert Campbell disclosed in an article in the *Boston Globe*[6] that during the investigation of the glass failure, an engineer had discovered that the building might, under certain wind conditions, topple over, and not on its side, as might have been expected, but on its end. The calculations involved were highly theoretical, but the threat was taken seriously. As a result, the building was, while still under construction, virtually disemboweled and rebuilt with an additional 1,650 tons of steel bracing costing some five million dollars. "It was like putting your socks on after your shoes," said Michael Flynn, Pei's main technical expert on the job. There was some question whether such drastic precautions were actually necessary. But at the time, the building's glass problems alone had created a crisis of public confidence. So close to panic were some Hancock people that rumors began circulating that the building might have to be taken down.

When the tower opened in 1976, four years behind schedule, the final cost stood at roughly $160 million, including legal fees. The sum was nearly twice the original estimate. And the reglazed, rebraced building was, even then, not without problems. Stunning as it was from a distance, it met the ground in an awkward fashion. So compelling was the purity of its geometry that a conventional entrance, no matter how grand, was bound to look out of place. Putting five clear acrylic domes, each nineteen feet in diameter, over the entrance pavilion did not solve that problem. Then there was the wind, which because of the tower's shape and position, gusted around the bottom with frightening force. To office workers trying to negotiate his architectural weather, Cobb's response was hardly satisfying. "I'm sorry people get blown off their feet," he said, "but we could not let that become decisive in the design. In order to achieve resonance between the tower and the church, we had to be single-minded."

For all its trials and faults, Hancock's overall power went far to wipe out the public image of the building as a technological disaster. It soon began to appear on postcards of Boston and on the covers of architecture books. It was mentioned in a short story by John Updike.[7] If it was not actually the last, best example of the Modernist skyscraper, it was at the very least a unique monument to that form. After Hancock, architects of tall buildings (including Cobb) were forced to find other avenues of expression, manipulating their forms in ever more complex ways or embellishing them with mock-Classical details and "hats" like the one Philip Johnson and John Burgee put on their headline-catching headquarters for AT&T in New York. Just as Mies van der Rohe had, with the Seagram Building in New York, brought one interpretation of the skyscraper to its logical conclusion, Cobb had, with Hancock, all but written finis to this building type as pure geometry.

If today the Hancock Tower is seen as a classic of Late Modern skyscraper design, it was for years after its completion remembered as a building that broke. And if the stigma of being "house architect" to William Zeckendorf had slowed the acceptance of I. M. Pei & Partners by corporate clients before Hancock began, its unhappy construction saga almost brought the I. M. Pei story to an end. When asked in 1978 about the impact of Hancock on the firm, Pei paused and said: "Immeasurable."[8] He did not elaborate. Cobb later conceded, "The impact was calamitous. We easily could have gone out of business."

For Cobb, the punishment was as much personal as it was professional. During the construction of Hancock, his father died. Some days later, the son was passing the construction site and came upon a senior member of the Trinity Church hierarchy, a man he had known for years through his family. The elder paused only long enough to say to Cobb, "Your father was a fine man. How could his son do such a thing?" He then turned abruptly and went on his way.

Years later, Pei still preferred not to discuss the building's problems in detail. He was, of course, bound by the restrictions of the legal settlement. But he conceded in 1984 that "during the 1970s, it almost cut off all corporate work from

Whatever its power from a distance, Hancock remains off-putting at street level, a condition not improved by the canopy over the front door.

our practice, and that was a very serious loss." Cobb was as terse, "We were virtually blacklisted from corporate and development work for a period of years." He added that a major Texas developer had told him at the time that he couldn't hire the Pei firm because his financial people would not have approved.

Quite apart from what the firm did not get because of their Hancock reputation, there was one prize they already had that was snatched from them. Before the Hancock problems began, Pei had been asked by IBM to design their new headquarters building in New York. It was not only one of the most important corporate commissions of the time (Johnson and Burgee's AT&T was the nearest competitor), it was to be located on the corner of Madison Avenue and 57th Street, one of the city's most important intersections. Pei accepted and began work on the design with James Freed.

At the height of the Boston upheaval, Pei was chatting in his office with the writer Peter Blake. They were interrupted by a call from Pei's friend Edward Larrabee Barnes, who had been a near-contemporary at Harvard's Graduate School of Design and was a formidable architect in his own right. As Pei recalled the moment years later, Barnes sounded apologetic but quickly got to the point. "I don't know if you are aware of this, I. M.," he said, "but IBM has asked me to take on their Madison Avenue building." Blake said Pei stiffened slightly, but showed no other emotion, and Blake left the room. It is characteristic of Pei's ability to put pain behind him that he was able to speculate years later that "we could have lost the building for other reasons." Barnes, himself a man of considerable reserve, was not surprised at Pei's restraint. "One thing I. M. doesn't do is wear his heart on his sleeve," Barnes said. "It was all very business-like."

The virtual blackballing of the firm caused by Hancock lasted for the better part of the next seven years, and it was made worse by bad economic times in the United States. The combination drove Pei to look for much of his professional sustenance abroad. Cobb was already working on a major project in Australia, and Pei had begun work in 1970 on a revised scheme for a commercial tower that had been designed by another architect for the Oversea-Chinese Banking Corporation in Singapore. Through that and other personal associations in Asia, he was able to win a number of additional commissions that, while they were not by any means the best things he or his colleagues had done, helped keep the firm afloat. (By far the biggest was an enormous commission for a multi-use project to be called Raffles City, also in Singapore.)

Like many American architects in those years, Pei also turned to the Middle East, embarking on projects in Iran and Kuwait. As one member of the team was preparing to leave New York for Teheran, Eason Leonard, the firm's chief administrative partner, took him aside and told him with a grim smile, "You've got to bring back a check." With unusual bluntness, Pei himself conceded years later that "we simply needed the money." (He insisted that he had pursued the work in Iran because he was drawn to the architectural heritage of Persia. Whatever his reasons for the choice, the overthrow of the Shah ended any hope that Pei would see anything into construction there.)

Cobb spent the better part of the years from 1972 to 1976 directing the remedial work on the building, and on diplomacy, shoring up Hancock's confidence in the Pei firm and trying to control the collateral damage from the crisis. Pei, in addition to the work for foreign governments, busied himself with smaller-scale work. "We did a lot of academic buildings and museums," he said. "They're all right, if there are enough to go around."

Painful and costly as the process of rebuilding the firm may have been, it did not seem to affect Pei's relations with his staff. One member of the firm remembered especially that the senior partner remained "immensely human; even then, he understood when you had family problems, or wife problems." For the firm as a whole, according to those who endured it, the Hancock episode proved to be a positive one in the end. "Going through this trial toughened us," said Pei. "It helped to cement us as partners; we did not give up on each other." According to Cobb, who had suffered on the front lines, the crisis never affected the partnership. But it had been a near thing, and people close to the facts claimed later that if Pei had not proved so resilient, the firm would indeed have failed.

As the immediate impact of the Hancock saga began to recede, Cobb detected a change in the attitude about the firm. The public seemed to feel, he said, "that if these people are still in business, they must be doing something right; they must not be the incompetents they have been portrayed as being." Looking back, Pei agreed. "We had quite a lot of things under way at the time, and the public felt that if they were still going, we couldn't be all bad."

It also turned out that when the controversy over the building's problems had passed, the professional admiration for its design began to grow. And if Cobb had suffered from the building's notoriety, he profited handsomely from its artistic impact. Indeed, although he had been functioning as an autonomous design partner in the Pei firm for some years, Cobb emerged after Hancock as an architect who now had his signature for all to see on a building of unquestioned aesthetic importance.

Not the least of the benefits to Pei of Cobb's increasingly high profile was the opportunity to concentrate more on his own buildings. In the case of the East Building of the National Gallery, it was the opportunity of an architect's lifetime.

8. THE EAST BUILDING OF THE NATIONAL GALLERY (1968–78): THE POWER OF ART, TASTE, AND MONEY

I f the travails of the John Hancock Tower threatened the very foundations of I. M. Pei & Partners as an artistic and business enterprise, the completion of the East Building of the National Gallery of Art in Washington, D.C., secured those foundations against virtually any further assault. Rarely in the twentieth century has so much attention been paid to a work of architecture, and rarely has it come from such a wide range of people. When the East Building's hard-edged assemblage of triangular forms opened in the spring of 1978, the leading architecture critics were all but unanimous in their praise. Nor was the enthusiasm limited to the professionals. Luminaries arriving for the event from around the world strained their vocabularies for superlatives. Schoolchildren who were brought to see the gleaming mass of pink Tennessee marble were moved to scribble Pei personal notes of praise in such number that his office finally had to give up answering them. Most telling, the public embraced the building with a warmth unprecedented for a work of American Modernist architecture; in its first two months, the East Building received more than a million visitors. Before leaving, thousands of them felt compelled to stroke the almost unbelievably sharp nineteen-degree angle formed by the marble at one of the corners near the entrance, staining it black in involuntary tribute to Pei's uncompromising geometry.

Until the unveiling of his expansion for the Louvre in Paris more than a decade later, the East Building remained Pei's most famous work. It will surely endure as one of his best. Here was the refinement he had felt unable to achieve in the detailing of the National Center for Atmospheric Research, the massing of the Dallas City Hall, and the spaces of the Kennedy Library. It combined the best of

As the design of the National Gallery's East Building proceeded, it grew increasingly complex, but it remained rooted throughout in the early sketches Pei had done of a trapezoid divided into a pair of triangles.

155

his planning experience gained under Zeckendorf with the full fruits of the later years of experimentation in geometric complexity and the exploitation of materials. More than any of his previous buildings, it was also informed by an inescapably Chinese sensitivity to light and space and a subtle control of how the user experiences a work of architecture. The building was at once monumental and animated, a mature expression of all that Pei had been moving toward as an architect.

It is not surprising that Pei should have reached a high point in his design career working on an art museum. After all, the project he selected as an exercise while studying under Gropius at Harvard had been a museum for the city of Shanghai. From his earliest days with Zeckendorf, Pei had shown himself dedicated to art—especially sculpture—and the growth of his discerning personal collection in subsequent years confirmed that dedication. Among his own buildings done after leaving Zeckendorf, museums had been among the finest. His first such undertaking, the Everson Museum of Art (1961–68) in Syracuse, New York, was a deft combination of brutalist forms handled with extraordinary grace. His addition to Eliel Saarinen's Des Moines Art Center in Iowa (1966–68) was proof of his ability to expand an existing museum without overwhelming its original identity. And while the Herbert F. Johnson Museum of Art at Cornell University in Ithaca, New York (1968–73), suffered somewhat from a small budget and a balky client, it had excellent moments, especially in the lobby. The East Building resolved the experiences of those museums into what is—despite some late-blooming criticism—a classic of its type and time.

There is no more compelling reason for this successful synthesis than the coming together in the East Building project of a particular architect and a most particular sponsor. Paul Mellon, who is as close to the aristocratic ideal of a gentleman and a scholar as the United States is likely to produce, was for Pei the perfect client.

Paul Mellon's involvement with the National Gallery went back to its beginnings. In 1937, the United States Congress passed an act authorizing a national gallery of art. The heart of the institution was to be a collection of 132 works of painting and sculpture donated by Andrew W. Mellon, the wealthy banker, former Secretary of the Treasury, Ambassador to the Court of Saint James, and Paul Mellon's father. Paul Mellon was made a member of the building committee and remembered years later that one of his greatest concerns at the time was that the blocks of Tennessee marble used on the exterior be carefully graded in color so that the walls would not look like "checkerboards" when darkened by rain.

The building that was intended to house the collection was to be located on a rectangular site formed by Constitution Avenue, Madison Drive, 4th Street, and 7th Street, and facing the Mall. It was designed by John Russell Pope and was paid for entirely by Andrew Mellon. Taken together with the value of the collection, the gift was the largest ever made by an individual to any government. The building opened in 1941, and although it eventually was recognized as one of the finest American examples of 1930s neo-Classicism, it was roundly criticized at the time for being, in what were the heady early days of Modernism, a retrograde work of architecture. But even then, the senior Mellon had his sights on the future and had the prescience to set aside the adjacent piece of land for future use. For years, it was occupied by tennis courts.

While the Pope building was under construction, a man named John Walker, a boyhood friend of Paul Mellon's, was studying in Italy. He had already been a student of the legendary art historian Bernard Berenson and had moved on to the American Academy in Rome. Mellon offered his friend the position of chief curator of the new gallery. Walker consulted Berenson, who suggested to Walker that, while the gallery was a worthy undertaking, what the United States really needed was an institution that would serve as "a great center of learning, like the library at Alexandria." Years later, when Walker had become director of the gallery, he and Mellon were discussing the future of the tennis court lot. According to Mellon, they were worried that "one day, somebody was going to take that land from us and build something else."

At the same time, the gallery's needs were rapidly outgrowing the Pope building. Apart from the lack of exhibition space, there was scant room for storage and conservation. Walker brought up Berenson's suggestion about an Alexandrian library, where scholars would have access to the art in the original building, as well as the support services needed to study it properly. Walker estimated that such a building could be built for about twenty million dollars. Mellon agreed to put up half, and his sister, Ailsa Mellon Bruce (who died in 1969), offered to provide the rest. By the time it was finished, the cost had risen to roughly ninety-five million dollars. That figure, which was covered by additional contributions from the Andrew W. Mellon Foundation, did not include operating expenses, which, as in the case of the original gallery, were to be paid for by the federal government.

This culturally magnanimous gesture was thoroughly characteristic of Paul Mellon. He was born in 1907 to one of those few American families of great wealth—the Carnegies, the Fricks, the Rockefellers—that have evolved to make as great a name in art and public service as in industry and finance. Mellon is a

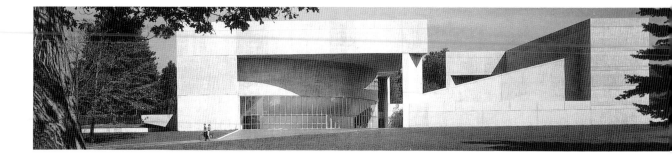

picture of upper-class elegance. His patrician head is embellished by a long beak of a nose, silver hair, and slightly watery eyes that often convey an expression of impish, almost childlike, mischievousness. His soft and rather high-pitched voice combines the tones of the Virginia hunt country and the high tables at Cambridge, where he studied after graduation from Yale. He wears understated clothes of the finest cut and material. Perhaps his most telling sartorial detail is his footgear. In the winter of 1989, while inspecting the muddy construction site of a science center he had funded for the Choate Rosemary Hall school (where he prepared for Yale), Mellon shunned galoshes and braved the duckboards in a pair of black toe-capped Oxfords that were highly polished, but cracked where they bent at the instep. This is a man who can buy the best in shoes as often as he likes, but prefers the comfort of old ones that have been perfectly maintained.

Mellon has spent his life pursuing many of the things that money makes possible. He has been a major benefactor of both Choate Rosemary Hall and Yale. Choate has two Mellon buildings—the science center he was inspecting in 1989 and an earlier one for the arts—both designed by Pei; Yale has three: Morse and Stiles colleges, both by Eero Saarinen, and the Center for British Art, by Louis Kahn. (The license plate on Mellon's metallic-brown Mercedes reads "Y1929," reflecting his Yale class.) He has a 4,000-acre estate in Virginia, townhouses in Washington and New York, and vacation homes on Antigua and Cape Cod. When he and his wife, Rachel, bought their Cape Cod house, they were disappointed by the lack of dunes nearby and had 2,000 tons of sand trucked in to rectify the situation. Mellon maintains three full-time pilots for his Gulfstream jet so that one will be ready to fly the plane at any time of the day or night.

Horses are a Mellon passion. In 1941, he joined the army as a cavalryman (but ended up in the OSS, the forerunner of the CIA, and won four Bronze Stars). Among the Mellon mounts that race in the gray-and-yellow silks of his Rokeby Stables, many have been named for landmarks at Yale or in England. (A definitive Anglophile, Mellon was named an honorary Knight of the British Empire in 1974.) Over the years, he has ridden many of his horses to triumph in competition. When his British Art Center opened at Yale, in 1977, Mellon was not at the ceremony, competing instead in the annual Hundred Mile Ride across the Blue Ridge Mountains of Virginia. (In the ways of such rituals, the rider doesn't win, the horse does, by finishing in the best condition. Mellon's mount, Christmas Goose, took the honors, as two other Mellon horses had in years past with him in the saddle.)

But for all the trappings of the horsey set, Paul Mellon is above all an

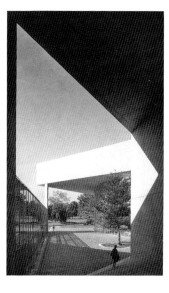

Aspects of the East Building's geometry were worked out during the design of the Mellon Arts Center at the Choate Rosemary Hall School (top). Like the Washington building, the arts center embraced different functions that were to be linked in a single building. At Choate, Pei left a gap between the main masses (above) to create a gateway joining two sections of the campus.

aesthete. Indeed, if he had not been born wealthy enough to buy virtually any work of art that struck his fancy, he might well have become an art historian. But because he was rich, he could buy at will. And he has done it with great discrimination and singleness of purpose. He is not interested in contemporary art, preferring the French Impressionists and the art of eighteenth-century England. He donated $100 million worth of British art to Yale as the nucleus of the British Art Center; the building cost him an additional eighteen million. Mellon never argues over the price of a painting. A story is told that when a dealer once offered him a Van Gogh for five million dollars, Mellon turned the man down. The dealer came back with an offer of four million, to which Mellon replied: "Frankly, if you offered it to me for $10,000, I wouldn't buy it. I just don't care for the painting." His favorite picture remains *Pumpkin with a Stable-Lad*, painted by George Stubbs in 1774.

Like Pei, Mellon was a banker's son who had a rather remote relationship with his father. (While an undergraduate at Yale, he wrote a short story for the *Yale Literary Magazine* about a businessman who pooh-poohed his son's interest in art.) Also like Pei, Mellon avoids confrontation, relying on indirection instead. When it comes to art, however, Mellon is likely to insist that a painting be moved a fraction of an inch to improve its position on a wall. When he decided to go forward with the addition to the National Gallery, quality came before cost. Reflecting on the project in 1988 from the understated luxury of his Park Avenue townhouse in New York, he said simply: "We thought that since it was the National Gallery, it ought to be the best of its kind."

Aiding Mellon in the pursuit of such excellence was J. Carter Brown, who was hired in 1961 as the heir apparent to Walker as the National Gallery's director but was, at the beginning of the East Building project, serving as his assistant. Brown, an angular Yankee with curly reddish-brown hair, was cut from cloth very much like Mellon's. A member of the distinguished Rhode Island family for which Brown University was named, he is a canny and energetic man who graduated first in his class at Groton in 1951 and summa cum laude from Harvard College, but had the real-world savvy to linger at the Harvard business school for an MBA. From there he did tours at the University of Munich, the Netherlands Institute for Art History, the Louvre, the Hermitage, and New York University's Institute of Fine Arts. He also studied with Bernard Berenson. In 1967, two years before Walker's retirement, Brown was detached to spend all his time on the development of the new building. When Walker stepped down, he duly became director of the National Gallery.

With Paul Mellon (left) as patron and Carter Brown (center) as director of the gallery, Pei had the luxury of two powerful and like-minded supporters for his ambitious plans.

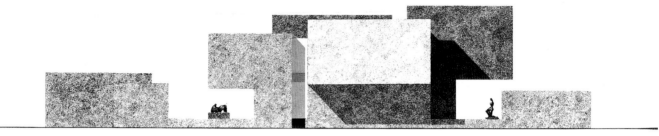

Among the buildings that most impressed Mellon in his search for an architect was the Everson Museum of Art in Syracuse. Although bunkerish on the outside (top), it had the sort of interior spaces (above) Mellon thought would be appropriate to his own museum.

In an article in the *Washington Post* magazine published in 1971, Brown reviewed the requirements of the expansion. It was intended, he wrote, to be "two kinds of building." One would provide exhibition areas for growth of the collection. "This should incorporate a major central space to allow the visitor to orient himself but to allow art to be exhibited in segregated spaces where the visitor will not be overwhelmed by architecture, and where the curator has total freedom." In addition, he insisted on "a different kind of building, one with great flexibility of office space, which will serve the scholars coming to the Center for Advanced Study, which will emphasize the library and photographic archive as being the central resource, and which will allow all the professional staff to move out of their highly inflexible quarters in the present building and operate cheek-by-jowl with the scholars at the Center."[1]

Not the least of Brown's intentions in all this was to provide the National Gallery with space appropriate to the display of large-scale modern art, something he felt was essential if the gallery was to remain competitive with other museums, primarily those in New York City. At a time when Washington was beginning to shed its reputation as a cultural also-ran, this was not a contest Brown intended to enter ill-equipped. As he told *Vogue* magazine some years later, "What we are banking on is the precedent of this building, which was given for a collection that did not exist."[2]

To accomplish the goals set by Mellon and Brown clearly required the services of a major architect, one who could deal simultaneously with Washington's daunting array of architectural restrictions as well as its well-earned and intimately related reputation for architectural mediocrity.

Louis Kahn and Philip Johnson were among the early contenders, but I. M. Pei soon emerged as the prime candidate. Brown and Mellon accordingly began to visit the relevant Pei buildings. They were impressed by the sensitivity of Pei's addition to the Des Moines Art Center, an especially delicate undertaking in light of the prominence of Saarinen. At the Johnson Museum, they got a sense of how Pei could integrate the demands of site, art, and public access. The hill on which the museum had been built was, according to Cornell lore, the very spot on which Ezra Cornell stood when he decided to establish his college, and as such had the quality of sanctified ground. Looking out over Lake Cayuga, it also

constituted an important opening in the fabric of Cornell's quadrangles. Pei's solution—a tall structure of raw concrete with an elevated sculpture court that doubled as a reception area for public functions—took full advantage of the view, but was deliberately perforated to continue the flow of space across the site.

More influential in making up the minds of Mellon and Brown, however, was the National Center for Atmospheric Research. During the visit to Boulder, Mellon was treated to a tour of the building and a picnic on the mesa by Walter Roberts. Mellon remembered later that the rugged building "fitted into the landscape very peacefully." But he was equally struck by the interior details, particularly the treatment of the bookcases and stair railings. What finally convinced Mellon that he had his architect was the enthusiastic testimony of the scientists who used the building. "That was the clinching thing," he said. Brown recalled that after the visit Mellon "turned to me and said, 'Carter, I'm impressed.' I knew then that in a sort of understated way, we had a decision."

Whatever doubts may have lingered in Mellon's mind about Pei's fitnesss for the National Gallery were dispelled by the subsequent visit to the Everson Museum in Syracuse. Located in what was then a bleak section of downtown, this small (130 by 140 feet above ground), but frankly sculptural building makes a forbidding first impression. It is essentially four boxes of reinforced concrete cantilevered out from a central core, or podium, and arranged in plan rather like the wings of a pinwheel. Each box houses gallery space; the core is devoted to a sculpture court, which serves as a focal point for the surrounding galleries.

The bunkerish exterior, which reflected the fortress mentality of many inner cities of the late 1960s, gives way on the interior to a remarkably airy assembly of spaces that include nine separate galleries of varying size. As he did at Cornell, Pei used slots of glass to separate the major concrete masses, creating an impression that they are actually hovering in space. The concrete is further lightened by diagonal bush-hammering, which exposed the aggregate and created a surprisingly warm corduroy-like texture. A circular staircase dominates the two-story sculpture court with rather too much authority, but it further animates the rectilinearity of the building with some welcome curves. Balconies and catwalks that open unexpectedly onto the central space add a note of asymmetry and exploit the movement of visitors along them as an element in the

Pei's addition to the Des Moines Art Center (left) demonstrated to Mellon an ability to expand an existing facility in a sensitive fashion, while his Johnson Museum (right) at Cornell showed skill at siting a building to maximum advantage in an older architectural context. Both qualities would be required in Washington.

composition. Mellon sensed from Everson that the architect had what the patron described as a "philosophical mean." He made it clear that for the National Gallery he wanted "a building to house art that would be a work of art in itself." After seeing Everson, he said, "I recommended Mr. Pei."

Delighted as Brown was with Mellon's decision, he was concerned that the National Gallery design, once through the conceptual phase, might be passed to other hands in the Pei office for completion. Pei assured Brown that he would remain personally in charge of the design. He had to. Everyone involved knew that the firm needed a triumph to restore its reputation in the aftermath of Hancock and could not settle for anything less than a maximum effort.

No one was more aware than Paul Mellon that American art museums and the way they were used had changed since his father's day. Like so many other of the nation's elite institutions, the great museums were opening their doors to the larger public. The advent of the "blockbuster" show—which concentrated great masses of art from all over the world and was accompanied by equally great masses of promotion and press attention—was attracting unprecedented numbers of visitors and putting correspondingly great strains on museum staffs and support facilities. Between 1957 and 1988, the number of visitors to the National Gallery increased 660 percent, according to a study by the National Endowment for the Humanities.[3] Brown reported in 1971 that attendance was already up fifty percent over the previous year.

But there were hazards in going too far to accommodate the increased traffic. These would become abundantly clear at the Centre Georges Pompidou, known as the Beaubourg, in Paris, designed by Renzo Piano and Richard Rogers and completed in 1976. The Beaubourg was intended as a national center of art and culture that would, through its "polyvalent" use of multimedia exhibitions and high-tech architectural expressionism, make the visitor an active participant in the building. According to its first director, Pontus Hulten, the Beaubourg was to be "totally open...emphasizing life and the event." But in its first year, only one-quarter of its six million visitors actually visited the exhibitions; the rest preferred to take in the dramatic views of Paris provided by the exterior escalators that rose past its multicolored maze of exposed pipes and ducts.

Mellon, Brown, and Pei all were after something more substantial for Washington. And yet it had to be something very different from Mellon's British Art Center at Yale, which was dedicated to a permanent collection and intended primarily for use by scholars.

In a way, Mellon was searching for something Pei understood at his core.

Among the constraints on the architect was a complicated set of requirements on heights and setbacks intended to preserve the scale of the low buildings in the vicinity. But the most controlling demand was that the East Building (left) have a clear relationship to John Russell Pope's neo-Classical original with its elegant columns and dome (center).

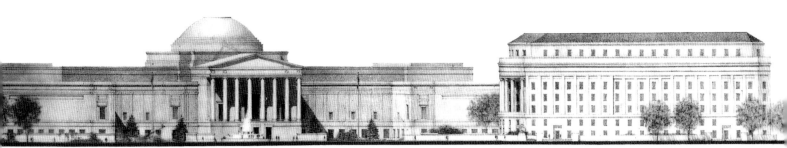

The architect had grown up in a culture that regarded art as a private matter. He remembered members of his family gathering in their villas in Suzhou to contemplate delicate scrolls that were normally stored away from view and were unrolled only for certain people and on special occasions. Yet Pei's own view of how art and the public interact grew far more democratic during his student days. And in his time with Zeckendorf, Pei had learned the importance of organizing buildings to accommodate masses of people. In a remark that later provided a text for some of his most vigorous critics, Pei said that his aim from the start in the East Building had been to design for a "mob scene. We needed to make the visit a pleasant one, so we built a circus."[4]

For all that, the scale required for the display of smaller works of art also had to be honored. Brown was particularly insistent on this point. "While our strategic position on the Mall called for bigness," he wrote at the time, "I hoped for smallness. The exhibition galleries must be on a human scale—intimate rooms in which visitors could absorb art without visual indigestion, where they would not be overwhelmed by architecture or suffer 'museum fatigue' from walking down endless corridors."[5] To study the problem, Brown traveled with Pei to a number of small European examples, including the Poldi Pezzoli Museum in Milan, which was, essentially, a house converted for the display of art. The problem Pei and Brown faced in their project was to find a formal solution that would simultaneously accommodate spaces for large and small works and the crowds that would want to see them. Whatever the shape of the new building, it would also have to fit in with John Russell Pope's original.

The problem was compounded by the site, which was an awkward trapezoid covering 8.8 acres on the Mall at the intersection of Constitution and Pennsylvania avenues. The odd shape was one of a number of leftover fragments created by L'Enfant's 1791 plan for Washington, which had created streets by superimposing a radial pattern on a grid. For a number of reasons, a conventional rectangular building on the site was out of the question. For one thing, it would have wasted a great deal of space at the unoccupied corners. For another, the axis through the center of such a building would have been off-center with the axis of the Pope building, and all agreed that there should be a symmetrical relationship between the two facades across the strip of 4th Street that separated them. The difficulties of the site were made no easier by the complicated restrictions on building heights and setbacks established by the National Capitol Planning Commission and the Commission of Fine Arts to maintain the low-rise character of the area.

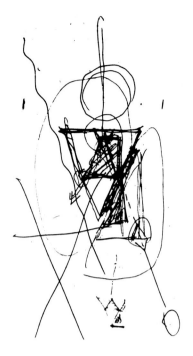

As in the case of NCAR, Pei decided not to fight the special character of the site, but to exploit it. According to the architect, the solution to the problem of fitting a building of the appropriate size onto the trapezoidal site emerged in a classic "back-of-an-envelope" moment. One afternoon in 1968, Pei was flying back to New York from a National Gallery meeting in Washington and began to sketch with a red ballpoint pen on a scrap of paper he had with him. The result showed a trapezoid inscribed within the outline of the site, leaving enough of a buffer to satisfy the city setback requirements. The trapezoid was divided by a diagonal line into two triangles, the larger one representing the museum, the smaller the study center of which Berenson and Walker had dreamed. The center point of the base of the larger triangle lined up precisely on axis with Pope's building, solving the problem of the relationship across 4th Street. Like so many of the best solutions, it was absolutely simple. "This," Pei said later, "was the beginning."

In due course, Pei presented the scheme to the board of the gallery. The board approved, and Pei promptly repaired to the home of his longtime friend Joseph Alsop, the veteran journalist, to celebrate. While there, Pei did another quick drawing of the plan, which Alsop saved and later sent to the architect. Inscribed on the back was a note: "In memory of a happy afternoon." Pei later returned the drawing to Alsop, having added to the inscription: "This sketch clearly shows the effects of bottles of Dom Perignon—and what vintages!"

Although the triangular geometry of the design accommodated the needs of the building, it also intrigued Pei from a purely aesthetic point of view. Its prime virtue, he felt, was that it provided not two vanishing points, as square and rectangular forms do, but three, making the spaces more active. A rectilinear space can be understood at a glance and is therefore largely predictable. In a triangular space, however, the view is constantly changing, surprising the beholder with unexpected relationships between the converging planes. The architect immediately saw the potential in the apparent disadvantage of the triangular form that the East Building site had thrust upon him, and he began to design accordingly, using permutations on the triangle as the organizing element of the entire structure.

But he was well aware of the potential hazards involved. In a 1978 interview, he put it this way: "Now there's a danger when you have this kind of richness—it is undisciplined—considerable confusion. And if the public, the viewer, cannot grasp the space, what good is richness? It creates confusion. We're stepping into an area where there aren't too many precedents."[6] But he was

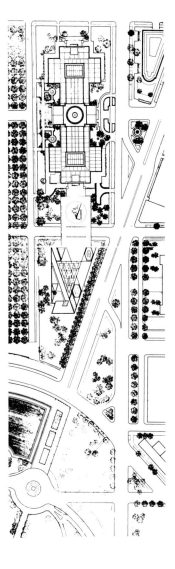

willing to take the risks. The levitating, interpenetrating forms that Pei had developed with such success at the Everson and Johnson museums could now be enriched with the added visual complexity of the triangle.

The geometry may have been compelling to Pei, but it struck some members of his team as overly simplistic. William Pedersen—who went on to become a partner in the firm of Kohn Pedersen Fox Associates—was fresh from MIT and a Rome Prize when he became the first member of the design team to work on the project. A freshly scrubbed Minnesotan, Pedersen was very much in Pei's thrall. Pei had been on the jury that selected Pedersen for the Rome Prize and had later asked the winner to come for a personal interview at the firm's offices. At one point during the interview, Pei's secretary, Leicia Black, came into the office and quietly reminded Pei that he was expected shortly at a meeting of the National Institute of Arts and Letters. Pei waved her off, saying, "That's not important," and continued to talk with Pedersen for another hour.

Pedersen was duly hired and quickly became one of those young designers with whom Pei established a special relationship. He was given an office near Pei's, and the senior man used to drop in on him to chat before work when both were in on weekends, which was often during the National Gallery period. But the young star learned quickly that whatever Pei saw in him as a designer took him only so far. Pei had assigned Pedersen to begin development of the two-triangle scheme. After studying it for some time, the young architect concluded that subjecting the display of art and the provision of scholarly resources to such rigorous geometry would eventually raise a number of problems and ultimately compromise the clarity of the original idea. Later, he raised the point with Pei at a meeting. When Pedersen had finished his presentation, Pei looked directly at him across the table and said, with a slightly paternal smile, "No compromises." According to Pedersen, Pei didn't seem angry at him for questioning the triangular theme. However, he said, "there was no longer any doubt about his wanting to pursue it."

Nevertheless, as the concept developed, Pei and his lead designers, who included Pedersen and Yann Weymouth, another of Pei's best young architects, found themselves wrestling with how to organize the larger of the two triangles into spaces that were appropriate both to art and to the handling of masses of people. Their struggle was suddenly made easier by Carter Brown, who had just returned from a museum conference in Mexico. At the conference, there had been a discussion of how much time the average museumgoer can effectively spend looking at art before fatigue begins to set in. The conclusion was that the ideal

The Plexiglas model (top) conveys a sense of the complex interpenetration of Pei's triangular forms in three dimensions. A site plan (above) reveals how the unorthodox shape of the East Building made the most of the irregular site.

CONCOURSE
LEVEL

GROUND
LEVEL 1

MEZZANINE
LEVEL 2

amount was about forty-five minutes. To get a sense of what that number meant for the design of a gallery, Brown estimated that, strolling at a comfortable pace, a visitor would cover an area of roughly ten thousand square feet.

Those numbers confirmed Brown's instinctive feelings about the appeal of "house" museums like the Poldi Pezzoli. When he raised them with Pedersen and Weymouth, both young architects reacted almost simultaneously. According to Weymouth, "Bill and I looked at each other and said, 'House? Ten thousand square feet? If we wall off the corners of the big triangle, we get a big central space for the public—and three ten-thousand-square-foot houses left over for galleries!'" The houses rapidly evolved into 110-foot-high towers, which were divided horizontally, creating what were almost freestanding buildings (and soon became known as "pods").

The towers produced problems of their own, however. They were shaped like parallelograms, and the two acute angles in each would have created some impossible spaces in which to hang pictures (which would have been face-to-face at the sharp ends). Again profiting from adversity, Pei decided to wall those angles off, creating three hexagons (each with six obtuse angles, all favorable to displaying pictures), and to use the leftover corners for elevators, staircases, and utility lines.

The gallery areas in the towers were deliberately left unencumbered so that curators would be able to customize them according to the needs of a given exhibition. (The director's insistence on this point earned him the nickname "Flexibility Brown.") The uppermost ceilings in the three towers were equipped with hoists so that they could be raised and lowered according to the scale of the art on display. Altogether, the aboveground portion of the new structure would provide the National Gallery with an additional 75,000 square feet to show art.

While work on the galleries was proceeding, attention was also focused on the study center. Its offices and a library for 100,000 books and roughly a million slides and photographs were to be wrapped around a full-height atrium in the smaller of the two triangles, which was to be separated from the larger triangle by a slot of open space. The clear distinction between the building's two functions was a problem Pei pursued during the design of the Paul Mellon Center for the Arts at Choate Rosemary Hall, a job that came into the office after the National Gallery project had begun. (A much less ambitious undertaking, it was completed six years before the East Building, in 1972.) In the school building, one portion of the structure contained studios and gallery space, while the other housed an auditorium. The two elements were set astride a pathway connecting

Floor plans of the different levels of the building (top) show how the triangular motif was divided and subdivided to provide the combination of large and small areas the client and the architect were seeking. The "house" museums were created by closing off the corners of the larger triangle, the center of which became the main public space.

 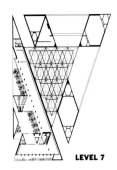

MAIN GALLERY
LEVEL 4   LEVEL 5   LEVEL 6   LEVEL 7

distinct areas of the campus and linked so that they would form a gateway. Pei hoped that the need to pass between the two pieces of the building would forcefully impress the presence of the arts upon the students. In a much more complex way, the cohabitation of galleries and research facilities at the National Gallery was intended to emphasize their interrelationship. But, as Pei said in 1978, "you can't just mix them all up in a building."[7]

Finding enough room for the study center in the space provided by the smaller triangle was a particular challenge. At the early stage of the design, Pei proposed cantilevering a boxlike protrusion out over the wall facing the Mall to increase the usable square footage. During a staff meeting on the problem, he explained his idea to his designers as something like what Le Corbusier had done at La Tourette and, to illustrate his point, sent a man off in search of a book by the master entitled *Creation Is a Patient Search* (the French title is *L'Atelier de la recherche patiente*). When the book was brought to him, Pei looked through it impatiently for a picture of La Tourette, but could not find it. One of the wags in the room observed, "Well, I. M., creation is a patient search." Pei didn't respond to the joke, and the rest of those present cringed with embarrassment, not so much at the humor, but because it had seemed for a moment that Pei was planning to crib a solution from another architect. (The cantilever was abandoned, and space was found elsewhere.)

One of the greatest challenges posed by the decision to put the gallery and the study center in the separate triangles of the East Building was how to give the result a sense of a coherent architectural whole. From the outset, the aim had been to have the functions intermingle, but the architecture was beginning to enforce a separation along the slot between the forms. The answer was to use the public space as the link. What emerged was yet another triangle, this one devoted to a 16,000-square-foot courtyard that emerged from the larger triangle and butted up against the smaller one. This extraordinary volume rose fifty-seven feet from ground level and extended fourteen feet below it; it was bridged by two catwalks, one thirty-two feet above ground level, the other fourteen, connecting the office and study wing with the galleries.

To reinforce the link between the old building and the new one across 4th Street, a two-story connector was to be sunk below the traffic. This passage was to contain temporary exhibition space, a pedestrian concourse, and a restaurant, as well as a gift shop, a 442-seat auditorium, a 90-seat lecture hall, loading docks, storage, workshops, and parking for 110 cars. The underground space—200,000 square feet—amounted to roughly one-third of the entire new building.

To provide the marble for the exterior, the same Tennessee quarry that had supplied stone for Pope's building was reopened. Mellon had been involved in checking the consistency of the stone color for the original gallery, and on one occasion he joined Pei, Brown, and (to Brown's right) Stoddard Stevens, a gallery trustee, to do the same for the new building.

To alleviate the potentially oppressive, tunnel-like aspect of the concourse, a portion of one wall was made of glass, against which light from the courtyard above filtered down through a cluster of glass tetrahedrons. The subterranean view was further embellished with a constant flow of water that splashed down across the concourse window from a fountain in the courtyard.

This portion of the project was made especially complicated by what lay beneath the site. The worst of the problems was the former bed of Tiber Creek; during heavy rains, water would rise almost to the surface. To secure the building, Leonard Jacobson, who was in charge of the construction, saw to the installation of forty-foot-long steel cables with concrete anchors that were attached to six-foot-thick concrete slabs. The slabs supported the building during dry periods when the ground would contract, while the anchors weighed it down when wet weather soaked the ground and threatened to "float" the building away.

The subterranean concourse provided one of the main entrances to the new building; visitors passing through it from the Pope building would surface by means of an elegant staircase leading to the courtyard. But entering the building at the ground level provided yet another difficulty. The entrance had to be on the 4th Street side, facing the Pope building, but it had to serve both the gallery and the study center. The solution was to create two ways in: a larger and appropriately public one, which lined up with the door of the old building across the street, and a lesser one to the right for the scholars. Because the entries are separated at the wall plane by the pointed corner of a marble triangle, they read to a passerby almost as a unit, while functioning as two discrete openings.

The public entrance receives added emphasis from an enormous bronze sculpture by Henry Moore that stands like a sentinel to the left of the opening. As part of the composition of the facade, the piece provides just the right amount of weight to balance the void of the study center door and might have been placed there for that reason alone. In fact, the position of the sculpture was something of an accident.

Pei had had a longstanding friendship with Moore, and one of the most pleasant of their exchanges took place over a sculpture Pei commissioned for the Cleo Rogers Memorial County Library (1963–69), in Columbus, Indiana. Pei had insisted to J. Irwin Miller, the client for the library, that the plaza in front of it required a major work of sculpture to "hold the space." Miller approved the idea, and Pei approached Moore, telling him about a trip he and his daughter Liane had made when she was young to the sculpture garden of the Museum of Modern Art in New York. Liane had delighted in running in and out under one of the

Intended to be both an extension of the original museum and a center for scholarly research, the East Building owed its inspiration to the great library at Alexandria.

The facade on the Mall (above)
creates an effective street wall,
but it also provides enough visual
access to prevent its becoming a
hostile neighbor. A roof court
(opposite) offers carefully
framed vistas.

Following pages: Alexander Calder's mobile, which was designed specifically for the East Building, is kept in constant motion by the ventilating system.

171

The apparently random visual collisions created by the repetition of the triangular motif (opposite) are underlain by a rigorous abstract order. Lest that order become overwhelming, Pei made such unexpected gestures as scooping out the wall next to the escalator (above).

175

Moore sculptures, and Pei thought that something similar would help enliven the open space at the Columbus library. He asked, however, that the piece be big enough for a grown couple to stroll through. ("I wanted to be able to get under it myself," he said.) Moore pondered the request and agreed, but only on the condition that the opening *not* be big enough to accommodate an automobile. During one of Pei's visits to Moore's studio in England, the two men discussed the matter further, and, after tea, Moore had his assistants make a Styrofoam mock-up. When the model of what was to become *Large Arch* was done to his satisfaction, a process that took only about two hours, Moore declared, "No car is going through *there!*"

In developing a piece with Moore for the National Gallery, Pei was less concerned about people interacting with the sculpture than he was about having a counterpoint to the mass of the building. He thought *Knife Edge Mirror Two Piece*, as the sculpture was called, would work best on the Pennsylvania Avenue side of the building. To persuade Moore of the idea, Pei and Brown met with the sculptor, and Pei went on at some length about the importance of the thoroughfare and how it was used for the parade during presidential inaugurations. Moore was unimpressed, announcing curtly, "I don't like it." Pei had rarely seen Moore so upset and was at a loss to explain his reaction. Finally, Brown asked Moore directly what the problem was. Moore declared, "It will get no sun there—no piece of sculpture should be without sun." To which Pei instantly responded, "We put it in front." Which is where it went.

The National Gallery's building committee had established at the outset that the material for the East Building be the same pink Tennessee marble that had been used by Pope for the original. Although he was a past master of architectural concrete, Pei had never done a stone building before. Nevertheless, he embraced the mandated material with characteristic enthusiasm. To get it, the disused Knoxville quarry that had supplied the marble to Pope was reopened, and, amazingly enough, the man who had overseen the earlier project, Malcolm Rice, was located and brought out of retirement in his seventies to perform the same service for the offspring.

The original building had been constructed of marble blocks more than a foot thick. This time, such extravagance was out of the question; the marble was cut instead into three-inch-thick panels that were hung as a veneer on a reinforced-concrete structure. One problem raised by the new technique was that the thinner marble was sure to expand and contract with changes in temperature, leaving unsightly gaps as it did so. (Pope's marble blocks were sufficiently heavy to

Opposite: More than in any other building he had yet done, Pei was able in the East Building to indulge his passion for the precise assembly of fine materials. Above: Pei with (from left) Carter Brown, Eileen Pei, and Henry Moore at the installation of Moore's sculpture *Knife Edge Mirror Two Piece* at the entrance to the East Building. The side entrance to the Pope gallery can be seen at rear.

177

prevent any such movement.) Pei's solution, worked out with the assistance of Jacobson, was to insert between the panels special neoprene gaskets that would absorb the changes in the stone without revealing them on the surface.

The panels themselves were selected by Rice and positioned according to color, shifting imperceptibly from the darkest at the bottom to the lightest at the top. The technique was the same used in the original building, but required additional attention in the new one because there was no longer sufficient marble in the quarry to provide the same selection of colors. Where Pope had as many as five different shades from which to choose in order to get the gradation in color he was after, Pei was limited to two.

An example of the attention to detail in the use of the stone is the handling of the knife-edge corners on the building's exterior. A standard approach would have been to miter the slabs at the point where they converged, but that would have meant a joint at the corner, revealing the thinness of the stone. Instead, the slabs were cut in such a way that their surfaces wrapped around the edge, creating the impression of solid blocks.

No less attention was paid to the concrete Pei used for the horizontal members that spanned the entrance and, on the interior, the doorways. Employing a technique similar to the one used at NCAR, the architect added to the concrete a mixture of marble dust produced by grinding bits of the stone used elsewhere in the building. The materials remained clearly distinct, but their close similarity in color made a sympathetic palette for the whole ensemble. The wooden forms used in the pouring of the concrete were, according to Pedersen, made with the same care as if they had been pieces of fine furniture—and were discarded after a single use.

The combination of great masses of marble and concrete assembled with such precision added to the building's overall sense of elegance and refinement. Admirable in its own right, it also helped create a delightful tension. There was something almost impossibly weightless about a structure that was clearly very heavy.

Nowhere is this more evident than in the great public space of the courtyard. The first designs for it included a coffered concrete slab for the ceiling. But such a massive element would, it was felt, have created an oppressive effect; something more delicate was needed to strike a contrast with the great expanses of

The early versions of the main space included a ceiling of coffered concrete. It was judged too oppressive and replaced by an enormous glass skylight.

178

marble wall. After considerable discussion, the team settled on a metal space-frame made up of twenty-five tetrahedrons; it measured 150 by 225 feet and supported hundreds of irregularly shaped panes of glass. Fabricating the metal and glass elements was a monumental task in itself, but the most demanding job was insuring that all of them would be able to expand and contract according to temperature changes without producing leaks.

The effect of the spaceframe on the central space was close to magical, lightening it in both senses of the word. To exploit the drama of the volume, the architect deliberately made the entrance to it as low as possible (the ceiling is only ten feet off the floor at the door), so that a visitor moves from a compressed environment to one that seems to explode. This device of compressing the approach is one Pei had used before—most notably at the Kennedy Library—but never with such effect. Although one can see the courtyard beyond, the full impact of its size is not clear until one emerges into it.

Large as the space is, it is more uplifting than overwhelming. The main reason is the quality of the light. Sunlight coming through the crystalline facets of the spaceframe is skillfully diffused by narrow aluminum rods set across them like space-age Venetian blinds. It is picked up by the pink marble and concrete, producing a rare warmth for such materials. The space is at its best when it is filled with people promenading along the balconies and catwalks, throwing moving shadows across the walls.

Yet Pei intended that the space be not only spectacular, but purposeful. And the main purpose, in addition to providing for the display of a limited number of large works of art, was to give visitors a place in which to orient and refresh themselves. Having been "welcomed" by the super-lobby, they were free to move off into the more intimate spaces of the house galleries to see an exhibit in relative seclusion. They would then be able to return to the main space to pause and digest what they had seen before moving on to the next house or through the underground passage to the old building. Although the initial impact of the space might seem simply exciting, it was deliberately fashioned to enhance the sorties into the smaller galleries.

Inevitably, one must look to Pei's experience as a child in the Suzhou gardens' subtly manipulated environments of light and shadow for a clue to his handling of the gallery's courtyard. But he claimed that there was another, rather

The irregularly shaped panes of glass (left) add to the geometric complexity of the main space, while washing it with a soft light created by the diffusing effect of screens made from aluminum rods. Shadows cast by the space-frame and the catwalks on the walls of the atrium (right) produce constantly changing abstract patterns.

179

surprising source for what he was trying to achieve. On his trips over the years to Germany and Austria, he had been intrigued by the intricate trompe-l'oeil effects of the simple Baroque churches he found scattered in small villages across the countryside. Rather than replicate them with plaster and gilt, he employed in the East Building a combination of light and the movement of people through it to bring about a comparable effect in a modern idiom. The happy tension created at Everson by bracketing heavy blocks of concrete with slots of daylight became in the National Gallery an exuberant quickening.

The space is further animated by the enormous mobile by Alexander Calder that hangs from the center of the spaceframe and adds its constantly changing shadows to those of the visitors, making of the marble walls a canvas for an abstract composition that is a work perpetually in progress. The mobile was Calder's biggest (it measured seventy feet at its widest point) and his last. (He approved its construction only a week before he died, in November of 1976.)

The first version of the mobile was to have been executed in steel and would have weighed about 5,000 pounds. The architects were worried, though, that it would be too heavy to move as they wanted it to in the air currents created by the circulation system. Paul Matisse (Henri's grandson), who was assisting on the project, had it made in aluminum, and the final mobile weighed only 920 pounds, a mass easily kept moving by the circulation of air flowing out of reveals in the walls and flush-mounted lights in the ceiling.

During the building of the gallery, construction costs rose approximately forty-one percent. As they did, there was considerable worry in the Pei office about just how much would be possible after all, and some serious trimming was called for. The marble floor intended for the cafeteria was done in terrazzo, and some facing on the interior that was to have been marble was executed in concrete. The panes of glass in the skylight were made smaller. The metal trim in the study center was to have been polished stainless steel to match that in the galleries; it became painted aluminum.

Over the seven years of the East Building's development, Paul Mellon never missed any of the seventy meetings of the building committee. Those meetings took place at Mellon's Manhattan townhouse, where the participants gathered under the gaze of the championship horses immortalized in the prints and statuary that embellished the serene second-floor drawing room. (James Freed, who sat in on several of the early meetings, remembered being struck that the martinis were mixed with gin that bore the juniper-berry label of Mellon's personal brand.)

Yet Mellon insisted years later that he had not been much involved in "the nitty-gritty" of the design decisions. "I was collecting and fox hunting; it wasn't like being somebody on the job day by day," he explained. But he was very much a participant in the strategic matters and stood by the architect in some risky choices. One was the cost of the underground connection with the original building, which could not be accurately predicted because of the uncertain ground conditions and was obviously going to be enormous. "Pei had some round figures," said Mellon, "but the matter was a little bit worrisome. We just decided to forget about it for the time being."

The only significant controversy was over the cost of the movable ceilings in the "house" towers that had been proposed so that there would be room for large sculptures. The numbers came in late, and they were, as Mellon put it with characteristic understatement, "a big change order." The cause prevailed, however. "To have a perfect building," Mellon concluded, "we ought to have that, too."

Mellon's restraint and support delighted Pei. But there was clearly more to his feeling for Mellon than the fact that he did not interfere with the design. Mellon was another of those "cultivated people" with whom Pei had always had the most successful relationships. In Paul Mellon, Pei got a unique combination of the qualities shared by all of them.

The occasion of the opening of the East Building was unlike anything anyone in Washington or any other American city could remember for a work of architecture. On May 30, 1978, two nights before the building opened to the public, 250 of the nation's most elegant and powerful arrived for a black-tie dinner party that ranked with the capital's best. Waiters wearing white gloves crisscrossed the marble floor of the courtyard carrying silver trays laden with pâté en croute, spring broth, and filet of beef with Béarnaise sauce. Light from the candles on the tables was refracted through glasses of champagne, throwing romantic shadows across the vast expanses of marble and concrete. The Mellons were there, of course, as were the Hammers, the Whitneys, and Mrs. Onassis. The list of artists included Anthony Caro, Willem de Kooning, Helen Frankenthaler, and Robert Motherwell. Music for the evening was provided by Benny Goodman's orchestra, which had been laid on in secret as a surprise for Mellon, who counted Goodman not far below horses and art among his passions.

When the doors opened to the public, the East Building was overwhelmed by crowds eager to see the new monument on the Mall. The country's leading commentators found as much to marvel at as did the visitors. The *Time* review carried the headline "Masterpiece on the Mall," and the critic, Robert Hughes,

Mellon regarded the movable ceilings specified for the "house" galleries as "a big change order," but finally agreed to accept them.

181

Pei's uncompromising Modernist geometry adds a new ingredient to Washington's architectural mix, but fits in spiritually with the most imposing of the city's neo-Classical monuments.

went on to describe the East Building as "a structure born of sustained and highly analytical thought, exquisitely attuned to its site and architectural surroundings, conveying a sense of grand occasion without the slightest trace of pomposity."[8] The building would, he predicted, "take its place among the great museum buildings of the past hundred years." Ada Louise Huxtable of the *New York Times* declared Pei's work "a palatial statement of the creative accommodation of contemporary art and architecture" and "the finest that informed connoisseurship and discriminating wealth can buy."[9]

Not everyone was so pleased, however. A number of critics pointed out with some merit that the angular glass skylights adjoining the fountain between the new and old wings were less than graceful and verged on the gratuitous. The underground passageway connecting the buildings came in for considerable criticism as pedestrian in more than the literal sense. So did the gallery spaces, which some faulted for their lack of natural light. And the insistence on carrying the triangular motif to such lengths struck some observers as obsessive. Christian Otto, the editor of the *Journal of the Society of Architectural Historians*, wrote in the English *Connoisseur* that "Pei has not challenged his initial intentions; he does not use the triangular proliferation that constitutes the East Building to explore a multiplicity of forming and meaning. In this fundamental sense, the project fails architecturally."[10]

There are grounds for each of these claims, but none is even remotely sufficient to qualify the building as a failure. What seemed to offend the naysayers most was the building's success with the public. The interior courtyard was dubbed "the poshest of suburban shopping malls."[11] A writer for the *Architectural Review* described the main space as a "superluxurious transit-lounge," an "artistic terminal building" that constituted "an empty monumental gesture."[12] A particularly vicious attack was mounted by Richard Hennessy, writing in *Artforum*, who sniffed that "the chorus of oohs and aahs which greeted this building at its opening left me completely unprepared for its shocking fun-house atmosphere, its deeply philistine unseriousness." The building, Hennessy declared, was "a true marriage of interests: the crowd, and those who offer it distraction. An aura of ancient Roman patronage hovers about this endeavor."[13]

Ironically, the very fervor of these critics proved that Pei had succeeded in his mission. While many might still wish that works of art be seen only in private settings like those enjoyed by Pei's forebears in Suzhou, most had come to understand that art—at least in the United States at the end of the twentieth century—could no longer be restricted to the elite. With few exceptions, those who found nits to pick with the East Building betrayed a measure of frustration, an almost desperate self-righteousness that seemed to grow from a fear that art would be somehow violated by excessive contact with the public.

Such a view, of course, directly ignored the very clear intentions of the program worked out so long before by Pei, Paul Mellon, and Carter Brown. But apart from their philosophical arrogance, many of the negative critics simply failed to appreciate another of the original goals of the East Building, which was to augment the Pope original by providing space and services the old building so badly needed. Indeed, the shrillest of the criticism faulted the building for being exactly what it was meant to be. If one goes back to the aims of the client, one can only wonder at the peevishness exhibited by the faultfinders. As Pei's experience with the Louvre was to demonstrate, it was not the last time in his career that the art mandarins revealed a level of envy that reflected their own failure to grasp the complexities of architecture as more than an aesthetic exercise.

As time went by, some of the original opponents came around. Carter Brown was particularly touched by one letter from a late convert. The writer was Allan Greenberg, an architect and a dedicated Classicist who had vocally criticized the design when it was unveiled. After visiting the building a decade later and listening to Brown explain its evolution, Greenberg wrote to Brown, "I am forced to admit that you are right and I was wrong! The building is a masterpiece."[14]

To be sure, the East Building of the National Gallery is not revolutionary architecture. Pei himself was candid about its being a refinement of what had gone before. And in that, he showed himself to be a quintessential conservative. But his conservatism was of a particularly deft sort. In his design for Mellon, he had retained the essence of monumentality and, through the innovative manipulation of mass, volume, light, and materials, had given the traditional definition of that term a meaning for its own time. In that sense the building showed a fundamental shift in Pei's priorities: it demonstrated more than ever before his ability to think experientially, to consider how people feel not just as they contemplate the formal aspects of a work of architecture, but as they pass through it. Pei himself realized that a change had taken place in his work. As he put it years later, "It was not until the National Gallery that I felt I had found a conviction about what architecture meant."

Of course, the sensitivity to such matters had been with Pei since childhood. And in his next major project, he found an opportunity to refresh his youthful experience at the source.

Pei being greeted by President and Mrs. Ronald Reagan and Mellon at a National Gallery dinner in 1983 honoring Andrew Mellon, Paul's father and the man whose largess created the original building, as well as the core of the National Gallery's collection.

9.

THE FRAGRANT HILL HOTEL (1979–82): YOU CAN'T QUITE GO HOME AGAIN

When the Fragrant Hill Hotel opened, in 1982, there was considerable clucking among some American Post-Modern architects. In their view, the foremost standard-bearer of Late Modernism had finally seen the light and embraced their vision of an architecture based heavily on historical allusion. And, on the surface, there was reason for their claim. Pei's building, in an old imperial hunting preserve some twenty-five miles northwest of Beijing, was unlike anything he had done before. There was no trace of the sculptural abstraction that had distinguished NCAR, the Dallas City Hall, and the Everson Museum. Nor was there anything of the relentless geometry or crisp planarity of the East Building of the National Gallery. This low-lying structure zigged and zagged across its site and was embellished with all sorts of what appeared to be un-Pei-like ornament. Diamond-shaped bits of masonry were scattered across the facade; lattice-work screens shaded interior hallways; and the windows in the off-white walls were given dark geometric outlines of an almost graphic power.

In fact, though, Fragrant Hill, or Xiangshan, as it is known in Chinese, had virtually nothing to do in Pei's mind with the Post-Modern movement as it had come to be defined in the United States. Far from being a revival, or even a reference to the architecture of the past, the design of Fragrant Hill was based on a rigorous distillation of what Pei felt were the best elements of a continuing tradition in Chinese architecture, one that had been stalled but not stopped by nearly a century of political upheaval and warfare. His real aim in the design was to pick up that lost thread of continuity and use it in the weaving of an architectural aesthetic for contemporary China.

If design were the whole story of Fragrant Hill, the saga of the building

Pei in 1979 with Chinese officials discussing his design for the Fragrant Hill Hotel. They had originally wanted a high rise in Beijing, but Pei's objections led to a low structure in a pastoral setting.

would be complex enough. But this project, more than any on which Pei had yet embarked, had a personal and, in the end, a slightly tragic dimension for the architect. Although there was no individual on the order of Walter Roberts or Paul Mellon involved in the commission, Pei's personal involvement was no less intense. The reason was that he saw the client for this building not as an individual or even as a national government, but as the Chinese people—*his* people. In Dallas, he had had to attend city council meetings to come to know the personality of the citizenry. For Fragrant Hill, his own past and his continuing identity as a Chinese provided him with a unique connection to the culture for which he was designing.

He was to discover, however, that memories were not sufficient as a source for his architecture and that the country for which he was making such a personal commitment was ill-prepared to build what he had designed. Worse, it was no better equipped to honor his inspiration. Fragrant Hill, said Pei after the building was finished, was the "most tortuous thing I've ever done."

What became the Fragrant Hill Hotel might be thought to have begun years before and far to the south at the Pei family villa in Suzhou. Indeed, it was while away from the turmoil of Shanghai playing with his siblings and studying with their tutor in the family garden that the young Ieoh Ming was imprinted with the basic forms on which Fragrant Hill would one day be based.

The road from Shanghai to Suzhou is straight, flat, and dusty. It passes through miles of rich, almost treeless farmland that has in recent years been scarred by grim clusters of small manufacturing plants that feed plumes of yellowish smoke into the sky. As one enters the city now, there are few clues that this was once a great center of industry and culture, turning out highly skilled

painters, embroiderers, and carvers of precious sandalwood fans. The silks of Suzhou were famous throughout the world, and the city's numerous canals gave it the sobriquet among Westerners of "the Venice of the East." Here, royalty as well as the wealthy and powerful families of Shanghai and their retainers had retired for generations in search of reflection and recreation in villas of surpassing elegance and complexity.

At its height during the Ming Dynasty, Suzhou had well over 100 such villas, a few of which have been preserved by the Chinese government as museums. They are hard to find now without a guide. But by threading one's way through bustling masses of pedestrians and bicyclists down a succession of back streets, one will eventually come upon the now-shabby reminders of a sumptuous past. Most of the buildings are hidden behind walls that also enclose fabulously complicated gardens. The gardens are, in fact, the most compelling aspects of these hideaways. They are not large, because even at the time they were built—most in the sixteenth century—there was little enough room for sprawling estates in the European or American fashion. For that reason, they are extremely dense. They were designed to create in miniature the sense of an entire landscape, so that the poets, scholars, and painters who used them might see, in the Chinese expression, "nature in a nutshell."

The origins of the Pei family garden, known as the Lion Forest, go back to the Yuan Dynasty (1279–1368), when a monk built a temple on the site to honor the memory of his master. The grounds and buildings grew steadily, changing hands many times over the centuries, and were restored by Pei's granduncle. The site covers only about two acres, but, like the others in the city, gives the impression

As a way of persuading the Chinese of the appropriateness of his unexpected design, Pei turned to collage, superimposing an image of the hotel on a traditional landscape drawing.

187

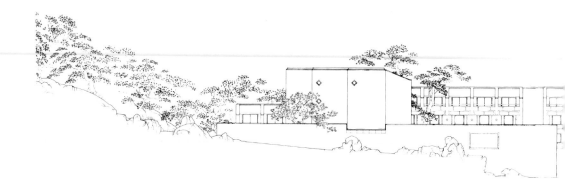

of being much larger because of the apparently rambling arrangement of low buildings, trees, water, and rocks.

In fact, nothing about the gardens is random. Every element in their design was considered with the greatest care, especially the rocks. Like those in most of the other gardens, the ones in Lion Forest are of a porous volcanic variety that were selected in the wilderness by "rock farmers" for their attractive shapes. The farmers would then "improve" them with hammer and chisel and lay them at the edge of a stream or lake where the action of the water would gradually erode the marks of the human hand, producing forms meant to evoke mountains and, in the case of the Pei garden, animals as well. The process could take generations; it was not uncommon for a particularly fine rock to be "harvested" and installed in a garden by the grandson of the farmer who had originally found it.

The willingness to wait so long for just the right sculptural effect is a central characteristic of Chinese art of the period and represents a reverence for time and continuity that is almost inconceivable to Western minds. Pei once told an interviewer, "My own development, when I stop to think about it, is very much in that spirit. I have been placed at the edge, or often at the center, of many different lakes and streams. And my buildings, like those of every architect, are always being pulled out of the flow of the water and put back in."[1]

Another key to the design of the Suzhou gardens is the arrangement of the rocks and other elements. The goal was to create the illusion of nature and to enhance it by subtly controlling the way in which the illusion was received. Thus a footbridge across a small pond would climb in an exaggerated arch or follow a zigzag pattern, providing to someone crossing it a greater variety of views than would be available from a straight or level span. Each of those views was carefully composed so that at each point in the crossing the visitor would be presented with a succession of compositions pleasing to the eye.

A similar technique was used in the design of windows and doors. Each opening was arranged as if it framed a painted version of the natural "picture" that lay beyond, and the approach to each was deliberately restricted so that the best view was inescapable. Even today, when the Suzhou gardens have become tattered and overgrown, the experience of walking through them is full of delightful "surprises" that, when one reflects on them, were clearly arranged for one's benefit. Enjoyable as the experience is while it still appears accidental, it is made more so by the realization that it has been secretly manipulated in one's favor. On a trip back to Suzhou, while Fragrant Hill was under construction, Pei

The site for the building included scores of mature trees. In order to preserve as many of them as possible—and immerse the hotel guests in the natural surroundings—Pei broke the building into a series of low forms that deferred to the landscape.

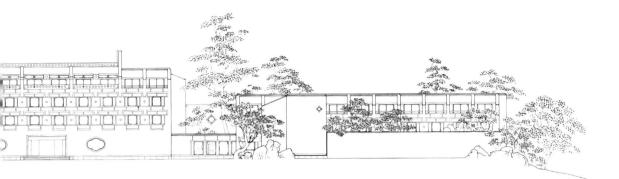

explained to a companion that the important part of the garden design was that "you see a bit, then you are led on—you never see the whole thing."[2]

Such subtleties had become a part of Pei's aesthetic consciousness at an early age, but he could not have imagined before 1974 that he would ever have a chance to explore them again in his homeland. In that year, Pei returned to China for the first time since leaving for the United States in 1935. He went as a member of a cultural exchange tour organized by the American Institute of Architects in the wake of President Richard Nixon's diplomatic "opening" to China in 1972.

Pei's reception was a warm one and included such extraordinary luxuries as a private railroad car. For such a welcome to be provided by a Communist government for the son of an archcapitalist banker might seem odd, even hypocritical, until one takes into account the country's special attitude to those of its sons and daughters known as Overseas Chinese. Historically, millions of Chinese have left their homeland under duress or in search of betterment. But regardless of their political or other allegiances before or after departure, they remain identified to their countrymen as Chinese first. Even today, the rigidly structured system of accommodations for foreign visitors to China gives Overseas Chinese—who may be the offspring of emigrants and have never before set foot on the mainland—access to hotels and stores that are off limits to non-Chinese. Of course, there was another reason. "The Chinese today are very pragmatic," Pei said by way of explanation, "and they regard the Overseas Chinese as a resource."

What Pei saw when he arrived in China impressed him. Although the social and economic class into which he had been born had vanished under the Communists, the desperate poverty and widespread corruption of the prewar years had also gone. And although the Cultural Revolution was in full swing, the architect noted approvingly that the people were well fed and well if simply clothed and that the trains, including his own, were on time.

But his appreciation of the strides made by the Communists in overcoming the material ills of an earlier time did not dull Pei's determination to speak his mind on an aspect of modern China he found repellent—its acres of faceless Soviet-style architecture put up since the 1950s. In a lecture during the AIA tour, Pei spoke out strongly against "slavishly following Eastern European patterns"[3] and urged his countrymen to look back to their own traditions for inspiration in modernizing their cities.

Despite the critical remarks he made on the 1974 trip, Pei was asked back by the Chinese government four years later—largely, he felt, because of the international impact of the East Building of the National Gallery. This time, he was invited to lecture on architecture and city planning. While in Beijing, Pei spoke on the issue of high rises, which the Chinese were especially eager to erect as proof of their emerging role in the international community. Although he had designed such buildings for an aborted housing complex in Teheran, where they would have been no less an assault on Iranian architectural traditions, he warned against them in this case. He was, after all, a native son, and this was not a foreign land from which he could walk away, at least not with a clear conscience. He was particularly concerned that tall buildings in the vicinity of Beijing's Forbidden City would destroy the awesome power of its great courtyards, from which nothing is visible beyond the walls but sky.

Not long after his return to the United States, Pei got yet another invitation from the Chinese, but the date was for late December of 1978, and he replied that he could not come because he always spent the Christmas holidays with his family. Not to be put off, the Chinese promptly suggested that he bring the family with him, which he agreed to do. (The group included Eileen, their four children, and two grandchildren, one of whom was only five months old.)

In the course of the third visit, Pei was invited to attend a banquet in the Great Hall of the People in Beijing. He had been given no specific agenda for the event, but recalled that everyone was expecting "something very important." Indeed, when Pei and his family arrived, they were greeted by a large group of high officials and a battery of television crews and reporters.

It turned out that the Chinese had a very clear idea of what they wanted their prodigal to do for them. Completely disregarding Pei's repeated warnings about tall buildings in the capital, his hosts announced that they would like him to design a group of high-rise hotels as part of a tourism campaign that required the construction of 100,000 rooms in two years. The flagship was to be a hotel in the center of Beijing.

Pei was flattered by the invitation, but horrified by its implications. He explained to his countrymen that the building they were proposing would "destroy the tranquility, the monumentality" of the great spaces within the walls of the Forbidden City. "I didn't want to commit a crime," he told a reporter later. [+]

This time, the Chinese had little choice but to accept Pei's opposition to tall buildings, but they were determined to have him do something. So they told him that they had some other sites available out of town. One was a former imperial hunting preserve. Not far from the Summer Palace, where the Dowager Empress had presided over the final days of empire in the 1920s, it included a small hotel that had fallen into disrepair. Pei agreed to investigate and was

immediately taken by the setting. Steep slopes rose up all around. They were thick with a rich variety of trees, some of them hundreds of years old. Pei first saw the site when it was covered with snow. Pictures of it in the autumn, with the leaves of the trees a blazing red, made it look even more spectacular. "It was perfect," Pei said.

After inspecting the site, Pei told the Chinese that he would gladly build in the old hunting preserve. Shortly afterwards, the government abandoned its intention of building high-rise tourist facilities in the vicinity of the Forbidden City. Moreover, they proceeded to establish guidelines for future construction in Beijing. There would be tall buildings, but they would be far enough from the Forbidden City so that they would not be visible from its great courtyards. It was never made officially clear that Pei was responsible for the guidelines, but he later said that if he had moved the government in any way toward the new policy, it was "my major contribution to China."

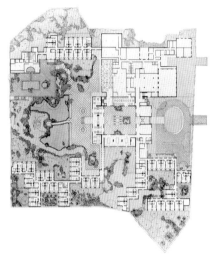

As a building type, a small-scale hotel was not the sort of thing to which Pei might normally have been drawn. But there was more to this undertaking than its type and scale. On a trip to Beijing not long after he had agreed to the assignment, Pei looked up an old friend who had been a classmate at Saint John's, Jing Shu-ping. As schoolboys, Jing and Pei had spent time at each other's homes, and Jing was a frequent companion on Pei's jaunts to the Shanghai pool halls and to the movie theaters to see the Bing Crosby and Betty Grable double features that so attracted the future architect to life in America.

Having survived the upheavals of war and revolution (as an intellectual and the son of an industrialist, he was condemned to two years of farm labor during the Cultural Revolution), Jing had become an important member of the government's foreign-trade department. A tall, birdlike man who had managed to travel widely in Europe and the United States, he had in the process developed a taste for things Western, including a wardrobe of blue blazers and button-down shirts that might have come from the most Ivy League of New York men's stores.

But for all his trials and travels, Jing had never lost sight of his country's traditions or their power to outride political storms. In a conversation in 1988 at the elegant executive restaurant of his Beijing office building, he reflected on the legacy that he and Pei shared as members of China's privileged classes. "People of our generation in China," he said, "had for so long felt humiliated by foreigners, whether British, American, French, or Japanese. We always secretly thought that we should 'stand up' for China, because her culture was so old. When I. M. and I got together, I sensed this feeling in him."

From the start, the design observed the Chinese tradition of making the architecture inseparable from the gardens.

During the early work on the hotel, Pei visited his family's former villa in Suzhou.

Although they had not seen each other for many years, Jing and Pei picked up very much where they had left off, meeting for a long talk at the old Beijing Hotel. "When I. M. told me about Fragrant Hill," Jing recalled of their conversation, "I knew it was more than just a hotel for him. Every Chinese is very proud of our ancestry, and he said that he wanted to develop some kind of architectural language to leave to our descendents."

The vocabulary of that language was not immediately clear to Pei as he embarked on the design of the hotel. He did not bring a preconceived stylistic idea to the project. Instead, he began to investigate what was best about what was already there. However, Chinese architectural history offered few guidelines for what he hoped to do. Indigenous architecture in any but the utilitarian sense had virtually ceased in the early nineteenth century with the arrival of foreign overlords and the onset of incessant warfare. The most enduring Chinese forms were those of the centuries-old imperial palaces and temples. Such examples, however, seemed inappropriate as a source for a building that was to serve a China so remote from their traditions. Of course, Pei could have relied on his own training and experience in Western Modernism, but that, too, seemed wrong for what he was after. He was looking, he said many times afterwards, for "a third way." If successful, Pei hoped, it would become a catalyst for nothing less than a new Chinese architectural style.

He found his first clues almost literally where he had started. To refresh himself in the aesthetic of his native land, he and several of his colleagues in 1979 made extensive trips throughout China, concentrating on the cities of Suzhou, Hangzhou, Yangzhou, and Wuxi, where there were still large stocks of traditional residential architecture. On those trips, Pei realized that, whatever might have happened in the years since he had left, "ninety percent of the Chinese people remain unchanged." The source for what he was seeking, he realized, was not to be found in the outmoded architecture of the emperors, but in the design of Chinese housing, a form that relied on principles and practices Pei felt were still applicable. "This is where the architectural tradition resides," he said. "It reaffirmed my belief in the importance of residential design as the best source—it was there one had to search."

Although the buildings in which the Pei family and members of their class had once lived were intended for the wealthy and the educated, they employed an architectural repertory common even to peasant dwellings. The interplay of wall and opening was central. The importance of gardens, no matter how small, was also primary, as was their relationship to the buildings. Indeed, the finest

examples of Suzhou's architecture create a sense that building and garden are totally integrated, with neither playing more of a role than the other.

As Pei began to develop his own design, he discussed it with a number of Chinese architects and officials. The younger ones were mostly opposed, hoping that someone who had so distinguished himself in the modern architecture of the West would bring something similar to China. "Many people thought I was being reactionary," Pei said. "It was not a very popular theme." But the older men with whom he spoke felt differently. "They appreciated history," said Pei, "and deep inside themselves, they liked it."

Not since NCAR had Pei been confronted with such a dramatic and demanding natural setting for a building. The trees alone were a powerful presence, and the Chinese were determined that as many of them as possible should be saved. As a first step, Pei's people conducted a detailed arboreal survey. The existing trees included cypress, chestnut, cedar, pine, willow, and ginko. At least two of the pines were as much as 800 years old, and one of them had provided shade to Mao Zedong as he negotiated the surrender of Beijing in 1949, sparing the capital what would have been a devastating assault.

The member of the Pei team most heavily involved in the planning of the site was Kellogg Wong, a Chinese-American architect whose parents had emigrated from Guangzhou. Wong had worked closely with Pei on the Everson Museum, as well as on all of the projects the firm had done in Singapore, but he had never been faced with the sort of delicate problems presented by the Fragrant Hill site. When the basic site plan was complete, Wong presented it to the government officials overseeing the project. He was in something of a rush, because he was scheduled to catch a plane to the United States the following day so that he could attend his daughter's high school graduation. The Chinese were in no such hurry and insisted on tracing the outline of the building on the ground with potash. When the outline was complete, they paced it off and promptly declared the plan unacceptable because it would eliminate 112 trees.

Wong was certain the Chinese had got the outline wrong and had it redone by his own team, who labored through a rainy night to finish it in time. The new layout, which was accepted as correct by the client, still meant removing sixty trees, which was more than the Chinese would agree to. So Wong patiently took them around to all the designated victims, discussing the "personality" of each and pointing out that most were either not healthy or small enough to move. Agreement was reached just in time for Wong to make his flight from Beijing. (Although his irritation over the incident lingered well into the job, it was

The architect with Chen Cong-zhou, the leading authority on Chinese gardens and Pei's close collaborator on Fragrant Hill.

One of Pei's main goals in the design of Fragrant Hill was to preserve the natural beauty of the site, which had once been an imperial hunting preserve.

mitigated somewhat three years later when he arrived at the opening of the completed building to be greeted warmly by his former antagonists as "Save-the-tree Mr. Wong.")

Although Pei hardly needed it, the mandate to preserve so many trees had given him a ready rationale for drawing on the rambling floor plans he so admired in the Suzhou villas. The one he created for Fragrant Hill was a meandering composition that wrapped around several interior courtyards and gave on an ornamental pond at the base of a hill. The building itself was to be focused on a four-story, 11,000-square-foot main reception space and provide for 325 guest rooms.

The walls of the hotel were finished in off-white stucco over reinforced concrete. (The color Pei wanted was not available locally, so he had it mixed in the United States from a Pratt & Lambert chart and imported.) What most attracted the attention of American architecture critics—and led to the declaration that Pei had finally succumbed to Post-Modernism—was the use of frankly ornamental window surrounds and wall details. They seemed uncharacteristic of the normally more restrained Pei, but were in fact refinements of devices he had seen in Suzhou and elsewhere on the trips he had taken to research the building.

Pei gave special care to the hotel's main entrance and to the windows, manipulating them and what one saw through them in very much the way the designers of the Suzhou villas had manipulated theirs, "borrowing" views by making picture frames of the openings. The atrium behind the lobby was in many ways an offspring of the interior court at the National Gallery, providing a central orientation space for the more intimate rooms surrounding it. Metal rods like those in the East Building were used to diffuse the light coming in through the glass roof.

Much as he had in Washington, Pei delayed the visitor's "discovery" of the main space, but this time, rather than lowering the ceiling of the lobby, he erected at the entrance a variation on a traditional ornamental screen, piercing it with a round opening that provided a glimpse all the way through the room to the back entrance and the garden beyond. Normally, such a screen would have been solid; penetrating it was an example of Pei's subtle alterations of traditional forms, something he did throughout the building in varying degrees. As in the Suzhou gardens, the aim was to reveal only fragments of the design at a time, creating a narrative procession that drew the visitor on to a continuing series of visual discoveries.

When the basic design was complete, Pei had a 220-pound model of it

Above: Chinese "water mazes"
developed from a legend about
poets who floated cups of wine
through the channel as they composed. In the Fragrant Hill garden, Pei rehabilitated such a
maze (foreground) to serve as a
centerpiece for his own architectural composition.
Opposite: The atrium combined
skylights reminiscent of those in
the East Building with aspects of
the traditional Chinese courtyard.

Drawing on examples in the
Suzhou gardens, Pei "borrowed"
interior and exterior views by
enclosing them in a variety of
"frames" in the form of windows
and doors.

shipped from New York to Beijing to help explain to the Chinese what he was doing. The reaction was puzzlement among some of the officials. This was not at all what they had expected from Pei. But none intervened to change it.

The building, of course, was only half of the design. The rest was made up of the gardens, which, consistent with the Suzhou example, were inextricably linked to the architecture. Exploiting the need to thread his building around so many trees, Pei created a series of interior courts, using the trees as compositional elements for small gardens. Ancient evergreens are seen against the stark walls as if they had been planted there for art's sake; in a sense, they had been, but Pei had given them an architectural frame. So thoroughly did he pursue the integration of architecture and landscape that every guest room in the hotel was given a view of some sort of greenery. The process brought back decades-old memories of his conversations with Gropius at Harvard about the class exercise on the Shanghai art museum. "Nature has always been part of my sensibility," Pei explained after Fragrant Hill was finished. "I didn't learn that in America."

Sensibility is one thing, but the technical knowledge to give it form is another. To help him design the large garden that would lie behind the hotel, Pei turned to China's leading authority on the Suzhou gardens, a man named Chen Cong-zhou. Chen and Pei agreed that, along with the important trees, another existing element on the site should be preserved. It was a water maze, called *liu shui yin* in Chinese, and had been part of the grounds of the old hotel that was cleared for the new one. There were only five such mazes remaining in China (one is in the Forbidden City), and both men were determined that this one should be restored.

These mazes developed out of an ancient legend about a group of poets who took to sitting by a country stream to compose their verses. As the story had it, the poets devised a game in which each man would set a cup of wine in a saucer and allow it to float down the slow-moving waterway. Each poet in turn was obliged to compose a poem in the time it took the wine to cover a prescribed distance. If he failed to do so, he was obliged to drink the wine, adding to the merriment, but making his next literary effort correspondingly more difficult.

No less important than the maze to the garden were the rocks that were to be positioned throughout it, also in the Suzhou manner. Contemporary designers of Chinese gardens still use such rocks, but Pei was not content with the available selection. By chance, he was looking through some tourist brochures and came upon a photograph of a spectacular rock formation in southwest China that seemed perfect for his purposes. His clients were taken aback by Pei's demand

The garden's phantasmagoric rocks were transported thousands of miles to add to the interplay of nature and human artifice.

that a selection of rocks from the remote region be prepared for shipment, but finally went along. The caravan of railroad cars that hauled all 230 tons of them the 1,500 miles to Fragrant Hill had the peasants in the fields staring in wonder as it passed.

An even more unlikely discovery solved Pei's problem in locating a traditional variety of dark gray brick that he wanted. Local builders had told him that the brick was no longer manufactured. With an uncanny luck that recalled the discovery of Malcolm Rice, the retired expert on marble who had solved a similar problem at the East Building, Pei found a craftsman who said he still knew the technique for making the brick and would be happy to take charge of providing enough for the hotel.

For all the similarities between the Fragrant Hill garden and those at Suzhou, there is a significant, and deliberate, difference. The Suzhou gardens were intended for the private use of individuals and small groups, whether scholars or wealthy patrons. The designs were accordingly compact, the paths narrow, the pavilions cramped. (The crowds of tourists who visit them today make it almost impossible to recapture the tranquility that was their fundamental reason for being.) Although the Fragrant Hill garden is not large, it is laid out far more generously than its forebears, and its borders are sufficiently obscure so that one feels it is part of the ancient preserve occupying the surrounding hillsides.

Pei's subtle alteration of the original model to accommodate more people, while still maintaining the reflective mission of the garden form, is closely related to the technique he used in the East Building. There, he combined the traditional experience of viewing art in intimate spaces—the "house" galleries—with the stimulation of a thickly populated atrium. In Fragrant Hill, he managed to preserve the contemplative experience while making it available to larger numbers. Once again, the key was a carefully disciplined disorientation, making the visitor feel at first surprised by the spaces, only to realize later that the experience had been precisely ordered to produce the effect for the visitor's delight. Neither building—which in the case of Fragrant Hill also means the garden—can be understood from a single perspective. They must be passed through, preferably at a leisurely pace.

The Pei office's earlier work on designs for Iran and Singapore had accustomed the staff to operating at long distance, but the spirit that pervaded the Fragrant Hill work in the Madison Avenue drafting rooms was unique. No doubt it had much to do with being the first major Western firm to design a significant building in China since the reopening of the country to the outside world. But

most of the excitement was generated by Pei himself, who got involved in the smallest details with an enthusiasm that was unusual even for him. It was, after all, a homecoming of sorts. He had been embraced by the country to which he had always intended to return, and he was doing for that country what he did best.

Pei's second son, Chien Chung, known as Didi, was put in charge of overseeing the design of the project and remembered that it produced a special esprit in the New York office. "When things get busy, we tend to throw more people at a job instead of asking the ones already on it to produce more," he said after it was all over. "This time, we didn't have to; everybody just worked harder." So eager were the members of the team assigned to the job that Eason Leonard, who, as usual, was responsible for the business end of the undertaking, eventually lost track of the hours his people were putting in. "They just kept working," said Didi. "There was a certain missionary zeal, a feeling that we were searching for the truth for China." One member of the team said later that he had never seen Pei so committed to a job.

For all his own enthusiasm, Pei appeared to have few illusions about what his team was facing by doing a twentieth-century building at long range in a Third World country. Despite the excitement generated by the restoration of normal diplomatic and cultural ties with the West, that country remained technologically far behind, still relying on manpower rather than machinery and working with inferior materials. At one planning session in New York, Pei warned his team, "We're going back to China, you know; we can't expect to do things our usual way."

In fact, the actual execution of the design at times drove those responsible for it on the site close to despair. One of them was Preston Moore, who had been a student of Pei's at Harvard and had joined the office in 1953. A tall, wiry man with a mustache that gave him a strong resemblance to a Battle of Britain fighter-pilot, Moore had worked on the Society Hill and Kips Bay designs, among many others. For Fragrant Hill, he was in charge of coordinating the drawings and overseeing the day-to-day operations once the construction got under way.

Moore's assignment to the job had a personal symmetry to it; as the son of an army officer who had been stationed in China, he had spent an afternoon in 1931 with his family at the very hotel the Pei building was replacing. More useful in his task than a fleeting familiarity with the site, however, was his prematurely white hair. The Chinese have a traditional respect for age, and although Moore was only sixty at the start of the job, he commanded additional

The graphic treatment of the windows creates a deliberate visual uncertainty about which are flat surfaces and which are three-dimensional forms.

respect by seeming to be older than he was. At one point, "the white fungus," as he was nicknamed—affectionately—by the construction crew, was offered a seat on a bus by a much older woman and was forced out of politeness to accept it.

In the United States, a job on the scale of Fragrant Hill would have required a construction force of perhaps 200 workers. At times on the hotel project, there were as many as 3,000 laborers doing with their hands and backs what would have been done in other countries by bulldozers and cranes. But the numbers could not compensate for lack of experience. The work was carried out by Beijing's Number Six Construction Company, which was not the best the Chinese had to offer. (The Number One Company was responsible for the major government buildings.) Early in the preparation of the site, Moore was inspecting excavation work being done with an aged steamroller, only to find that the roller, which should have been filled with water to give it sufficient weight, was empty.

As the work progressed, things got no better. When carpet was specified for the hotel guest rooms, the Pei team brought in a Japanese manufacturer, who demonstrated his wares by using a small-scale working model of his company's enormous new machines. They turned out carpet in strips fifteen feet wide, and the Japanese, who had just traded up from machines that turned out twelve-foot-wide strips, were eager to sell one of the old versions to the Chinese. The Chinese, in order to save money, insisted on buying not the machine the Japanese were offering, but the model, which turned out sample strips only thirty inches wide. Platoons of women were then assigned to sew the strips together by hand. The carpet was laid before the painting began, and when it did, the painters routinely rested their dripping paint cans on the new surface, leaving scores of circular stains. When the first shipments of coal were delivered for the hotel furnace, the lumps turned out to be too big. More workers were detached to hammer the lumps down to size. In the end, the budget of twelve million dollars ran to more than twice that. Such an increase was not unheard of on Pei jobs, but normally it would have reflected extensive design changes agreed to by the client. On this job, incompetence canceled out virtually every attempt to economize.

The missteps caused increasing rancor between the architects and the laborers, and at one point Moore was taken aside by a Chinese foreman who complained that a member of the Pei team had blown up at him. "You've got a crazy person working for you!" blustered the foreman. When Moore investigated, he had to sympathize with his own man's frustration, but nevertheless pulled him off the job for a week so that he could cool down.

Although Pei himself was on the site only rarely after construction began, the constant problems finally got to him, and at a meeting with a group of officials, he totally broke character. As he told the tale later to his friend William Walton, who had been so instrumental in keeping the troubled Kennedy Library project afloat, he found himself "shouting and pounding the table like any good American businessman who thinks he's being ill-treated by foreigners. The Chinese bureaucrats were aghast. But suddenly I got what I wanted. I guess I'm not as completely Chinese as I thought." Pei's pain at having such an emotionally compelling job short-circuited at almost every turn was not a pretty sight for the men who had watched him weather the Kennedy and Hancock storms with such control.

As the opening of the hotel neared, Pei, who had arrived to inspect the last phases of the work, could stand it no more and left for Japan with his wife to visit their friend the sculptor Isamu Noguchi. Kellogg Wong said he'd never seen his boss so exhausted.

Pei quickly recovered and returned to Fragrant Hill for the final preparations. But even the finishing touches became a trial of his restored equanimity. On the eve of the event, Pei and his wife were both seen scrubbing floors in the guest rooms and filling the lobby planters with the bamboo trees that should have gone in weeks before. The rest of the Pei family was making beds and cleaning windows. "I was so tired at one point that I burst into tears," Eileen recalled. Pei very nearly lost his composure for a second time when he saw a Chinese maintenance crew standing idly by while Eileen struggled with a vacuum cleaner. She had to do it, she explained later, because the crew insisted on using the machines without filters and burning them out.

On October 17, 1979, the Fragrant Hill Hotel finally opened. Present were some of the campaigners who had been with Pei for the opening of the East Building, including Carter Brown and Jacqueline Onassis. Armand Hammer and Thomas Hoving, the former director of New York's Metropolitan Museum of Art (which was later to install a replica of a Suzhou garden designed by Chen Cong-zhou), also made the trip for the occasion, which went off well enough for most of those present to remember it warmly. One participant who remained thoroughly unimpressed was Eileen, who felt that the shoddy and inefficient execution of the hotel's design constituted a personal betrayal of her husband. At the time, Pei had already done some preliminary work on plans for a new (and ultimately unbuilt) American embassy in Beijing. "I don't think they

Wall surfaces are used as backdrops for trees, producing the illusion of a graphic composition. On the garden side, these "still lifes" are amplified by reflections in the pond.

deserve another building by him." Eileen said afterwards. "I'm bitter."

Things did not improve after the glittering entourage of Western guests left. Over the next few months, maintenance of the building grew steadily worse. The man who was made the manager of the hotel knew nothing about his business, having won the job in recognition for his role as one of the first revolutionary soldiers to have entered Beijing with Mao. Pei tried to put the best face on what was happening. As he told an interviewer a decade later, when the gardens had been allowed to deteriorate and the strips of Japanese carpet had become stained with innumerable spills: "It's not like putting a child in an orphanage where he is beaten. They aren't doing the wrong thing on purpose. They are taking care of it their way. But the people running it don't have the sensibility; they are once removed from the farms and the trenches. And the bureaucrats refuse to let it go, but don't know what to do about it." Nevertheless, he turned down several subsequent invitations from the Chinese to return for a visit. Didi went and came back with a bleak report on the hotel's condition. "How do you tell someone who lives on a dirt floor at home that the bathrooms in a $100-a-night hotel aren't clean enough?" he asked rhetorically.

Perhaps more painful for Pei than the lack of care for his building was that it did not attract the sort of attention he had hoped for from Chinese architects. In 1988, the chief architect for the Beijing Institute of Architectural Design, a Pei loyalist named Zhang Kai-chi, confessed that the young people in his office were more interested in learning about the works of Michael Graves and other American Post-Modernists than they were in studying the building Pei had designed very much for their benefit. (The prospect of their pursuing virtually anything of American origin was made instantly more remote by the suppression of the fledgling prodemocracy movement in the summer of 1989.)

Pei later expressed a rather wan hope that, as time passed, the message of the design might sink in and that the building itself would be rehabilitated. Kellogg Wong, for one, remained optimistic about the prospect. "I. M.'s legacy to Chinese architecture is one China will one day awaken to," he said. "Eventually, an approach, a style, will evolve whose roots are seen to be uniquely Chinese. And somebody will say, 'But isn't that what that man Pei was trying to tell us?' In the meantime, though, they still want to prove that they can do Western architecture."

Perhaps Pei was wrong to try to change that determination single-handedly. After all, the kind of building China continues to need most is housing. Would it not have been wiser in the long run for him to divert the Chinese

government's demand for hotels, as he had diverted the demand for high rises next to the Forbidden City, and insist instead on a prototype for apartment houses? Given his years working on low-income housing with William Zeckendorf, Pei was more qualified than any other American architect—perhaps any other architect—to provide guidance on the subject and thus to make a fundamental and far-reaching contribution to the welfare of his native land.

One of Pei's close friends thought the architect had done precisely what he had had to do. Jaquelin Robertson is a product of the Virginia establishment who spent part of his youth in China (his father was a diplomat) and studied at Yale and at Oxford as a Rhodes scholar before spending several years working for the New York City government as an architect and urban planner. He had come to know Pei in New York, when they served together on a planning committee, and later traveled with him in Europe on a project for the American Institute of Architects to draw up a report on what were then being called "new towns." Robertson had been doing work in Iran when Pei's abortive high-rise housing project there got under way and was appalled that a man he so admired as a deeply civilized architect would design such Western buildings for a land with such a strong architectural tradition of its own.

When Robertson learned of the Fragrant Hill design, he was delighted and concluded that the weight of Pei's own traditions had, in this case, overcome the sort of demand he had evidently been willing to carry out for his client in Iran. Having followed the Fragrant Hill saga, Robertson was no less disappointed than his friend at the way the building was treated. But he said years later that he felt Pei, being the man he was, had had no choice. "Countries must be made aware of their culture even if they don't want to be," said Robertson, who had gone on to serve as dean of the school of architecture at the University of Virginia. "Fragrant Hill was exactly right for China, even if they wanted something else."

The Fragrant Hill saga was Pei's deeply sensitive attempt to set an example for his native land's architectural future; yet, what came through even more was an image of the architect that he rarely allowed the public to see. Beneath the cool exterior of the consummate American corporate architect emerged a romantic expatriate whose heart had, perhaps, overtaken his head. It was something his wife understood, even if his clients did not. In the elegant scrapbook Eileen prepared for her husband to commemorate the opening of the building that had caused them both so much personal pain, the inscription read "Love from Eileen." The first "O" was formed with a red leaf from the slopes of the hill behind the hotel.

No modern hotel can survive without a swimming pool. Pei managed to make the one at Fragrant Hill an integral part of the traditional aesthetic. The semicircular opening allows swimmers to enter the hotel's gymnasium without leaving the water.

10.

THE JACOB K. JAVITS CONVENTION CENTER (1979–86): THE WAGES OF POLITICS AND TECHNOLOGY

Having suffered so much from municipal incompetence in trying to advance architecture in his native land, Pei might have been forgiven for hoping that he would get a better reception in his adopted city. Since the Zeckendorf days, the firm had done a number of projects in New York—University Plaza, the Bedford-Stuyvesant "superblock" in the borough of Brooklyn, the National (TWA) Airlines Terminal, and a commercial office tower—but none approached the scale or prominence of what was originally to be called the New York City Exposition and Convention Center. It was a perfect chance for the Pei firm to make a major mark on its own turf.

But Pei's hopes for this building—which was renamed in 1986 in memory of Jacob K. Javits, a longtime United States Senator from New York—were to be almost as abused as were those for Fragrant Hill. Indeed, the center was to combine some of the technological trials of the John Hancock Tower with the incompetence of Fragrant Hill and add to the mixture a peculiarly New York brand of contentiousness.

The convention center also marked a further step in the evolution of the firm of I. M. Pei & Partners. Henry Cobb had, with Hancock, emerged in the public consciousness as a "name" designer in his own right and had since been operating with increasing autonomy within the Pei firm. Among his most significant buildings during that period were Wilson Commons at the University of Rochester (1968–76), the Johnson & Johnson World Headquarters in New Brunswick, New Jersey (1976–82), and a Texas office tower called One Dallas Centre (1977–79).

Although Pei was the principal partner for the Jacob K. Javits Convention Center, James Freed (left) was given primary responsibility for the actual design work. Together, the architects and their client Richard Kahan (center) weathered a storm of controversy that on more than one occasion threatened to halt the building.

A similar development now took place for Pei's other lead designer, James Freed. Born in 1930 in Essen, Germany, Freed had been taken by his parents to France and then Switzerland to escape the Nazis. In 1939, he and his sister were sent to the United States and settled in Chicago. Freed studied architecture under Mies van der Rohe at the Illinois Institute of Technology and, after military service, moved to New York to work with Mies and Philip Johnson on the Seagram Building. In 1956, after a falling-out with Johnson over the design of the ornamental fountains in the Seagram plaza, he signed on with Pei.

Freed worked with Pei on Kips Bay, the pioneering New York apartment complex that had done so much for the firm's reputation as experts in architectural concrete, and when the firm left Zeckendorf, was given a major design role on University Plaza. Having designed a number of other projects in Nebraska, Texas, and elsewhere, he also did 88 Pine Street (1968–73), a strongly Miesian office building in lower Manhattan, and 499 Park Avenue, a rather nondescript black-glass tower finished in 1981 for a New York developer.

Although he was not widely known to the public, Freed had become well established in architecture circles as a highly respected designer, and he was now eager to consolidate his emerging reputation. With his extensive experience at working in New York City, it was appropriate that he take overall responsibility for the design of the convention center. And in that role, Freed, as Cobb had before him, began at last to assume a public identity independent of the senior partner's. (He became a partner of the firm in 1980, along with Leonard Jacobson and Werner Wandelmaier.)

Pei was quick to acknowledge Freed's role in the convention center. Indeed, he said after the building was completed that "the working out of the concept was Jim's; he was the chief designer of the whole building." But whereas Pei always gave full credit to Cobb for Hancock, he continued to list the convention center as one of the buildings for which he had been the principal partner. The reason was that, while Pei participated only marginally in the design work, he had secured the commission and remained involved in the tortuous political and personal efforts required to see the building through to completion. In any number of cases before, Pei had played the role of "Mr. Outside," locating the client and landing the job, while passing the execution of a building on to his colleagues. He might well have done the same in the case of Javits, but this time the delays and assorted other difficulties grew so great that he was forced to use his influence as the firm's elder statesman to keep the project from being derailed.

If Hancock had become notorious for its windows, the focus of the controversy that was to engulf the Javits Center was its "nodes." These looked rather like steel bowling balls with extra finger holes drilled in them. The holes were designed to receive the tubular members of the vast spaceframe that was the basis of the center's design. As construction of the spaceframe was about to begin, the nodes that had been fabricated for the job were found to be flawed, a discovery that required scrapping many of the originals and replacing them with new ones made by a different manufacturer. The process helped set the project back by more than a year and cost millions of additional dollars. As in the Hancock case, the failure of the material led many to believe that the Pei firm had been responsible. In fact, the structural problem was an almost inevitable consequence of the maddeningly complex organizational process to which the architects were subjected from the outset. "The complications exceeded even my expectations," said Pei after the building was finished.

Although there had been several stalled attempts at building a convention center in New York, planning began in earnest only with the decision in the mid-1970s to close the old Coliseum, at the southwest corner of Central Park. Built under the reign of Robert Moses and finished in 1956, the Coliseum, a work of no architectural distinction whatsoever, had a mere 300,000 square feet of exhibition space. With the enormous growth of trade shows, the Coliseum's limited space meant that New York could no longer compete with other major cities for the most important exhibitions. New York officials hoped that a new and larger building would restore the city's competitive edge in the trade-show and convention business. At the same time, they were eager to use the new building as a catalyst for the redevelopment of a shabby portion of Manhattan's West Side roughly one mile south of the obsolete Coliseum.

The planners' vision called for a building that would be the biggest municipal project in New York City since the completion of the World Trade Center's twin towers in the early 1970s. Big as it was, the project took on an even larger importance because the city was at the time struggling back from its fiscal crisis of 1975, which had left New York on the edge of financial collapse. This building was intended to prove that New York was still capable of construction on a grand scale. The *New York Times* described the undertaking as "a symbol of the city's future."[1]

To manage this extraordinarily ambitious project, a joint venture—later to be described caustically as a "Rube Goldberg contraption"—was set up between two governmental agencies, the Triborough Bridge and Tunnel Authority, which had strong bond ratings, and the Urban Development Corporation, which had powers of condemnation and was exempt from city zoning requirements, but had a history of shaky finances. To bring what was thought to be the best attributes of both agencies together, the Convention Center Development Corporation was formed, providing representation for both bodies. But city and state officials wanted their own representation on the board as well. Without them, the enabling legislation for the project could not go forward. So yet another, separate, body was created, the Convention Center Operating Corporation, which would presumably manage the building after completion. With that compromise in hand, the legislation was passed, in April of 1979.

A site for the new building was then laid out on the old Penn Central rail yards. It covered roughly twenty-one acres and stretched for five city blocks between 34th and 39th streets and between 11th and 12th avenues. The area was best known at the time for its fast-talking prostitutes who hawked their services to passing truckers among the disused factory and loft buildings.

The person who became head of the Convention Center Development Corporation, and therefore the person most responsible for getting the construction going, was a combative young graduate of the Columbia Law School named Richard Kahan. A compact man with close-cropped dark hair and a rapid-fire speaking voice, Kahan was a fitness enthusiast whose impressive physique amplified his bantam rooster image. But for all his macho manner and carefully selected vulgarities, Kahan retained from his days as a student activist in the 1960s a sincere commitment to the public good and to government's obligation to serve it. He was an ardent admirer of Robert Moses, the high-handed New York City construction czar who had built the original Coliseum (and had crossed swords with William Zeckendorf), and of Edward Logue, who had hired the Pei firm to remake Boston's Scollay Square for the Government Center. With such instincts and heroes, it was not surprising that Kahan had developed a reputation as someone who could get things done; he had already proved himself an effective head of the powerful Urban Development Corporation. What he wanted to do in this case was to build "a great civic world-class" building. "I saw this as my biggest shot at doing something for architecture in New York City," he said.

Not everyone involved in the convention center effort was so optimistic. Opponents attacked the proposal as too big and, at an estimated $375 million, too expensive. There was also widespread concern that the site of the building was too far from the commercial heart of the city and from the main public-transportation routes. Undaunted, the planners decided to press forward and select an architect. The process was overseen by James Stewart Polshek, an architect with wide experience in New York who at the time was dean of the Columbia University School of Architecture and Planning. (He had also worked

HUDSON RIVER

WEST SIDE HIGHWAY

12TH AVENUE

34TH STREET

11TH AVENUE

briefly for Pei during the early Zeckendorf years.) Polshek's screening committee, which was appointed by New York City Mayor Edward I. Koch, reviewed submissions by twenty-four architects and finally recommended that the job should go either to Pei or to the firm of Philip Johnson and John Burgee. The recommendation was later extended to include a team made up of Gruzen & Partners and Davis, Brody & Associates, both firms with solid reputations and extensive experience negotiating the political mazes of construction in New York City.

The committee's recommendation then sat for nearly a year while the leadership of the project was worked out. When it was turned over to Kahan, he decided that, rather than restart the selection process, he would accept the original recommendations. (He knew and admired the work of all four firms.) But before making a final decision, he asked Polshek to draw up a master plan and develop a detailed description of what the building should contain and how it should be laid out.

The Johnson-Burgee firm had a high profile in design circles, but its recently unveiled scheme for the Madison Avenue headquarters of AT&T, with its pink-granite cladding and ornamental "Chippendale" top, was getting mixed reviews, and Johnson himself—who could be quirky and imperious—was pronounced "odd" by the committee. His chances did not improve when he announced that, if chosen, he would not abide by the committee's guidelines. Kahan was being urged to choose the Gruzen–Davis, Brody team, which could be expected to do a thoroughly professional, if possibly unglamorous, building. Pei, Kahan's advisers reminded him, might have had a hit with the East Building, but he had had problems with Hancock in Boston. When Kahan chose Pei anyway, the decision was seen by some as a compromise between the flamboyant approach of Johnson and the workaday product expected of the Gruzen team. Others saw the choice as trouble in the making. As one community leader put it: "I. M. Pei buildings are notoriously expensive and hard to maintain; they aren't Volkswagens."

At the time of Pei's selection, in April of 1979, Kahan had not yet seen the East Building. He later traveled to Washington with Pei and got a personal tour. "I almost cried with joy," said Kahan. "When I saw that building, I knew I had done the right thing." As a modern-day populist, he was particularly impressed when during the visit several awed museumgoers came up to the architect and said, "Thank you, Mr. Pei."

Despite his enthusiasm for what Pei could do, Kahan was not without his

The site for the center lay on the western edge of Manhattan in a rundown neighborhood. In addition to providing convention facilities, the city hoped the building would serve as a catalyst for new development. The darkened portion of the plan above shows the main public areas of the center; the "great hall" is at bottom, linked to the river side of the building by the ill-fated "galleria."

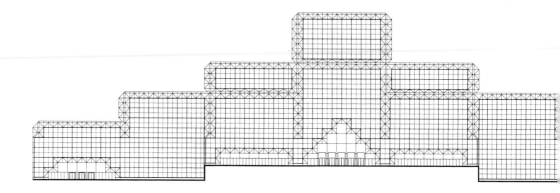

own worries about what might be involved. "Pei had a reputation for doing exactly what he wanted," said Kahan. "I was worried that the public sector wouldn't be able to control him; he was clearly a force to be reckoned with." But Kahan was the sort of man who was intrigued by a personal challenge, seeing it almost as an athletic opportunity, and he was confident that, whatever the experience of others might have been, he would be able to put a rein on this architect.

The qualities that attracted Kahan and Pei to each other were not unlike those that had animated some of Pei's most constructive past collaborations. Kahan was neither the offbeat poet-scientist in the Walter Orr Roberts mold, nor the quietly forceful patrician of the Paul Mellon stripe. But he shared with them a similar intensity, and he had a Zeckendorfian taste for large-scale undertakings. And for all his tough-guy exterior, he retained a sincere commitment to working in the public interest, something that had drawn Pei to Erik Jonsson in their conversations about the larger purpose of the Dallas City Hall. Above all, Kahan was energetic in a way that may have reminded Pei of himself in his earlier days. "He was young, and I was idealistic," said the architect. "Without Richard, we never would have been selected."

To bring themselves up to speed on what was being done in convention center architecture, Kahan and Pei took a wide-ranging trip around the country. (At the time, Freed was somewhat in the background, and he did not make the trip. As far as Kahan was concerned, the architect who had been hired to design the convention center was Pei himself. Kahan remembered that he saw little of Freed in the early stages of the project, but was not surprised when he began to emerge as the main participant. "I didn't expect I. M. to actually draw the building," Kahan said. "I didn't feel the need to have him involved day to day.") As they traveled from city to city, Pei and Kahan discussed their views of the purpose of the convention center and agreed that it should be something more than the standard anonymous shed of the sort they were seeing. It should, they concluded, be a truly public work of architecture that would provide a ceremonial place for the citizenry of New York as well as a commercial facility for the conventioneers from out of town.

Having visited a number of faceless halls, Pei and Kahan stopped off in Atlanta to pay a call on John Portman, the commercially successful architect-developer of hotels whose favorite architectural devices were brightly lit glass-clad elevators rocketing through enormous atriums. Although he was no admirer of Portman's glitzy decor, Pei had confessed to Kahan that he did appreciate Portman's sense of theater and his technological skill. Portman had done a design

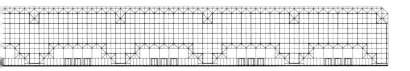

for a convention center in Atlanta, and although the building was never built, the visitors thought they might be able to learn from Portman's experience. They didn't get much that they didn't already know, and as the visit was ending, the populist Portman declared to Pei, "Just once, I'd like to do something like the East Building." According to Kahan, Pei replied with a smile, "Just once, I'd like to make the kind of money you do."

From Atlanta, Kahan and Pei continued on to Florida for a look at Disneyworld. Again, art was not the object, technology was. The vast Orlando amusement park had a well-earned reputation for the efficient handling of great masses of people and traffic. Disney officials had planned a tour of the park's behind-the-scenes infrastructure, but when it was time to start, Pei was nowhere to be found. Assuming that he had been only temporarily held up, Kahan, who had been joined by Freed, proposed that the tour be delayed to wait for him. The Disney people brusquely announced that they were starting without him. Kahan later concluded that Pei had been given the wrong starting time and speculated that it was not an accident. "They were paranoid about trade secrets, and seemed especially worried about what Pei might do with them," said Kahan. (When Pei caught up with Kahan and Freed later in the day, they repaired to the park's faux-Western saloon for some refreshment. The only available drink aside from beer was sangria, a concoction Pei had never sampled. He gamely ordered some, but when the frosty pitcher arrived and he sampled a glass, he discreetly asked the waiter to take it away. Bordeaux it was not.)

Once back in New York, Pei and Freed paid two visits to the site of the new building. Freed also felt strongly that the center would have to be more than a purely architectural statement. He remembered saying to his colleague during one of the visits that any convention center must necessarily be a "dumb" building—a collection of barnlike spaces for the display of vast quantities of wares—and that they would have to come up with something very special to give this one any real distinction. Pei agreed. "It bothered me enormously that buildings built with public money make so little public contribution," he said. "No public building can afford to ignore the impact of architecture on its community. We should give the public something back. We should at least give them a big room." Although Pei had comparatively little to do with the design work as the job progressed, his early perception of the fundamental issue was critical. "That's where his genius lies," said Freed.

Right from the start, the architects fixed on a compelling image for their building. It was to be a "crystal palace" in the tradition of the huge glass-clad, cast-iron pavilions built in Europe and the United States at the turn of the century for the great industrial expositions of the day. To create a similar effect with modern technology, Freed decided against a standard column-and-beam structural system and chose instead a lightweight spaceframe made up of interlocking tubes not unlike the ones used to support the skylights at the East Building and Fragrant Hill. There were many reasons for the decision, but among the main ones was that such a system would permit maximum use of glass. That way, they reasoned, the building would allow passersby to see in, while allowing users of the building to see out, creating what Freed hoped would be a "festive" atmosphere. "For a long time I felt like the little Dutch boy with his finger in the dike arguing for the glass," Freed said. "The construction manager wanted an opaque building to save on heating and ventilating."

The spaceframe had another advantage, which was that the intricate tracery of the structural members could be exploited as a decorative device, creating visual interest in what was essentially an enormous hangar. Moreover, there were the structural advantages: the spaceframe would provide the same volume as a column-and-beam system with only about twenty percent of the materials and be easier to put up.

The spaceframe was to extend over 1.7 million square feet and be made up of 76,000 tubes plugged into 18,700 nodes of several different diameters, rather like a gigantic Tinkertoy. It was to be covered with 4,155 panes of glass. Roughly 750,000 square feet of the area it enclosed would be devoted to exhibition space.

At the time, New York City was planning to redevelop the highway running along the Hudson River to the west of the center into a massive boulevard called Westway. Although the project did not go through, Freed had to assume that it would, and he concluded that such a thoroughfare was not the sort of thing he wanted at the front door. Accordingly, the main entrance to the center was placed facing eastward, toward the center of the island. At the entrance would be a "great hall"—Pei's "big room"—rising 160 feet (the atrium of the Kennedy Library was only 112 feet) and measuring 270 feet square, making it higher and wider than the concourse in Grand Central Terminal. As the promoters rather breathlessly described it, this grand space would be tall enough to accommodate the Statue of Liberty (without the base) and wide enough to handle two Boeing 747s wing tip to wing tip.

The main architectural problem posed by a building of the size proposed—both on the inside and the outside—was how to keep it from being

Having survived its structural travails, the Javits Center went far toward transforming a seedy section of New York by adding to it a monumental piece of civic sculpture.

Used at such large scale, the spaceframe (above) became a decorative as well as a structural element of the design. Slicing off the corners of the component masses to produce "facets" (opposite) added to the crystalline effect the architects sought.

monotonous. To enliven the massing, the architect arranged the enormous bulk of the building asymmetrically. The boxlike forms housing the great hall were stacked up toward one end, their corners chamfered to create what were intended to appear as facets of a crystal. Notches were then cut into the low-lying portions of the facade to break up the remaining expanses of glass. Freed predicted confidently that, especially when the interior of the building was lit at night, the effect would be of "an elephant dancing on its toes."

On the inside, the designer stratified the longer spaces horizontally and then "skewered" them with the vertical ceremonial space, which penetrated from basement to roof. The most powerful stratifying device was a freestanding concrete concourse—a "building within a building"—that ran the length of the center's northern end, providing conventioneers with a place to congregate, make deals, and keep an eye on the exhibition floor, which stretched out beneath them on either side. A large circular opening in the floor of the mezzanine provided natural light to a portion of the floor below and created a dramatic contrast with the powerful rectilinearity of the rest of the building.

One of the elements to which Freed, Pei, and Kahan were most committed was the sixty-foot-high "galleria," an interior promenade running westward toward the river from the great hall. It was to be lined with shops and restaurants—as Freed put it, "like a New York street"—representing the city's ethnic and commercial diversity and was to terminate in a large public space providing sweeping views of the river beyond the highway.

To add to the allure of the front entrance, Freed included a block-long public park. Because Kahan was confident that taxis and shuttle buses would be able to handle the convention traffic (conventioneers, he contended, didn't use public buses and subways), he deliberately left out provisions for parking. (He also feared that large parking lots on the site would have caused emission problems that might have threatened approval of the project's environmental impact statement.)

When the basic design was complete, Freed presented the drawings to Kahan, who had seen little of what was developing since the process had been set in motion. When Kahan saw what the architects had wrought, he was thrilled. "I loved it right away," he said. A $150,000 scale model of the center was then prepared, and the design was made public on December 11, 1979. "What Lincoln Center and the Kennedy Center were to the 1960s and 70s," Jerry Lowery, the executive director of the Convention Center Operating Corporation, declared, "this will be to the 1980s."

Above: The spherical nodes used to join the members of the space-frame became notorious when some developed cracks during manufacturing.
Opposite: With those problems solved, the transparency permitted by the structural system afforded dramatic views of the surrounding metropolis, especially at night.

Ground for the building itself was broken the following April. Faced with the financial uncertainties of high inflation, Kahan and the architects decided to "fast-track" the job, meaning that construction would go forward on completed portions of the design before the rest was entirely finished. It was a common but somewhat risky approach, and the risks were compounded by a local requirement that the construction work be assigned to the lowest bidder. Kahan fought the requirement, arguing for a modified bidding system that would have allowed him more negotiating room, but to no avail. The process was complicated even more by another local regulation requiring that the contractors for plumbing, electricity, and heating and ventilating all be on an equal footing, rather than coordinated by a general contractor, which was the more common practice. By the time the full work force was in place (and Kahan's demand that it include a maximum number of minorities was satisfied), there were sixty prime contractors working on the building, an unusually large number even for a project of this size.

The various labor requirements—well intentioned as some of them may originally have been—proved costly to the project from the outset. According to Werner Wandelmaier, Pei's partner in charge of managing the project, working with so many contractors was "a nightmare, a jungle, a Tower of Babel." To make matters worse, the entire construction climate in New York had changed. In the wake of the fiscal crisis of 1975, when virtually nothing was being built, the city was experiencing a boom in office construction. That meant demand for contractors was at a peak, and few of them wanted public-sector work of the sort the convention center offered when more lucrative private jobs were available. Not surprisingly, those willing to do the job presented the highest possible "low" bid. Concrete provided the best example. Kahan was expecting to get as many as four bids on that aspect of the job; he got two, one for thirty million dollars and one for forty million. It was widely assumed that the local concrete suppliers had simply agreed in advance on what their services would cost.

To further complicate matters, there were problems with the site itself. The architects had to thread the foundations around two of the tubes of the Lincoln Tunnel, which links Manhattan to New Jersey under the Hudson River. The ground was found to be wetter than expected. "I can't imagine a foundation type we didn't use," recalled Wandelmaier. Suddenly, the forty-million-dollar contingency fund Kahan had created to take care of unexpected hurdles was beginning to evaporate.

The problems produced considerable friction in some quarters. Kahan, a man who preferred a face-to-face confrontation even if it meant raised voices, was

Promoters made much of the fact that the main space was big enough to shelter the Statue of Liberty (or two Boeing 747s wing tip to wing tip).

upset by the flurry of paperwork flowing out of Wandelmaier's office. "He was building a file for litigation," Kahan said. "There was a lot of hostility when we could have been working things out across a table."

To keep costs from getting out of control, Kahan reluctantly ordered a number of cutbacks. The building's two northernmost bays were eliminated in August of 1981, saving an estimated seventeen million dollars, but losing 60,000 square feet of exhibition space. (The trimming was especially painful because the complicated foundations for the space had already been prepared.) For Freed, the worst cut was the funding for the skylight in the galleria. Replacing it with a solid roof saved almost three million dollars, but meant the space would lose the open-air feeling he had hoped for. The sacrifice, said Freed, was "penny-wise and pound-foolish." Meanwhile, political changes in the state capital began to affect the progress of the building. Mario Cuomo was elected governor, succeeding Hugh Carey, who had been one of the center's prime movers and political protectors.

While Freed struggled to minimize the impact of the cuts on the design, he and Pei were called in repeatedly by Kahan for emergency meetings on how to deal with the budget problems. As usual, Pei's courtliness and diplomacy did much to calm the contending factions, but if those qualities were stretched to the limit, the strain—also as usual—didn't show. "Most normal mortals would have been outraged with frustration," said Kahan, "but Pei was totally under control."

Another player who helped keep things from getting out of hand was Polshek, whom Kahan had retained as an adviser throughout the process. It was he to whom Kahan turned for confirmation on what could be cut and who acted as a sort of ombudsman between the Pei firm and the client. But the decisions were rarely easy. "Polshek stood up for the design all the way," said Kahan. "He was the one who defended the architecture against the construction people."

By September of 1981, the major budget problems seemed to have been resolved, and the building was proceeding in what appeared to be an orderly fashion. But to the surprise of many of those involved, Kahan announced that he was giving up his post at UDC and his position as head of the Convention Center Development Corporation to go into business on his own. "The project was half finished, and ninety percent of the bids were in," he explained. "The State Comptroller was satisfied that the building was on time and on budget, and I felt that the main problems were behind us. After all, I wasn't an indentured servant, and it looked like a good time to leave." Some time later, Kahan told a reporter for *New York* magazine: "The job I was uniquely qualified to do was pretty much

By "skewering" one end of the main horizontal expanse with a circular opening, the design allowed light from the public space to be passed to the floor below.

done. I had put together the deal, negotiated the contracts, made the revisions. All that was left was the construction, and there were others who were better qualified to supervise that than me."[2] Although Kahan remained on the Development Corporation board, the leadership passed to George Shoepfer, who had worked for Robert Moses and was regarded as one of the best construction people available.

Construction of the spaceframe was to begin in late 1982. In specifying the materials to be used, the Pei office had called for something called the Mero system, which used balls of forged steel for the nodes. Another system was available, the P.G. system, which used cast steel for the nodes. However, because the client was concerned about cost—and wary of Pei's reputation for going over budget—they asked that specifications be written for both systems. The bid on the P.G. system was made by the Karl Koch Erecting Company of Carteret, New Jersey, and was lower than the Mero bid by about $1.5 million. The Pei office was not particularly concerned. Both Mero and P.G. were proven systems, and Koch had done the steel work for the World Trade Center. Besides, said Freed, "Nodes are basically an off-the-shelf item, like nails or screws." The Koch company picked Goltra Foundries of Chicago to produce the nodes.

When the nodes began to arrive, they were examined under X rays. To the alarm of everyone concerned, many showed hairline cracks and porous sections, the result of air bubbles trapped during casting. Fully 12,000 nodes, or a year's production, were rejected. The architects complained to the client, declaring that "we have no confidence in the quality of the product." They were told that the manufacturer could make new nodes, using a different formula. The new ones began arriving in December of 1982. They, too, were flawed. By this time, the convention center's ills had become public, and the press had a field day comparing its plight with what had happened to the Hancock Tower. Freed's balletic elephant—by this time at least a year behind schedule and running well over budget—was rapidly becoming known as the "beached whale on the Hudson."[3]

Matters deteriorated further when Governor Cuomo appointed his former campaign manager, William Stern, to head the Urban Development Corporation. A self-styled "man of the people," Stern rejoiced in his disdain for high-design architecture and had no affection for Richard Kahan, on whom he promptly began to blame the growing disaster. As Stern saw it, the whole thing could have been avoided if Kahan hadn't been allowed to play around with the public's money in pursuit of art. As he put it to *New York* magazine: "I would have built a very large building with four walls, a nice steel roof, and some doors."[4]

Relief finally arrived in late 1983, when Thomas F. Galvin, a veteran of major building projects in Texas who had been involved at the earliest stages of the convention center planning, was made president and CEO of both the Convention Center Development Corporation and the Operating Corporation. At the time, he said, "You could barely hear the pulse of the beached whale." Galvin rapidly set about applying life-saving measures, which included reorganizing some of the corporation staff and implementing a proposal that a Japanese manufacturer produce new nodes. (According to Galvin, "Whereas two American foundries couldn't produce more than 1,800 nodes in a week, the Japanese could produce 1,000 in three days.") He also doled out $11.2 million in overtime and bonuses to meet a revised deadline for opening the center on April 1, 1986.

At one point, it seemed that even these efforts might be frustrated. As the construction momentum began to pick up, weather forecasters reported that a hurricane was on the way. To the delight of Galvin and everyone else, the storm changed course. But then a fire broke out on the roof, causing $200,000 worth of damage, and a subsequent test of the firefighting system went awry, producing a minor flood. Meanwhile, local law-enforcement authorities had subpoenaed the center's records for an investigation of possible bid-rigging by contractors. When disagreements persisted about the color of the terrazzo for the floors, Galvin called in the architects and got tough. "Nobody leaves this room until we decide which one we're going to use," he declared. A color was promptly selected. The center opened at 9:30 A.M. on April 3, 1986. "With any major building," Galvin told a reporter, "the toughest part is the final two percent."[5]

When New York's modern "crystal palace" opened for business, it was not without its share of shakedown problems: electrical failures, inadequate staff, confusion at the loading docks. But there were some larger causes for criticism. The reflecting glass used for the greater portion of the building's skin proved darker than expected, making the enormous mass seem almost opaque under bright sun, rather than semitransparent, as the architects had originally intended. (They had favored a lighter glass, but were overruled on cost.) The galleria, which was to have been one of the key gestures to the public role of the building, remained unfinished, a sadly leftover space instead of the vibrant artery it was meant to be. And for all the nips and tucks in the facade and the manipulation of form and volume on the interior, the building still had the feel of, well, a convention center.

But to the degree that the effect could have been mitigated, it was. The stacking of the boxes at the entrance did indeed provide sufficient focus to lessen

Contrary to charges by those opposed to the design that the structural system was experimental, the spaceframe (top) was in fact a commonly used system for enclosing large volumes. The main columns supporting the superstructure (above) were treated as pieces of Minimalist sculpture.

the potential monotony of such an elongated mass. And at dusk or at night, the glass skin was far more transparent than during the day, allowing a view of the brightly lit interior that was every bit as festive as Freed had hoped. Inside, the combination of the crisply geometric concrete elements—especially the concourse—with the lacy filigree of the structure created a dynamic contrast, each pulling at the other but ultimately in balance.

Surely the greatest achievement of the building was the decorative effect of the much-maligned spaceframe. As Freed had predicted, the enormous scale of the main spaces required a visual leavening, and his hopes for the system were fully realized. Although, looked at straight on, the patterns formed by the steel tubes of the frame seemed symmetrical and predictable, when viewed at an angle, their intersections created the illusion of curves. The patterns changed constantly as one moved through the building, and they were amplified by the shadows they cast on the floor. Thus what remained essentially an assemblage of "dumb" spaces, as Freed had said to Pei years before, became highly active, indeed theatrical.

If there were in the Javits Center links to Pei's atrium space in the Kennedy Library and his National Gallery courtyard, there were clear signs of Freed's sensibility in control of the whole. The building is far more axial and spatial, and more overtly ordered, than a Pei design would probably have been.

Under the circumstances, Freed and his partner had also fulfilled many of the hopes they and their original client had entertained when they undertook the building. The Javits Center nearly tripled New York City's exhibition space, and even with the cutbacks, it could accommodate all but the fifteen largest of the country's 150 top trade shows. The first show turned out to be the seventh annual International Fur Fair, which had shunned New York for two years in favor of Las Vegas because the old Coliseum was so inadequate. "It has raised questions about whether there's a place for public construction of this scope," concluded Shoepfer, who had by then stepped down as president of the Convention Center Development Corporation. "But it's a beautiful building, and it will serve the purpose well." In the architects' minds, however, that purpose had always included more than an efficient setting for fur shows. And when the doors opened to one of the truly grand urban interiors of its time, they had reason to feel that the public, too, had been well served. Here was a monumental space in which the city could take aesthetic as well as commercial pride.

So painful had the political process been, though, that the designers were all but ignored in the public celebration. Although the major governmental

participants were all listed on the huge sign erected outside the center in the closing stages of construction, the firm of I. M. Pei & Partners was not. And while, in his speech at the opening, Governor Mario Cuomo thanked a long list of contributors to the building's saga, neither Pei nor Freed was among them.

For Richard Kahan, who by then had his own development firm, the center had become a bitter memory—so much so that he would tell his taxi drivers to avoid the site even if it meant an expensive detour. It came as no surprise to him that he was not invited to the opening ceremonies. Pei and Freed were, and when they heard that Kahan was not on the list, they called him to insist that they tour the building alone beforehand. They arrived at the center as the last fragments of the construction debris were being cleaned up. "It felt like I was home again," said Kahan when he saw the finished product. "'This is very good,' I thought. 'It will stand up to the ugliest trade show and still feel dignified. The architecture is so strong that you can't contaminate it.'" His spirits rose even higher when he met a construction worker who had been on the job from the start. "It's too bad the wrong fucking guys will be cutting the ribbon," the laborer said. "That was all I needed to hear," said Kahan.

Pei was, as usual, philosophical about the bittersweet conclusion to the extended drama that had been played out so close to his office. "New York is a city of transients," he said. "At the time, it was undergoing a change from being an American city to being an international city. The people aren't boosters the way they were in Dallas; tomorrow they may be going back to Switzerland, and you can't expect them to take up the cause of good architecture. It is not a welcoming environment."

In addition to its impact on the city of New York, the Javits Center had an important effect on the future of the Pei firm. According to a friend of both Pei's and Freed's, Javits was, after Hancock, "the first big building in which Pei went so far in acknowledging other hands at work." As a result, virtually all the reviews—most of them positive—gave Freed his due as the lead designer. However well known he may have been among his colleagues, Freed now had achieved a level of public recognition that had long been lacking. The immediate effect was an invitation for him to design an expansion of the Los Angeles convention center, as well as a commission to do a museum in Washington, D.C., honoring the victims of the Nazi era.

Pei, meanwhile, was undergoing a liberation of his own. It came in the form of a commission that would make the politicking over the Javits Center seem like reasoned debate.

Freed positioned the main entrance (top) facing midtown Manhattan, both to avoid an unsightly view of a planned (but ultimately unbuilt) highway and to stimulate activity in the then-bleak neighborhood. If the glass was more opaque than hoped for when seen from the outside, it admitted more than enough light (below) to justify the original image of a "crystal palace."

11. LE GRAND LOUVRE (1983–89): THE BATTLE OF THE PYRAMID

In May of 1988, François Mitterrand was running for a second term as president of France. On the night of the voting, as was his custom at the end of a campaign, he chose to await the results at a quiet inn outside Paris. This time, the innkeeper had prepared a special treat in anticipation of his customer's all-but-certain victory. When the reports indicated that Mitterrand was securely ahead, the innkeeper brought in his creation. It was a cake, but there was nothing unusual about that. The surprise was the complicated little structure made of icing on the top. Rather than a French flag or the Arc de Triomphe, as might have been expected, it was, unmistakably, a pyramid.[1]

The inspiration for the miniature ornament was the seventy-one-foot-high glass structure that Pei had recently erected as the new entrance to the ambitious renovation of the Louvre museum in Paris. Mitterrand had selected Pei personally for the job five years before, and together they had weathered a firestorm of criticism to get it done. Under the circumstances, the fact that a work of architecture should have come to symbolize a political triumph was only fitting. "At the base of all politics," Mitterrand had declared after visiting the construction site of the pyramid two months earlier, "is the politics of culture."

Perhaps only in France could a head of state make such a pronouncement without risk of pretension. For in France, culture—especially as it is expressed in architecture—remains inseparable from national pride. The country's kings for centuries raised monuments to embody the power of the state, and after the Second World War the tradition was continued with unflagging *élan*. Georges Pompidou commissioned the national arts center in the Beaubourg district of Paris, and his successor, Valéry Giscard d'Estaing, redeveloped the disused

Although the public furor that greeted his plan for the Louvre focused almost entirely on the design of the pyramid, Pei approached the project from the start as a planning problem. In addition to reordering the museum, he intended to reanimate what had become a backwater in central Paris.

markets of Les Halles and transformed the old Orsay railway station into an art museum. "Louis XIV had his Versailles," observed a French member of the Pei team. "President Mitterrand has the Louvre."

For Mitterrand's architect, the aboveground portion of the Louvre project (the part that caused most of the controversy) was one of the smaller buildings he had done. But by the time the entire undertaking was finished, it had become the single most demanding—and rewarding—commission he had ever received. It involved not only architecture, but art, politics, planning, diplomacy, and sheer grit in a unique admixture. It subjected him to unprecedented strains and gave him his greatest victory. "It was the most important project of my life," said Pei shortly after the building was opened to the public. "It's unnerving if I look back on it."

If French heads of state have dedicated themselves to great building programs for their personal *gloire*, they have also been serving a public trust. Unlike the United States, France does not leave its cultural monuments in the hands of private philanthropists; the state is by far the major patron. And by the early 1980s, no French cultural landmark was in greater need of patronage than the Louvre. Its royal builders had never intended it to be a museum. Indeed, the Ministry of Finance had occupied roughly half the building since the 1870s, and the last important work on the building had been done in the 1880s. Since then, it had come to sustain an annual flood of nearly three million visitors, who had to negotiate its confusing layout and vast galleries with a minimum of modern museum aids and amenities. (There were, for example, only two bathrooms and a meager cafeteria available to the public.) According to some Parisians, the most frequently asked question about the Louvre was how to find the front door.

If visitors were suffering, so were the works of art. While the Louvre's collection had grown over the centuries to include hundreds of thousands of items, only a fraction of them could be displayed in its limited gallery space; the rest were in storage or on loan to other institutions. And while most modern museums set aside approximately fifty percent of their interiors for nongallery use, the Louvre's needs for gallery space left only about ten percent of the museum's square footage for such critical functions as administration, storage, conservation, and research. Museum people were fond of referring to one of the world's greatest museums as "a theater without a backstage" and "a masterwork of incoherence."

Despite its lamentable condition, the Louvre's age and prominence had long been enough to make it an obligatory tourist attraction. But since the completion in 1977 of Pompidou's Beaubourg cultural center, the new building

Pei meeting with François Mitterrand in June of 1983. The President of the Republic felt so strongly about the importance of the Louvre that he abandoned the customary practice of holding a competition to select an architect.

had snatched first place from the Eiffel Tower by a considerable margin. Of those who continued to come to the Louvre, only thirty percent were French and only ten percent Parisians, an embarrassing tally for such a national treasure.

Shortly after Mitterrand's election as president in 1981, the combination of the Louvre's institutional decay and the resulting cultural loss of face began to have an especially strong impact on his new Minister of Culture, Jack Lang. "I would pass by the Louvre every day," Lang said. "I thought how awful was the presence of all the cars and buses, how stupid that the Minister of Finance occupies part of the Louvre. So I wrote a note to the president asking why not a 'Grand Louvre,' without the finance ministry there. It could be a beautiful symbol. Culture will win against finance."[2]

Mitterrand was impressed, and in September of 1981, he decided to act, declaring at his first presidential press conference that the Ministry of Finance, which occupied the Louvre's northern, or Richelieu, wing along the Rue de Rivoli, would be moving to other quarters and that its space would be turned over to the museum. The goal was to turn the L-shaped museum into a larger and more workable U-shaped one, something the museum's administrators had proposed often in the past but had never been able to accomplish.

The decision to convert the Richelieu wing meant that the entire Louvre could be reorganized. But tampering with the building was a daunting proposition, especially because so much more than architecture was involved. Indeed, the building had long ago become a semisacred place for the French, embodying as it did so much of the history and spirit of the nation. It was begun around 1190 as a fortified castle by King Philippe Auguste in a forest where wolves once roamed. In 1365, Charles V transformed the fortress into his royal residence. François I later razed the fortress and erected on the site a new group of buildings, which were added to by Henry IV (who ordered the construction of the gallery along the Seine), Louis XIV (who turned the Louvre into an institute for advanced study), Napoleon I, and Napoleon III.

Over the years, parts of the complex had served variously as barracks, prison, academy, administrative offices, and art school. In 1793, the revolutionary Convention decided to use one of the galleries to exhibit the royal art collections to the public, and so was born the idea of the Louvre as a museum. Thus the building has always meant much more to France than, say, the National Gallery has to the United States. It is almost as if the White House, the Capitol, and the Lincoln Memorial had all been combined with the gallery in a single structure.

Pei and Mitterrand on the construction site with Emile Biasini (center), the determined civil servant who backed the plan through all its crises.

When Mitterrand took office, he already had several *grands projets* in mind. Ultimately, they would include an enormous office building, known as the Grande Arche de la Défense, behind the Arc de Triomphe, the multipurpose Parc de la Villette on the northern edge of Paris, and an opera house to take over the functions of Charles Garnier's 1875 triumph of gilded excess. Considered together, these and Mitterrand's other undertakings would make him the most ambitious builder in modern French history. But the Louvre was the first of his projects, and clearly the one that mattered most.

Pei's first contact with the French president took place on December 11, 1981. He had recently been awarded a gold medal by the French academy of architecture and was invited to meet personally with Mitterrand. During the meeting, which took place at the Elysée Palace, Mitterrand told Pei that he had visited the East Building and had admired an earlier, ill-fated Pei proposal (done with Araldo Cossutta) for the office complex at La Défense. He expressed his hope that Pei might participate in some of the projects he was planning for Paris. Pei replied as gracefully as he could that he had no time to enter competitions. To which Mitterrand answered, "Well, we are flexible." There was no mention of the Louvre.

Not long afterwards, Mitterrand began assembling a team to oversee the architecture projects he was contemplating. For the Louvre, the president turned to a leathery civil servant named Emile Biasini. A veteran of fifteen years in the French colonies in West Africa, Biasini had been a cabinet member under André Malraux, De Gaulle's Minister of Culture, and a director of French national television. With close-cropped gray hair and a nose that reflected the rigors of the rugby he had played as a youth, he radiated a compelling sturdiness, a quality he would need as Mitterrand's right hand on the Louvre. In the fall of 1983, he was given the title of president of the Etablissement Public du Grand Louvre, the government agency set up to handle the job. His first task was to look into the selection of an architect. "I wanted someone capable of respecting history, but innovative enough to attack anew," he said.

Biasini was well aware of the hazards of his assignment. Indeed, in 1665, when Louis XIV had invited Bernini—the most celebrated architect, sculptor, and designer of his time—to do for the Louvre what he had for Saint Peter's in Rome, the Italian's flamboyant proposal ran afoul of Louis's finance minister, Colbert, and the leading French architects, and he was sent home. No less a talent than François Mansart, probably the greatest of all French architects, had had fifteen projects for redesigning the palace rejected. The Louvre is "part of the cultural patrimony of the world," said Biasini of the building he was charged with renovating. But, he added, "if it was to continue as a museum, it was absolutely necessary to do something. The Louvre was in a grave condition. It was the world's most miserable museum."

The common practice in such a situation was to set up an architectural competition. To educate himself about possible candidates, Biasini spent nine months touring museums in Europe and the United States. Among his stops was Pei's East Building, which made a strong impression. "I asked many people which architect they would choose," Biasini said. "Pei was on every list." As a Chinese, he had "an understanding of an ancient civilization" and, as an American, "he had a taste for the modern."

Biasini subsequently asked a friend of Pei's who was living in Paris, an expatriate Chinese painter named Zao Wou-ki, to introduce them. Pei and his wife shortly thereafter were visiting Paris, and a meeting was arranged at the Hotel Raphael, which was much favored by publicity-shy luminaries for its discreet location on the Avenue Kléber. Biasini told Pei that Mitterrand had asked him to make recommendations about the Louvre and that two or three other architects were being considered, but that he himself had been impressed by Pei's work. Pei reiterated that he no longer participated in competitions.

A few weeks later, Biasini called Pei in New York to say that he was coming to the United States and would like to meet again. Pei agreed, and at their meeting Biasini asked him if he would accept the Louvre project if it were offered. According to Biasini, Mitterrand had concluded that, despite the danger of the precedent, the Louvre was too important an enterprise to leave to the uncertainties of a competition. Pei said that "it was probably impossible" to alter the Louvre, but that he would look into it. He would have to study the possibility of doing such a thing before responding officially, and he thought he would need at least four months. The loss of the La Défense project had been painful, he pointed out, and he was not about to embark on another effort in Paris—and especially not this one—without proper preparation.

Biasini agreed, and Pei subsequently made three trips to Paris, staying for periods of a week to ten days at the elegant Hotel Crillon, on the Place de la Concorde, a short walk from the museum. He read widely on the history of the Louvre and the history of France and was given a laissez-passer to go anywhere he wanted in the Louvre. Lest Pei's real mission become known, only one man in the museum, Jean-Marc Gentil, then its secretary-general, knew why he was there.

So far, Pei had not mentioned the project to anyone in the office. He had not even spoken with his partners about it. The only person in New York who knew of it was Eileen, with whom he talked about it at length. No foreign architect had ever left his mark on the Louvre, and Pei was still not at all certain that trying to do so was either possible or prudent.

Originally, Pei had been planning to make four visits to Paris, but after the third he was convinced that some sort of intervention was not only workable but necessary, and he decided that he would go forward. He then returned to Paris, meeting with Mitterrand and Lang. They made a formal offer of the job, and Pei agreed. "I would not have accepted it if I hadn't studied the problem for months," he said later. "I concluded that it had to be done, and that I would be able to do it."

In the course of the meeting, Pei explained in general terms his ideas about the expansion, pointing out that the additional space required by the museum could be added by excavating the Cour Napoléon, the open area between the two wings built by Napoleon III. How the space was to be organized and entered was not then clear. Nevertheless, Mitterrand was encouraged. He seemed particularly impressed by Pei's sensitivity to the history of the Louvre as well as by the architect's determination to make the museum a more vital part of the city fabric. Finally, Mitterrand nodded and said, *"Très bien."* For emphasis, he repeated it twice.

Back in New York, the project was treated with all the precautions due a military secret. "The idea of doing *anything* to the Louvre would have been killed if it had leaked out," Pei said. A room was set aside on the eighth floor of Pei's offices, and although few of the rooms have locks on the doors, Pei made sure this one did—and that it was used. Soon after agreeing to take the job, Pei quietly contacted Yann Weymouth, who had worked with him as a young designer on the East Building before leaving to set up his own firm. Weymouth's mother was from Brittany, and he had lived for long periods in France and spoke the language fluently. In addition, felt Pei, Weymouth "had the right spirit." Weymouth agreed to rejoin the firm for the duration. Pei's son Didi, another architect on the East Building, was also assigned to the project, not least because he, too, spoke excellent French. Later, Pei picked yet another veteran of the East Building, Leonard Jacobson, to be the managing partner. Having given Jacobson only the bare outlines of the project, Pei finally telephoned him during a trip to Paris and asked him to phase himself out of his other assignments. "I told him: 'The job is real. It's going to go; get yourself ready.' I could feel the glee in his voice on the other end."

Although Mitterrand and Biasini would both have qualified as the sort of powerful and interesting clients with whom Pei had traditionally done his best work, the Louvre itself became the true client for this project. Biasini said at one point that the Louvre "occupies the subconscious" of France, and it came to occupy Pei's as well. Throughout the project, Pei and his French counterparts constantly labored in the shadow of the building's history; it was almost a tangible presence guiding their intentions.

At one point during a meeting held at the Pei office to discuss the re-distribution of works of art in the museum, Pei, Jacobson, and the Louvre's director, Michel Laclotte, were struggling with the fate of the museum's collection of paintings by Peter Paul Rubens. "There are many ways of solving this problem architecturally," said Pei, gesturing at the enormous roll of plans spread across the table. "You must tell me how you wish to do it from the museological point of view." To which Laclotte replied, "What is more important is whether the solution fulfills *l'esprit du Louvre.*" Pei and Jacobson both nodded. "Of course, of course, *l'esprit du Louvre!*" they exclaimed almost simultaneously.

As Pei understood it, part of that spirit had to do with change. The building had undergone so many alterations and reincarnations over the centuries that he felt another chapter in the saga was perfectly appropriate to sustain the monument's vitality. And as he had done increasingly in recent years—especially in the East Building and with Freed at the Javits Center—he began to concentrate on how the Louvre was to be used, in this case, by even greater masses of people than it had accommodated before. "Something had to be changed to involve the public," he said.

The scope of that change appealed to him. Clearly, much more was at stake than mere architecture. Here was one of the great treasure houses of Western art and civilization. Having studied not only the Louvre's history, but its position at the center of Paris, Pei saw the challenge as one that also involved urban design, not to mention high-level trans-Atlantic diplomacy. As his thinking proceeded, Pei briefly discussed the project with his former client Richard Kahan. "I. M. was approaching the problem like a real estate developer," Kahan said. "From the outset, he was planning the political strategy as well as the building."

One of the fundamental early design issues was how to enter the re-organized museum. A superficial analysis might have suggested using the three existing entrances, one in each wing. That solution, Pei concluded, was not prac-tical. The one in the northern wing was too small, another was cramped by histor-ic staircases, and the third—on the Seine side—had already proved inadequate.

Because of the Louvre's location, any alteration to it would have an impact on the heart of the city. Among Pei's challenges was deal-ing with the fact that the wings of the museum are slightly off the axis of the Voie Triomphale, which links the Louvre to the Arc de Triomphe.

Denied those options, Pei concluded that logic all but demanded an entrance at the center of the Cour Napoléon, where the museum's center of gravity would eventually lie. An entrance in the center of the court would, by bringing visitors equally close to all three wings, eliminate one of the old Louvre's worst features, the need created by the main entrance on the Seine to walk long distances if the art one wanted to see was not in that wing. Few would mourn the loss of the courtyard, which had long ago become a parking lot for the finance ministry during the day and an unsavory trysting place at night; in any case, it was not one of the Louvre's more distinguished architectural spaces.

But having settled on a site for the new entrance, the question arose of how it would be housed. Pei ruled out a freestanding masonry building, which would have obscured the facades of the embracing wings. He could go down into the spaces he had been planning from the start to excavate, but because the river was so close, he could not dig very deep, and simply decking over such a hole would produce an inhospitably shallow space for a proper entrance. "I didn't want to create the effect of a subway station," he explained. There had to be "a room of importance, and there had to be light."

The idea of a glass pyramid at the center of the court emerged almost as much from Pei's study of classical French landscape design as it did from the need to get a roof high enough to avoid the subway station effect. Pei had read widely on the works of Le Nôtre, the greatest of French landscape architects, and was intrigued by the crisp geometry of his arrangements of plants, pathways, and water elements. One of Le Nôtre's common devices was to distribute plantings in a square pattern divided diagonally. Viewed from above, such a pattern resembled the floor plan of a pyramid. The pyramid form had much to recommend it. It was stylistically neutral and would therefore neither ape nor compete with the existing buildings. It was a basic geometric shape, which would blend with the classical symmetry of the Louvre and the gardens of the Tuileries to the west. And if it were clad in glass, it would, Pei hoped, be virtually transparent and intrude only minimally on the view of the existing architecture. It would also provide both the space for the "room of importance" below and the light with which he wished to flood it. Pei predicted that the glazed surface would, as a bonus, reflect "the changing moods of the Parisian skies."

As Pei developed the idea, he extended subterranean passageways from the proposed underground space to each of the three wings of the Louvre. These would allow visitors to go directly to any of the museum's wings without making the traditional trek through galleries they had no interest in. He then added three

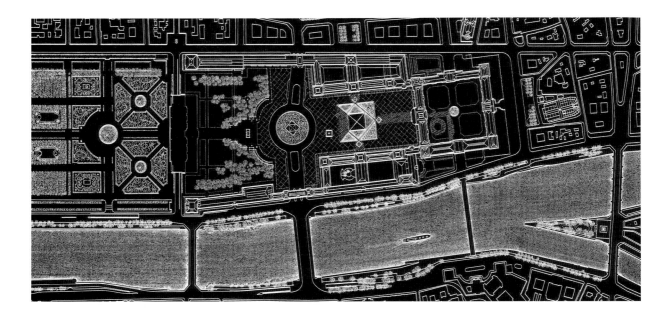

smaller glass pyramids above the passageways both to bring in light and to allow visitors to orient themselves as they moved from one wing to another. ("The measure of a large museum," he said, "is the clarity of its organization.") Back on the surface, Pei flanked the main pyramid on three sides with reflecting pools that were pierced by fountains. The effect was to further lighten the form by making it appear to float on the water.

The rightness of the scheme seemed equally compelling as architecture and as landscape architecture. Explaining it to a colleague in his New York office, Pei produced a copy of a book on Le Nôtre. Tapping the table with an almost boyish delight, he pointed to the elegantly ordered layout of one garden after another. "Look at this!" he exclaimed. "The love of geometry!"

The final design called for a main pyramid extending 116 feet on a side and rising to a peak of seventy-one feet, roughly two-thirds the height of the surrounding buildings. The three smaller pyramids were twenty-six feet on a side and sixteen feet high, and the reflecting pools reached out into a 7.2-acre public plaza that was to be paved with granite. Reaching back through Fragrant Hill to the convictions that had allowed him to persuade Walter Gropius of the merits of his Shanghai art museum project, Pei declared, "Architecture and landscape architecture cannot really be separated. In fact, some would say they are one and the same." According to Michael Flynn, Pei's resident expert on curtain-wall construction, "If I. M. had had his druthers, he wouldn't have used any glass at all and just made a beautiful trellis. But unfortunately, you have to keep the rain out."

When Pei had settled on the scheme to his satisfaction, he invited Biasini to New York for a visit. He had already prepared an elaborate wooden model of the existing Louvre and had had four pyramids—one large and three small—made from polished Plexiglas. After Biasini had studied the wooden model, Pei, with full appreciation of the drama of the moment, casually produced the Plexiglas pyramids and positioned them in their proper places at the center of the model. "*Diamants! Diamants!*" Biasini exclaimed. Then, switching to English, he declared, "I like it! Let's go!"

By removing the finance ministry from the northern, or Richelieu, wing (at top in plan), an L-shaped museum would become U-shaped. Pei argued that a new main entrance should be created at the center of the Cour Napoléon to facilitate access to all parts of the reorganized space.

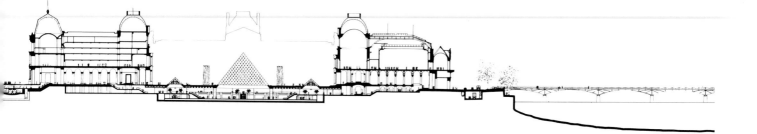

For all the architect's insistence on the origins of the pyramid solution in Le Nôtre, it was vintage Pei. In fact, variations on the form had been with him since the early schemes for the Kennedy Library, which was to have included a truncated version. It had all the qualities that most appealed to the architect: it was geometrically pure, minimal, and sculptural. According to Theodore Musho, Pei's long-suffering collaborator on the Kennedy Library, the Louvre pyramid was for Pei "a form waiting to get out." Nevertheless, it had a special appropriateness in the new role Pei proposed for it. In addition to satisfying the practical requirements of the program, it had direct links to the French Beaux-Arts tradition in its strict symmetry and unshakable rationality. (Despite his Harvard training under a Teutonic Modernist, Pei had never entirely lost touch with what he had learned at MIT, which was the last of the major American architecture schools to abandon the Beaux-Arts.) And while there were obvious links to Egypt, they clearly had provided confirmation rather than inspiration for the design. As Pei pointed out, the Egyptian precedent was about mass and impenetrability, while his pyramid was about lightness and transparency. As for the proportions, which turned out to be the same as the Egyptians': "We decided experimentally that they had been right 4,000 years ago. A few degrees steeper, and it's too aggressive; a few degrees less, and it seems to melt away."

While the positioning of the pyramid at the center of the Cour Napoléon may have satisfied the demands for symmetry imposed by the Louvre itself, it created a conflict in the larger Parisian scheme. The Louvre lies at the eastern end of the Voie Triomphale, the triumphal way that extends westward in a straight line through the Tuileries Gardens and the Place de la Concorde, up the Avenue des Champs-Elysées, and through the Arc de Triomphe. It is the most famous urban axis in the world. But the open arms of the Louvre wings are slightly off this grand axis, meaning that the pyramid, which Pei planned to position symmetrically in response to them, would seem askew when viewed from the west. (The problem had existed since the late nineteenth century, when the Tuileries Palace, which had terminated the axis from the west, was destroyed.)

This discontinuity had bedeviled many French architects, but having settled on the pyramid, Pei had virtually no choice about its relationship to the museum. The sense of order that dominates within the Cour Napoléon required that the new structure be aligned with the old. In any case, to align the pyramid with the grand axis would have put a corner of the structure inside the Louvre's south wing and disrupted the organization of the underground spaces on which the entire design was predicated. With a wry appreciation of the axial conun-

drum, Pei came up with a way to camouflage it. He proposed that a cast be made of an equestrian statue of Louis XIV by Bernini and that it be installed west of the pyramid. By aligning the statue with the triumphal way, Pei hoped that "it would ameliorate an incoherent composition."

Urban questions of another sort came into play when the project was looked at on its north-south axis. Because the passage through the Richelieu wing had long since been reserved for the finance ministry, there was no easy way for the public to get through that portion of the Louvre from the north or the south. This made it a major obstacle to the flow of pedestrians in the heart of the city during the day and virtually guaranteed that the Cour Napoléon would be abandoned by all but the adventurous at night. By opening that passage, which lay across the Rue de Rivoli from the Palais-Royal subway station, Pei could not only provide an additional entrance to the museum (by dropping escalators into the underground corridor), but also ease the movement between the two banks of the Seine. (His main ally in this effort was Biasini, who fought so hard for it that the architects informally dubbed the space the *"passage Biasini."*) Lighting the pyramid and its pools and fountains at night would, Pei was sure, reclaim the courtyard as an active urban space after hours. If his pyramid resonated with his classical schooling at MIT, his understanding of a museum renovation as an urban-planning opportunity could be traced directly to his practical experience with Zeckendorf.

While the public would come to focus on what Pei proposed aboveground, the officials at the Louvre were most concerned with what was going to happen below the surface. This, after all, was where the planning had begun, and what Pei proposed was no less Zeckendorfian in its ambitions than the "tip of the iceberg," as the pyramid itself became known. The entire excavation was to provide for approximately 600,000 square feet on two levels. The focus was the space beneath the large pyramid. Here visitors would buy their tickets and be given information about the museum and where to find what they wished to see. From the central space, the three passages would lead them north, east, and south directly to the galleries, without the marathon journeys required by the existing layout. Another corridor would ultimately extend west, lit toward the end by a skylight in the form of an inverted pyramid and culminating in a vast underground terminal fed by a depressed roadway and intended to absorb the legions of tour buses that had for years clogged the nearby streets.

Surrounding the public spaces would be an auditorium, shops, and restaurants. And embracing all this would be two parallel tunnels served by

The corridor leading westward along the river toward the Arc de Triomphe would accommodate a "street" of shops and a link to a subterranean bus terminal (extreme right).

239

electric carts and used for the transport of artworks (which formerly had to be winched in and out of gallery windows, weather permitting) and supplies for the other services. (Louvre officials insisted that the art and the food for the restaurants not share the same tunnel.) One level below would be offices, laboratories for the maintenance and repair of works of art, and storage facilities. With total understatement, Weymouth described the complex as a "seven-acre basement with a fancy roof." When complete, the added space would bring the Louvre's total area to more than two million square feet, making it the world's largest museum.

The scope of the Pei plan proved too much for the Louvre's director, André Chabaud, who resigned, saying that the reorganization was "unfeasible" and that "architectural risks" lay ahead. Pei, not surprisingly, had no doubts. "I sometimes have to pray hard that I'm correct," he said. "But this time, I was confident that we were on the right track."

Mitterrand shared the architect's confidence, but urged Pei to move fast, because there were only five more years left of his seven-year term as president. "It is a great pleasure," Pei said, "to work with someone who knows what he wants and will act on it."

The atmosphere in the New York office when Pei returned from his meeting with the president was close to euphoric. Ian Bader, one of the younger architects assigned to the Louvre team, said that Pei was convinced his design would be as well received by the French public as it had been by Mitterrand: "I. M. was sure that everybody would join in his vision."

As a formality, the proposal had to be presented to the Commission Supérieure des Monuments Historiques, an advisory group that had no binding authority, but carried considerable moral force in matters of Paris landmarks. On January 23, 1984, Pei, Weymouth, Didi, and Biasini arrived for the presentation, which was held at the Ministry of Culture. But although the details of the project were supposed to have been kept secret, the architects could tell from the muttering as the room began to fill that things were not going to go their way. The lights were dimmed, and Didi, who was operating the slide projector, put up the first image. His father, who had been given a bamboo pointer that was so long he had to break off a piece to get it down to a comfortable size, began speaking with the help of a young woman who had been asked to translate. "You could sense the hostility," recalled Weymouth. "It was palpable."

Gradually, the muttering grew louder, until the "delegates," including some reporters who had been alerted to the event and slipped in under cover,

Much of the early local opposition to Pei's project for the Louvre
focused on the fact that the architect was a foreigner.
In the end, converts concluded that the rigorous rationality of the executed
building could be interpreted as classically French.

Pei drew much of his inspiration
from seventeenth-century
French landscape design, but his
use of water (above) and framed
vistas (opposite) reveals still
more references to the Suzhou
gardens.

242

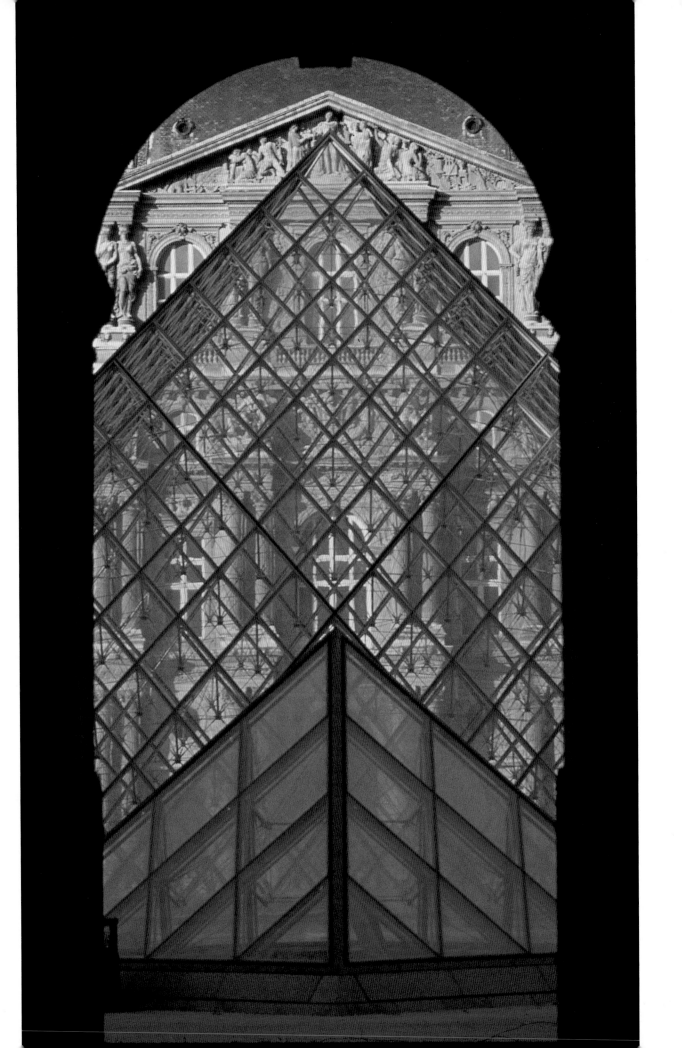

Having decided to put the ceremonial main space underground,
the architect countered the
potential for a "subway station"
effect with light-colored stone
and a frankly theatrical staircase.

If the pyramid is less transparent
during the day than Pei had
hoped, it becomes a see-through
jewel when lit at night. Its position
slightly off the axis of the Champs-
Elysées (opposite) is wryly
mitigated by the addition of a cast
of Bernini's statue of Louis XIV
(above) to anchor the line of sight.

Ever the precisionist, Pei outdid
himself in bringing the pyramid's
steel and glass into a crisp alliance with the stone and water of
its setting.

began attacking the design with abandon. The insults grew to such a pitch that the translator began to cry and said she could not go on. A member of the audience volunteered to replace her, but the verbal assaults continued unabated. Finally, when the lights went up, three of the members of the committee rose to read prepared statements condemning a project they were supposed to be seeing for the first time. The committee's former chief architect, Bertrand Monnet, denounced it as something that was "outside our mental space" and would prove to be a "gigantic, ruinous gadget."

With the presentation in a shambles, Biasini gathered up the Pei team and repaired to Chez Pauline, a classic Parisian bistro on the Rue Villedo, to assess the damage. Pei was less discouraged than angry at being treated unfairly. "None of us had expected the vehemence of the opposition," he said later. Weymouth suggested that they had been somewhat naïve and should have lobbied members of the committee before the meeting. With black humor, those present took bets on the margin of the committee's vote on the pyramid. (Didi, who predicted it would be unanimously negative, ultimately won.) Biasini, meanwhile, put the best face on matters by saying that since Mitterrand was behind them, the opinion of the committee didn't necessarily matter.

The public didn't see it that way. Parisians had become increasingly hostile to the incursions of modern architecture on their city. The dark hulk of the Montparnasse office tower that had gone up some years before on the southern edge of the city loomed as a reminder of the damage a single high rise could do to the Paris skyline, and the faceless spires of the new office buildings of La Défense showed what could happen when such towers were assembled as a group. The latest attempt at low-rise Modernism, the tacky structures that had replaced the once-bustling markets of Les Halles, were scarcely better. In light of such intrusions, it was perhaps predictable that almost anything new—especially in the bosom of French cultural patrimony—would be received by Parisians with skepticism at the least.

The Pei project was treated to much worse. Two days after the meeting of the historical monuments committee, a member of the French Academy, writing in *France-Soir*, predicted that the pyramid would be "an atrocity" and accused Mitterrand of "despotism."[3] The only proper response, he declared, was "insurrection." *Le Quotidien de Paris* carried a piece warning that the design "goes against the nature of the Louvre. It contradicts its biological development, its historic continuity."[4] *Le Monde* headlined one story "The House of the Dead" and compared Pei's proposal to "an annex to Disneyland."[5] Several critics insisted that

249

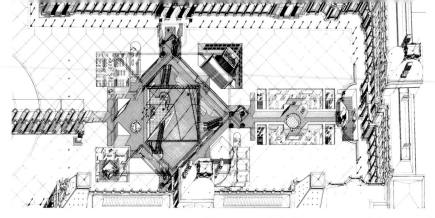

a pyramid was by definition a closed form and that there was no aesthetically satisfactory way to put a door in it. A writer for *Le Figaro* condemned it as simply "inadmissible." Declared the paper, referring to Napoleon's campaign in Egypt, "A new battle of the pyramids is about to begin."[6]

A hasty poll taken by *Le Figaro* indicated that while ninety percent of its readers supported a renovation of the Louvre, only ten percent supported the pyramid. A public petition was circulated asking, rhetorically, "Will the Louvre be disfigured?" The fact that Mitterrand had dispensed with a competition in selecting an architect moved one prominent art historian to intone, "It is unbecoming for a socialist president to act like a prince." Many of the attacks combined French cultural chauvinism with a thinly veiled trace of xenophobia. "I am surprised," sniffed one opponent, "that one would go looking for a Chinese architect in America to deal with the historic heart of the capital of France." The art magazine *Connaissance des Arts*, which backed the pyramid from the start, received for its pains a stream of what approached racist mail. "It was very unpleasant," said the managing editor. "There were letters saying the architect was neither French, nor even really American."

While Biasini was confident that the president's blessing would be sufficient to carry the battle, he was enough of a veteran of French cultural clashes to realize that a counterattack was called for, and he proceeded to rally his troops. In a matter of days, he rounded up the Louvre's seven departmental curators and shuttled them and the design team to Arcachon, a small coastal resort west of Bordeaux, to frame a response. Once the group had assembled, Pei and his people put on a full-dress presentation, to which the curators—who were, after all, the people with the greatest artistic stake in the project—gave their unanimous support. Laclotte (who was then the Louvre's chief curator of paintings) insisted that the group produce a public statement of their views.

It was published on the last day of January and concluded, "In the context of the Grand Louvre, it seems to the Curators-in-Chief . . . that Mr. Pei's pyramid for the entrance to the museum, far from being (as has sometimes been said) a 'modernist gadget' or at best a 'gratuitous architectural gesture,' is on the contrary an audacious concept that contributes to an architectural ensemble that for coherence and quality alike has been universally approved and accepted."[7]

The authority of the curators' statement did much to slow the momentum of the attacks, but it by no means halted them. Michel Guy, a former Minister of Culture, promptly founded the Association for the Renovation of the Louvre to mobilize resistance. He was less worried about the perceived threat posed by Pei's

For all its notoriety, the pyramid was only the "tip of the iceberg." The rest spread out in all directions below the surface of the courtyard.

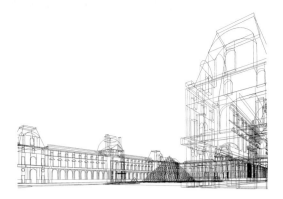

architecture than about the plan of reorganization that underlay it. He favored instead spending the money earmarked for the excavation and the pyramid on restoring the existing building and rearranging it into a loose conglomeration of "mini-museums" that would concentrate on artistic themes and styles. Again invoking French cultural superiority, Guy told the Associated Press, "I don't like the idea of everyone being treated like a tourist, that schoolchildren or you or I should be obliged to follow the same trail as the Japanese who come only once."[8] Even the American museum community eventually became alarmed, so much so that the French ambassador to Washington, Emmanuel de Margerie, had to call Pei in for a briefing to deal with the local protests. (Things were not made easier by the fact that the project involved the removal from the Cour Napoléon of an equestrian statue of Lafayette that had been donated by the Daughters of the American Revolution.)

The debate went well beyond both architectural and museological issues. Some observers saw the opposition to the pyramid as a focus for the resentment felt by many on the political right for Mitterrand's socialist policies. As one French sociologist and historian, Jean-Paul\Aron, described the situation, "I see it as a manifestation of the hatred that the opposition holds for the left. For the left to take power in France has always been seen by the right as a monstrous possibility, as something that went against the laws of nature."[9] Mitterrand's support was not strong at the time, and many expected him to lose control of the government in the parliamentary elections scheduled for 1986. Many of his harshest critics suspected him of trying with the pyramid to enshrine his administration before he left office.

The ideological crisis over the Louvre engendered a behind-the-scenes struggle at the highest levels of the Parisian world of art and society. Pierre Boulez, the renowned orchestra conductor, played a vigorous role lobbying his friends in favor of the pyramid. One of those friends was Claude Pompidou, the widow of the former conservative president. Madame Pompidou was arguably the most powerful woman in France and was widely considered its unofficial cultural ambassador. Despite the fact that her husband had been on the political right, he had broken with tradition in commissioning the controversial Pompidou Center, and his widow was now willing to put her own influence behind the pyramid. In a magazine interview, she declared (with an imprecision about authorship that would have wounded Henry Cobb), "I am convinced that Pei's pyramid will be very beautiful. I have seen a magnificent tower he built in Boston, and a project for the Bank of China in Hong Kong; truly, one can have confidence in this

Computers were used to generate drawings that helped the architect assess the impact of the pyramid on the semisacred monument.

251

architect!"[10] One of her friends went so far as to say, "It was a Mitterrand project, but there is no doubt that her support clinched it."

Happily for the Pei forces, Madame Pompidou was regarded with special affection by Jacques Chirac, then the mayor of Paris and the president of one of the two leading opposition political parties. It would have been politically correct for Chirac to condemn the pyramid, but following a discreet meeting with Pei himself, he announced that he was "not hostile" to the project. However, he did ask Pei to have a full-scale mock-up of the pyramid erected on the site so that the public could get a more accurate idea of the impact it would have on its surroundings. This overtly populist gesture was seen by the architects as particularly important because, as Weymouth explained the situation later, "We didn't have one client, we had fifty-five million clients, the entire population of France!"

In the spring of 1985, a crane was moved to the position in the Cour Napoléon where the pyramid was to stand, and from its extended arm four cables were stretched outward to simulate the ridges of the pyramid. Because the glass of the real pyramid's walls was to be clear, the architects explained, the outlines alone provided an accurate impression of what the building would look like when finished. They were well aware that the finished building would be only partially transparent, but if the truth about that was shaded for public consumption, the cables did convey a fair idea of the size of the structure, which many people were surprised to see was not as large as they had feared. The cables were left in place for four days, during which time an estimated 60,000 Parisians trooped by for a look. Almost overnight, the tide of public opinion began to turn. *Le Figaro* and several other newspapers that had opposed the pyramid suddenly fell silent on the issue.

But the debate continued to rage elsewhere. The American architecture critic Charles Jencks, a vociferous supporter of the Post-Modern movement, mounted an especially sharp attack in the September 1985 issue of the British magazine *Art & Design*, declaring that Pei had succumbed to "megalomania." Jencks, who felt Pei had redeemed himself for his earlier Modernist "malaprops" with Fragrant Hill, accused him of backsliding in Paris: "It is well known that Boulée and Le Corbusier suffered from this, occasionally; for Hitler and [his architect Albert] Speer the disease was chronic. It is also known that the ego is most likely to be infected near the centre of great cities, such as Paris, so when Mr. Pei went to talk to Mr. Mitterrand about adding a few new entrances to the Louvre one could guess the dreaded disease might strike again. . . . Now Pei and Mitterrand have succumbed to the same virus, and for much the same reason: they want

Pei with the cable mock-up that was intended to show the public what it could expect when the pyramid was finished. Although somewhat deceptive, the exercise proved convincing and turned the tide of criticism.

a memorial to their memory which one cannot avoid."[11]

Having wrested the momentum from the French antipyramid forces, Pei's supporters were dispirited to see the English-speaking press take up the attack. Nevertheless, Pei responded with characteristic determination. According to Ian Bader, who worked closely with him at the New York end during the entire period, the pressure in the office was "mind-boggling, shells were landing all over, but I. M. never showed it for a moment."

Even though the French public seemed to be coming around, the possibility that Mitterrand might be crippled politically in the next elections cast a lingering shadow over the project. Conceivably, the work already done might still be shelved. Jean Lebrat, the buoyant French *fonctionnaire* who had been put in charge of the construction phase of the project, urged all parties to speed things up so that it would be *"irréversible."* By the end of April 1986, the central excavations in the Cour Napoléon had been finished. There was no turning back.

Picking up the pace proved to have been a wise precaution, for in short order, politics again intervened to threaten the plan. In the parliamentary elections, Mitterrand's socialists suffered precisely the reverses Pei and his people had feared, losing power to a conservative coalition led by Chirac, who became prime minister, leaving the president to share power with a right-wing government. Although Chirac had earlier declared himself "not hostile" to the pyramid, Edouard Balladur, his finance minister, was not so sympathetic. From the very beginning, the plan had been to remove the finance ministry from the Richelieu wing. Pei had said often that he would probably not have accepted the Louvre commission if the ministry was going to remain in place. New accommodations for the ministry were already under construction on the banks of the Seine in Bercy, a section of eastern Paris that had been until recently the center of the wine trade. The main finance offices had already been vacated by the former finance minister, Pierre Bérégovoy, who transferred his people to temporary quarters on the Boulevard Saint-Germain on the Left Bank, and were in the process of demolition. (Bérégovoy, a supporter of the pyramid, had gone so far as to make sure that a hole was put in his roof before he left to encourage further demolition.)

But Balladur, a little-loved civil servant who served as Chirac's second-in-command, after nearly three months in office decided that he didn't want to be so far away from the center of the city—and power. After all, the ministry had been in the Louvre since 1873, having moved after its own building was destroyed by fire during the Commune. Its accommodations on the Rue de Rivoli included high-ceilinged offices furnished with red velvet chairs and embellished with gilded moldings, crystal chandeliers, and marble fireplaces. Quite apart from the loss of such luxury, the move would break what the Parisians call the "sacred triangle," the link between the Elysée Palace, home to French presidents since 1873, the Hotel Matignon, the prime minister's headquarters since 1958, and the Louvre. So on July 29, 1987, Balladur announced that his civil servants would remain in the Louvre until "appropriate space can be found for them in the center of Paris," a process expected to take as long as ten years. He then ordered the Richelieu offices restored (at a cost of some twenty million dollars) and moved his senior people back into the Louvre. Without the Richelieu wing, of course, the entire rationale for the pyramid would be compromised, since the wing was to account for most of the eighty-two-percent overall gain of exhibition space. Many saw Balladur's move as an insidious attempt to derail the entire project.

Yet again, Pei refused to buckle, or even to complain openly. "I was very sad at that moment," he said, "but the logic of the plan was so strong that I was sure it would prevail."

In fact, Balladur's high-handed manner did little to help his own cause, and the press took to needling him for such imperial gestures as having white-gloved footmen in his dining room and decorating his office with antiques from the museum's collection. Chirac at this point had his eye on the presidency, but his chances were fading as Mitterrand rebounded at the polls. Meanwhile, Balladur's stand against the Louvre expansion was costing him support among his own colleagues in the cabinet. In January of 1988, having been advised to face the increasingly likely prospect of a conservative defeat in the May presidential elections, Balladur finally agreed (after a quiet lunch with Pei and the Minister of Culture) to have half of his people out by the end of the year.

By this time, Biasini had reached the mandatory retirement age of sixty-five and was succeeded by Pierre-Yves Ligen, who had worked with Biasini in the Ministry of Culture under Malraux and had been director of urban planning for Paris under Chirac when he was still mayor. Meanwhile, Michel Laclotte, the curator of paintings who had played such an important role in framing the Arcachon statement, had been named by Mitterrand to be director of the Louvre. In the past, the post had been held by administrators rather than art historians and had always been subservient to the division of the Ministry of Culture that oversaw all national museums. But the job was now redefined to give Laclotte an authority comparable to that of Carter Brown at the National Gallery. Laclotte found Pei somewhat "obstinate," but conceded that "all great artists are like that" and put his new power behind the pyramid, which was no longer a mere cable mock-up, but a fully glazed presence gleaming beneath a film of construction dust outside Balladur's windows. At a "soft" opening on March 4, arranged with an eye to the elections that were only two months away, Mitterrand conferred on Pei the Légion d'Honneur—and made a conspicuous point of holding the ceremony inside the pyramid.

In May, Mitterrand prevailed at the polls, forcing Chirac and Balladur to resign. Bérégovoy again became finance minister and promptly turned to repacking his people's bags for Bercy. Almost two years had been lost in combating Balladur's rearguard action. Pei, who had never doubted that time would bring him victory, joked that "the Chinese invented bureaucracy, but the French perfected it."

Two months after the elections, Pierre Boulez conducted a concert at the pyramid for the benefit of *le tout Paris*, who by their well-heeled presence gave the project an indelible social imprimatur and hardly seemed to mind that the second half of the performance was rained out. Said Pei, flanked by Eileen and Didi and grinning widely beneath his umbrella, "I've been waiting a long time for this." (It wasn't quite long enough for Leonard Jacobson, who had been instructed to have the reflecting pools filled and the fountains playing for the occasion, whatever the costs. The machinery later had to be drained and disassembled so that it could be fine-tuned. "I was purple," Jacobson confessed.)

On October 14, 1988, Mitterrand cut a tricolored ribbon leading to the Cour Napoléon, officially opening the courtyard to the public, and thousands of Parisians streamed in for their first closeup look. The following March 30, at 4:30 on an unseasonably hot afternoon, the president cut yet another ribbon, this one to mark the opening of the "room of importance" beneath the pyramid.

What the first unofficial visitors to penetrate the interior saw was a spectacle of engineering as well as design. Pei and his people had created an almost sublimely simple object with the most sophisticated of means—and occasionally against what seemed to be insurmountable technological odds.

Acquiring the right glass was a saga in itself. Pei had insisted from the outset that it be absolutely clear in order to make the pyramid as nearly transparent as possible. Virtually all the glass available on the market, however, was made with small amounts of iron oxide, which gave it a slightly greenish tint. In hopes of finding something more suitable, the Pei team approached the centuries-old French firm of Saint-Gobain, the country's biggest glass manufacturer. Pei's people were told that Saint-Gobain, too, had abandoned the technique

At the heart of Pei's plans for the pyramid was the hope that it would be nearly transparent. Here, the architect (wearing a hard hat bearing the Chinese character for his family name) demonstrates the clarity of the specially fabricated glass to President Mitterrand (left).

for making totally clear glass years ago. What they wanted was simply *"impossible."* That answer was not good enough for Michael Flynn, who had handled the design of the skylight at the East Building. He tracked down a German firm which, while it had not done such a thing in recent memory, said it would be willing to resuscitate the craft for such a prestigious use. Flynn took the Germans' information back to the people at Saint-Gobain, who quickly appreciated the threat to French manufacturing pride. After extensive consultations, the firm concluded that it could, after all, produce the material Pei wanted by using a pure white sand from a quarry in Fontainebleau. "They came around when they realized how deadly in earnest we were," noted Flynn. As it turned out, the German product would have cost less, but buying French prevailed.

A similar exchange ensued over the subject of polishing the glass. If treated in the normal way, the sheets required for the pyramid would show minor variations in their surface. These would be invisible under ordinary circumstances, but, again, these were not ordinary circumstances, and even the slightest imperfections would compromise the crystalline effect for which Pei was striving. In this case, the French were not able to provide the service and agreed to have their glass shipped to an English factory that could.

The 675 diamond-shaped and 118 triangular panes that were eventually installed were held together by a structural system that involved some major innovations on the designers' part. Again to minimize any obstructions to the view through the pyramid, Pei called for a solution that made the spaceframes in the Kennedy Library and the Javits Center seem almost clumsy. "There were twelve other ways to do it, but I. M. pushed for a large number of small structural members," said Jacobson, who was responsible for making the whole thing work. The result was a steel spiderweb made up of 128 crisscrossing girders secured by sixteen thin cables. Unable to find any European source for nodes and struts of sufficient strength and lightness for this "bowstring" tensioning system, Pei turned to Navtec, a maker of rigging for America's Cup yachts, in Littleton, Massachusetts. (One of the few low-tech solutions for the problems posed by the pyramid was the one used for cleaning the glass. Because the exterior surface was so pristine, and the interior surface so difficult to reach through the spiderweb, the designers hired a team of trained mountaineers who were able to negotiate the structure without damaging it.)

Since the political uncertainties made it necessary to get the pyramid itself up faster than they would have liked, the members of the construction team were also faced with the problem of how to support the metal frame while the work that normally would have preceded it continued below ground. The problem was solved by erecting concrete columns from the foundations up to ground level at an early stage of the excavation. They were later connected by 150-ton box girders that were bowed upwards in anticipation of their ultimate load by cables attached to the ends. The cables were gradually loosened as work on the pyramid progressed, until, when the superstructure was finished, the girders were allowed to return to the horizontal. So accurate were the advance calculations for the process that not a single pane of glass in the pyramid broke when the last cable was released.

For all its technological complexity, the pyramid itself was, of course, only a relatively small part of the total undertaking. The combined area of the underground construction was larger than the entire floor space of the East Building. In the course of excavating for it, the architects came upon an additional opportunity. Just below the surface of the Cour Carrée—the enclosed courtyard to the east of the Cour Napoléon—were found the remains of an earlier Louvre. They were the twelfth-century foundations of the fortress erected by Philippe Auguste and portions of the palace of Charles V. Archeologists had long known they were there, but were surprised to find them in such good condition and proposed that they be restored. A crew of fifty-eight specialists promptly went to work, and their discoveries ultimately led to the largest archeological operation ever carried out in France. Altogether in the Cour Carrée and the Cour Napoléon, some 25,000 historic objects were found, ranging from ceramic shards and a cooking pot with pigeon bones still in it to a ceremonial helmet thought to have been stolen from the palace and abandoned by the thief. Plans were immediately made to link the foundations to the Pei design as a separate exhibition area, using the covered moat of the original fortress as a subterranean passageway.

With that behind them, the architects returned to work on the new construction. The floor plan of Pei's main space, christened the Hall Napoléon, shows a large square rotated beneath the square of the pyramid to form what appears from above to be an eight-pointed star. Its walls and floor were faced in a creamy limestone quarried at Chassagne in the Burgundy wine country and similar in color to that of the facades of the old building. To give the concrete of the coffered ceiling a comparably warm tone, special sand was brought in from the Nièvre valley and added to the mixture. The attention paid to the finish of the concrete exceeded even that in the East Building; ironworkers who were installing reinforcing elements were obliged to wear slippers so that the wooden forms would not be marred by their boots. The goal, said Pei, was to make it

Although the pyramid was the focus of public attention, the plan for the Louvre included a vast network of public areas and support facilities to be inserted in the space excavated from the Cour Napoléon.

appear as if the underground space had been "carved out of a single block of stone."

Protecting this extraordinary labyrinth from the elements was another formidable challenge. When the Seine floods, water can rise to within a few feet of the surface of the ground, so a drainage network was designed capable of pumping out even the worst floods. To satisfy French fire regulations, twenty-six fire exits were threaded to the perimeter of the Cour Napoléon, where they were covered with three-ton cast-iron grilles designed to open automatically in an emergency.

Pei had always involved himself in many of the minor details as well as the major decisions of buildings under his direct responsibility. For the Louvre, he was even more attentive than usual. The helicoidal staircase leading from the entrance platform to the floor of the main space is a typical example. Pei was eager that the metal supports for the stone steps be as thin as possible at the outside edges. But his advisers told him that a minimum thickness was required to keep the steps from bouncing under the anticipated traffic. Pei promptly trimmed back the steel to get the visual effect he was seeking, but then increased the weight of the stone treads to dampen any vibration of the steel. Both aesthetics and engineering were perfectly served. According to a French specialist working on the project, "We were always doing the impossible to cope with the architectural design. People have never seen anything so closely detailed."

Jean Lebrat, who had overseen the construction of the Les Halles complex, among other major Paris projects, was particularly impressed by what he called the "inevitability" of Pei's architecture. As he put it, "The rigor of the geometry ruled out *souplesse*—there was no chance for a multiplicity of solutions. With other architects, one changes the design to correct for what is possible, to accommodate the unbuildable elements of the design. But with Pei, it had been so well thought out that we could not build any other way. He has a complete vision, which he lets others discover on their own. It took me a long time to understand that. It was *diabolique!*"

Even though the project as a whole had been made *irréversible*, Mitterrand maintained an intense personal interest in its progress. On several occasions, he would slip away from the Elysée at night and, accompanied by Pei and a few bodyguards, inspect the site in secret. On one of the visits, Pei saw Mitterrand bend over and almost reverently touch the water from one of the reflecting pools as it glided in a perfect, thin sheet over one of the granite weirs.

By the time the Hall opened to the public, the agonies of the early days

Because window-cleaning machinery would have been cumbersome if not hazardous to the sheer surface of the building, expert alpinists were hired to deal with the inevitable urban fallout.

had been all but forgotten. For those determined to keep up the attack, the thrust shifted from the pyramid to the reorganization of the collections and the prospect of making the museum too popular. (To which the prickly Laclotte, sounding very much like Carter Brown at the National Gallery, was quick to reply, "This is the way we experience art today, en masse, and architecture must accommodate it.")

Some of the very newspapers that had devoted so much space to condemning the Pei design now found that it wasn't so bad after all. Conceded a writer in *Le Quotidien de Paris*, "The much-feared pyramid has become adorable." [12]

A few observers with a taste for history noted wryly how the flip-flop in official opinion resembled the one a century before over the Eiffel Tower. In 1887, *Le Monde* had run an article representing the views of some 300 French writers and artists protesting, "in the name of art and the threatened history of France," the plans to build "the useless and monstrous Eiffel tower." The artists insisted that the construction would "crush with its barbaric, factory-chimney weight" the "pristine beauty of Paris." No less a figure than Emile Zola condemned it as "a pile of iron junk." [13] The original supporters of the pyramid took special delight in the turn of the historic wheel, pointing to a Louis Harris poll taken after the opening that showed fifty-six percent of those surveyed in favor of the pyramid, with only twenty-three against, an almost exact reversal of the numbers four years before.

Congratulations poured in from around the world. *Le Figaro*, one of Pei's sharpest early critics, hastily reserved the pyramid to celebrate the tenth anniversary of its magazine supplement. (Amazed at the paper's cheeky loss of memory, Biasini asked Mitterrand if he didn't also think it a bit much. The president replied that he considered it "droll.") Dignitaries lined up for escorted tours. Among them was Britain's Prince Charles, who had made a name for himself as an amateur architecture critic by attacking most of the recent modern buildings in London. With unexpected enthusiasm, he pronounced Pei's work "marvelous, very exciting."

The building was not without its problems. The main one was that, for all the efforts to make the pyramid an intangible crystalline presence, it was sufficiently opaque under some weather conditions to disappoint even the architect. (And no one had quite anticipated the amount of dirt that would accumulate on it in a short time, despite the best efforts of the alpinists.) The air conditioning proved inadequate on a hot day, and the escalators were balky. Some visitors

Top: Having won both his political and his architectural campaign, Mitterrand cuts the ribbon at the April 1989 opening of the pyramid.
Above: Mitterrand and Pei tour the central space with culture minister Jack Lang.

found the acoustics of the main space excessively harsh. And the public excitement over the building produced such crowds that long lines formed at the main entrance despite all of Pei's planning for increased capacity.

One shortcoming that was as much a disappointment to Pei as it was to visitors who knew about it was the absence of a piece of sculpture atop the concrete column that rose in the center of the Hall Napoléon to support the reception platform inside the front door. From the beginning of the plan, Pei had hoped fervently that he would be able to secure the *Winged Victory of Samothrace* for this proud spot. Indeed, it appeared in all the early drawings. But its position at the top of the famous flight of stairs in the old building was so much a part of the Louvre's traditions that even Laclotte decided he could not risk the reaction to moving it. Several other candidates were considered and rejected. A replica of Rodin's *Thinker* was one possibility, but the anatomy didn't lend itself to a view from below. Another was a cast of an abstract rooster by Brancusi, who had died leaving only the plaster version. (Disputes over casting it put an end to that idea.) For an architect who had made such enthusiastic use of sculpture as a counterpoint to his work (and who had won virtually every other gamble on this project), the failure to secure the *Samothrace* for the pyramid was particularly painful.

There was much else for the Pei people yet to do. In a future phase of the project, the entire Richelieu wing would have to be rebuilt on the inside to transform it from offices to galleries. Landscaping of the gardens west of the pyramid, including the installation of a "ghost" outline of the foundations of the vanished Tuileries palace, would take months. So would the cleaning of the museum's limestone facades. The completion of the underground parking facility was years off.

Yet the structure that opened in the spring of 1989 was in every way at the heart of Pei's work. His fundamental love of geometric precision had found precisely the right setting. So had his feeling for landscape and the relationship of a building to the life of a city. His Modernist rigor had rehabilitated a neo-Classical monument through a form that resonated with history reaching back 800 years—or 4,000, if the Egyptian precedent is included—and yet pushed at the limits of contemporary technology.

And it worked for those who used it. As he had in the East Building and at Fragrant Hill, Pei exploited the movement of people through his volumes as a way to animate the crisp joints and satiny finishes of his forms. Eerily correct as the uninhabited Cour Napoléon looked with its glass centerpiece and equally glassy pools, it required pedestrians to make the space complete. Shortly before the

Pei had hoped to install the *Winged Victory* atop the column supporting the entrance platform, but the Louvre officialdom felt the public outcry over moving it would be too great and left it where it was.

courtyard opened, Weymouth, who had worked with Pei to find just the right stone for the spherical bollards on the edge of the space, noticed a young couple taking in the view with their child. Suddenly, the little girl walked up to one of the gray balls, studied it for a moment, then wrapped her arms around it and kissed it. "I broke into tears," said Weymouth. "We had worked for that for six years."

Here, Pei had found the equation that had been missing in the plaza of the Dallas City Hall and others of his overly abstract public spaces. The day before the opening, the architect was spotted across the street that penetrates both wings of the Louvre at the western edge of the Cour Napoléon, surveying the crowds surging around the new building. He had been there for some minutes, unrecognized by all but a few of the visitors. When an acquaintance joined him on the narrow strip of curb left by a construction fence, Pei told him that he had just seen a dog leap into one of the reflecting pools for a swim. "It's so festive," the architect said to his surprised listener. "I didn't mind at all."

The profit gained from the contrast between inanimate forms and human activity proved even more effective inside. Indeed, the helicoidal staircase with its lighted treads—which took its spiral forebear in the Everson Museum to unthought-of levels—verged on the theatrical, especially with the freestanding, piston-like elevator in its center. And by creating such startling views of the old buildings through the glass from below, Pei overcame the traditionally negative associations of being underground and actually amplified the appreciation of what had gone before. The old Louvre was no longer just an aged enclosure, but an active element in a redefined architectural composition.

Shortly before the gala dinner celebrating the opening, Pei was seen bustling around the hall giving last-minute instructions to museum employees in their new Yves Saint-Laurent uniforms on the arrangement of the planters for the ornamental trees. It was the same ritual he had performed hours before the opening of Fragrant Hill, but here it was not to conceal shoddy workmanship. It was to perfect the experience for his guests, who included much of the trans-Atlantic cultural elite and most of his family, who had come both for the opening and for Didi's wedding the next day. Halfway through the dinner itself, Jack Lang rose to toast *"notre ami, Pei."* The architect was then ushered to the microphone and said a few words in his heavily accented French. He paused, evidently searching his vocabulary, and then, in a voice that betrayed a rare tremor, added, *"Merci pour tout."*

Reflecting on the occasion some weeks later, Pei said, "I hope to do many more things, but never again will I have another opportunity like the Louvre."

Although Pei's renovation of the Cour Napoléon is no less abstract than the design for the pyramid itself, the space is far more inviting than many of the architect's previous plazas.

12.

1989: "THE YEAR OF PEI"

Looking back over I. M. Pei's career from the vantage point of late 1989, it was clear that the architect's remarkable trajectory had been marked by four distinct phases. The years with Zeckendorf had given him a unique practical exposure to urbanism on a grand scale; the commission to design the Kennedy Library had launched his public reputation as an architect; the East Building of the National Gallery had established him as a master of his art; and the commission for the expansion of the Louvre had secured his position as an architect of unchallenged international stature.

But while the Louvre may have attracted more attention than any other building he had done, it was only one of five Pei designs to be completed in 1989. It was followed in quick succession by an office building for the Creative Artists Agency, one of Hollywood's most powerful talent-management organizations; the Morton H. Meyerson Symphony Center in Dallas; a science building at the Choate Rosemary Hall School in Wallingford, Connecticut; and a seventy-story tower for the Bank of China in Hong Kong.

It was not merely the number of buildings, but their variety that made the year so extraordinary for Pei. Here was a man of seventy-two producing almost simultaneously an expansion of the world's most famous museum, a corporate headquarters, a concert hall, a school building, and a skyscraper. It was a bravura performance by any measure, demonstrating that Pei could do virtually anything he turned his hand to, and do it surpassingly well.

Pei's five buildings were the only ones actually completed by his firm in 1989, but they represented just a portion of its activities. Indeed, Pei's partners were also busier than ever. Henry Cobb was in the midst of a major renovation and

The architect contemplating the Bank of China tower under construction.

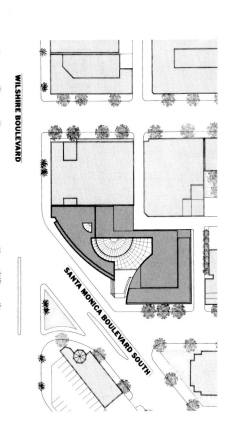

expansion of New York's Kennedy Airport, as well as an international trade center in Barcelona and an office complex in London, while James Freed was proceeding with the Holocaust Memorial in Washington and his convention center work for Los Angeles. With roughly 300 employees, the firm was ranked as one of the largest architectural offices in New York. In a deft display of timing, Pei took advantage of this high-water mark to change the firm's name from I. M. Pei & Partners to Pei Cobb Freed & Partners, formalizing the tripartite design arrangement that had existed for some time and creating an identity that would, he hoped, endure well past his inevitable retirement. But while the name change prepared the public and clients alike for the gradual withdrawal of the senior partner from the overall management of the firm, it also liberated Pei to pursue architecture at a more intimate scale than ever before.

The only cautionary note in what the journals quickly dubbed "the year of Pei"[1] was that none of the great American architecture firms had ever succeeded in perpetuating itself after the departure of the original talent. McKim, Mead & White had deteriorated artistically, as had Skidmore, Owings & Merrill, to name only the two most prominent examples. Pei clearly hoped that by giving his firm a sufficiently powerful burst of his own energy he could endow the organization he had created with enough momentum to avoid a similar fate.

The media coverage of the Louvre had only just begun to die down when Pei's Morton H. Meyerson Symphony Center opened in Dallas. Although nothing like the Paris project in scale or international impact, the building had been in the works even longer.

With the assassination of President Kennedy nearly twenty years behind them, the leading citizens of Dallas in the late 1970s were eager to crown their commercial success with a monument to their cultural aspirations, so that the city might be taken seriously as an arts center of national importance. The impulse began to take physical form with the designation of the so-called Arts District, an idea that had started with a 1977 study recommending that several major arts facilities be concentrated in the northeast quadrant of the city's downtown area. The first element of the plan to be built was the Dallas Museum of Art, designed by Edward Larrabee Barnes. The Dallas music community was no less eager for a proper facility of its own, and although the local symphony had been in such bad condition that it had to cancel its 1973–74 season, a campaign was set in motion to replace its shabby quarters with a new hall. It was meant to be, in a phrase repeated throughout its development, nothing less than "world class."

The backers of the new hall faced a number of obstacles, not the least of

them a lingering local suspicion in some quarters of high culture as "elitist." As one of the main patrons of the proposed hall, Stanley Marcus of the Neiman-Marcus department store chain, put it, "The people of Dallas regarded the arts as all right as something to attract corporate headquarters, but at heart they were not very enthusiastic." Moreover, the city had changed since Pei designed the City Hall. The minority population had grown in size and influence, and many people argued that development money should be devoted to solving the city's social ills rather than to providing places for the entertainment of the wealthy.

Nonetheless, the project continued to gather momentum. In 1980, a committee was established by the symphony association to select a team that would make the building a reality. The committee was headed by Morton H. Meyerson, a close friend of the well-known Texas entrepreneur Ross Perot and president of Perot's Electronic Data Systems. To get an idea of the sort of concert hall they wanted, Meyerson and other members of the committee visited twenty-one halls in North America and Europe. All of the committee members agreed that the most attractive were the Musikvereinssaal in Vienna (completed in 1870) and the Concertgebouw in Amsterdam (1887), both of which were relatively small, "shoebox" halls containing fewer than 1,700 seats, but had outstanding acoustics. "We didn't want just a 'now' hall," said a participant. "We wanted a building for the ages." With characteristic Texas confidence, they set aside until later a consideration of what such a building would cost. "In those days," said a member of the concert hall committee, "everything was doable."

In August of 1980, the committee contacted forty-five architects considered capable of handling the job. Pei was on the list, but, concerned that the troubled history of the City Hall might affect his involvement, he was not among the twenty-seven who replied. However, after the committee had reviewed the submissions by the other architects, they were unable to decide on a winner. So Stanley Marcus, who had come to know Pei during his work on the City Hall and remained an enthusiastic supporter, made a personal appeal. This time, Pei responded, coming to Dallas to discuss the project. He pointed out to the committee that he had never designed a concert hall, but said that he was eager to try. It was, after all, one of the few building types he had not already done, and he regarded it as a challenge. The committee voted unanimously to retain Pei; one member of the group commented, "We were convinced that we would get the world's greatest architect putting his best foot forward. We felt that the fact that he hadn't done a concert hall was an advantage."[2] The decision was announced on December 31, 1980.

Like his earlier building for the arts at Choate Rosemary Hall, Pei's science center at the school was intended to link formerly isolated areas of the campus.

Despite the protracted difficulties he had experienced with the City Hall, Pei retained a genuine affection for Dallas and its people, whom he had found to be refreshingly authentic, if not as sophisticated as some of his other constituents. Adding a building for the arts to those the firm had already done for government and commerce was an attractive proposition. But built into this assignment was an unexpected hazard. The symphony association was all too well aware of the humiliation suffered in 1962 by New York City when the acoustics of the new Philharmonic Hall in Lincoln Center had proved disastrous. (The hall had to be gutted and virtually rebuilt.) Determined to avoid a similar experience, the association had decided to divide the responsibility for the hall equally between an architect and an acoustician, so that aesthetics would not overwhelm the sound. The man the committee picked to take charge of planning the hall itself and caring for its acoustics was Russell Johnson, a 1951 graduate of the Yale School of Architecture who had made his firm, Artec, one of the most respected in the field. Extensive as his experience was, he had never worked on anything as ambitious as the hall Dallas was proposing. Johnson's selection was announced in February of 1981.

The arrangement might have worked smoothly if there had been one strong figure overseeing it, but there was not. From the outset, the hall was to be a joint project of the symphony association and the city. But Morton Meyerson, although he remained chairman of the symphony association committee throughout the project, was away for extended periods looking after his business affairs, and none of the other members had sufficient authority to make the major decisions. It rapidly became a case of what one city official called "mass confusion—we had five quarterbacks, not one."

The leadership vacuum created special problems for Pei, who had always done his best work when there was a strong and committed client in charge. The vagaries of command were compounded by a lack of firm financial control. The city of Dallas had agreed to provide roughly sixty percent of the money for the hall, while the symphony association was to make up the difference from private sources. But there, too, the chain of command was not clear, a particularly risky situation in light of the fact that none of the major participants had ever undertaken a project of such scale and complexity. The original financial estimate—$28.6 million from the city and $20.9 million from the association—was at best a guess. And although in light of the overruns on the City Hall the backers had extracted a pledge from Pei not to go over budget, the diluted management of the project virtually guaranteed money trouble in the future.

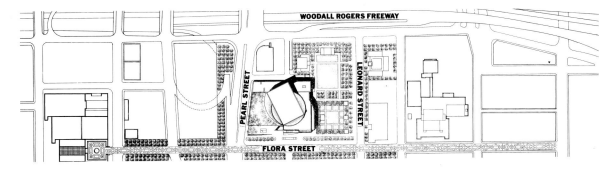

Despite the slim budget and the lack of clear oversight, the design process began. At the core was Johnson's version of the classic "shoebox," a 2,065-seat auditorium based on the European examples the committee had so admired. Anything larger, Johnson felt, would compromise the intimate qualities of sound and space Dallas was seeking. The box provided for a simple, narrow space with balconies and boxes rising on three sides. But around and over this conventional-looking hall were scattered a number of modern devices designed to prevent the sort of acoustical catastrophe suffered by New York.

Acoustics remains almost as much an art as a science, but Johnson made full use of every technological aid to create the best possible conditions for a variety of music. There was a double roof of concrete to keep out noise from airplanes passing overhead. Between the hall itself and the public space that was to surround it, Johnson provided a "sound lock" made up of antechambers. Above the balconies, he called for a vast "reverberation chamber," basically an attic space faced with enormous concrete doors that could be adjusted on pivots to absorb or reflect sound rising from the stage. Above the stage was to be suspended a U-shaped canopy that could be raised or lowered to further refine the musical effect. So mightily did Johnson strive to protect the Dallas hall from acoustical embarrassment that one participant in the process described the design as wearing "a belt and suspenders."

Pei, for his part, was not about to settle for a mere embellishment of Johnson's basic box. On the contrary, he saw in it an opportunity to go beyond his earlier work on the City Hall, which he had always felt lacked finesse. "Geometry has always been the underpinning of my architecture," he said. "And in the early work, it was relatively simplistic." This time, he was going to give the city something far more sophisticated. He began work on the design in earnest while he and Eileen were in the Caribbean taking one of their rare vacations.

In designing the East Building, Pei had been intrigued by the visual possibilities of the triangular forms suggested by the irregular site. For Dallas, Pei took matters a step further, looking to the even more complex effects achieved by the great Late Baroque architects, particularly Balthasar Neumann, the preeminent German architect of the period, in his pilgrimage church of Vierzehnheiligen (1743–72). There, arches, balconies, and vaults intersect in a dizzying combination of curvilinear forms, leading the eye ever onward to new spatial discoveries. In this architectural tour de force, the vanishing points have become virtually infinite. "There is something mysterious about the space," Pei said. It was precisely the effect he was hoping for.

By rotating the main mass of the Meyerson symphony hall (above, center) off the Dallas street grid, Pei intended to make simultaneous gestures to the nearby Dallas Museum of Art and the downtown business district.

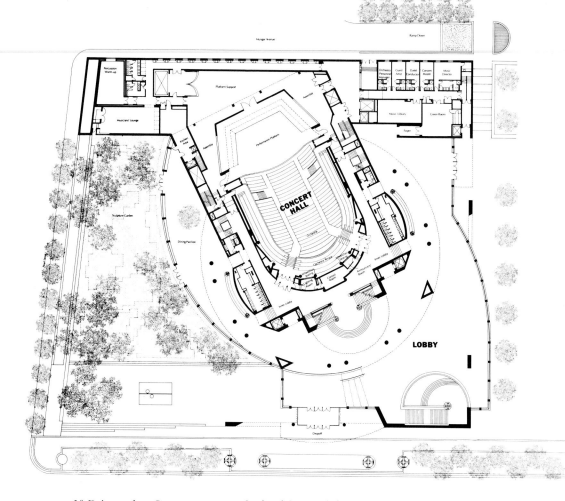

The rectangular core of Pei's building (above) was occupied by the "shoebox" of the concert hall itself. Its complex acoustical requirements were worked out by Russell Johnson, with whom Pei had frequent clashes. Pei modulated the exterior (opposite) by extruding unorthodox skylights called "lenses" and draping the lower portion of one wall (at left in drawing) with a glazed "conoid."

If Pei used a German example for his spatial inspiration, he turned to France as a source for the overall impact he was seeking. The "burghers of Dallas," as he had called the city's leading citizens, had never been known for restraint when it came to public gatherings, and in Charles Garnier's 1875 building for the Paris Opéra—that exquisitely garish monument to social excess—Pei thought he had just the building to convey the spirit of what he was prepared to do. For all its gilt, the Opéra was a fine work of architecture, and one he could be sure his well-traveled clients knew well. The Parisian precedent, Pei felt, had the right appeal for the leaders of a city determined to move itself up in the sociocultural world.

But there was more to the choice than canny salesmanship. Indeed, as he had been in the East Building and the Javits Center, Pei was genuinely eager to create a grand space that would attract people to the building in an act of celebration. In words very close to those he had used to describe his goal for the East Building, Pei told an interviewer in 1982: "I want to convince non-music lovers to love music, and the first step has got to be getting them intrigued about coming in."[3]

The design went through several incarnations, changing most often for reasons of budget and because of the nature of the site. The plan for the final building revealed a rectangle (which included Johnson's "box") rotated off the axes of the street grid to intersect a narrower rectangle (housing offices and rehearsal areas) and embraced on three sides by segments of circles (which

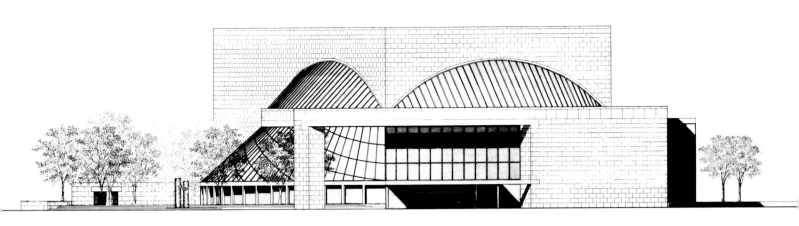

contained the lobby spaces). The rotating of the main form was done so that the most public aspect of the building would face toward the downtown area, while making a simultaneous gesture to the nearby Art Museum. According to Ralph Heisel, an architect in the firm who worked closely with Pei on the early stages of the building, "The whole conversation about the design started off with how it could be related to its surroundings." Whatever the urbanistic intent, however, the plan was classic Pei geometry, recalling especially the overlapping forms in the plans for the Kennedy Library.

The most dramatic part of the exterior was the glass, which was used for what Pei dubbed the "lenses," three curved skylights that seemed to have been extruded from the hard-edged forms of the limestone-clad box. They were amplified by a so-called conoid, a sloping, skirtlike glazed form that swept around and below the southernmost lens, giving the rectilinearity of the rest of the building an overt sensuality that Pei had rarely permitted himself. While skylights of various sorts had long been a part of his design vocabulary—in the Kennedy Library, the East Building, and the Fragrant Hill Hotel, for example—their primary role had been to enliven the interior spaces. In Dallas, Pei made the skylights themselves a sculptural embellishment of the exterior mass.

The interior spaces illuminated by the skylights expanded significantly on the precedent of the East Building. While in Washington the excitement of the interior court had been generated by premeditated collisions of triangles, the plan for the Dallas lobby seemed to flow sinuously around the anchoring mass of the hall. The curved steel members supporting the thousands of glass panes (each of which was a unique shape) intersected with the stone verticals and horizontals in such a way that the glass appeared to have been draped rather than assembled. The composition was made even more fluid by the insertion of a freestanding balcony in the form of a catwalk that curved gently through the main space and disappeared out of sight to both sides. These curves were echoed by others in the staircases, creating a spiderweb of lines that were constantly leading the eye to the discovery of new perspectives.

Intriguing as the view was intended to be from the street level entrance, the most inviting vista was reserved for the staircase that led from the basement, where, appropriate to the Dallas reliance on automobiles, a second major entrance was provided to permit access from an underground garage. Rising out of the drop-off area, the visitor was to be almost literally swept up into the lobby's maelstrom of curvilinearity. It was an arrival of which Balthasar Neumann would have been proud.

During the development of the Dallas design, elements of it were tested and refined at the Choate Rosemary Hall Science Center in Wallingford, Connecticut (begun in 1985), and the Creative Artists Agency in Los Angeles (begun in 1986), which served in certain respects as study models for Dallas in much the way the Mellon Arts Center had for the East Building. (Like the Arts Center and the East Building, the Science Center was paid for by Paul Mellon.) At Choate Rosemary Hall, Pei, working closely with his associates George Miller and Ian Bader, turned to brick, a much warmer material than his signature limestone and travertine, but the manipulation of the masses was no less crisply geometric. Here, he focused them on a semicircular courtyard overlooked by a two-story curved glass enclosure not unlike the one in Dallas. At CAA, a three-story gem of a building for which Pei's son Sandi oversaw much of the design, the similarities to Dallas were even closer. Here, too, was the familiar interpenetration of crisp geometric forms. But the links were particularly evident on the interior, where another curving glass skylight illuminated a public space remarkably like a smaller version of the Dallas lobby.

But the symphony center took all these devices to a higher plane. So complicated was the geometry that Pei himself remained somewhat unsure of how it would work out in built form. "I can imagine only 60 percent of the space in this building," he told the *Dallas Morning News* during the course of the design process. "The rest will be as surprising to me as to everyone else. That's what makes the project so exciting."[4] It was one of the rare occasions on which Pei turned to a computer during the design phase, if only, he said, to "confirm the spaces, to show me if I was right."

Although, as the symphony center progressed, Pei found himself increasingly tied up in the tortuous demands of the Louvre, he gave the Dallas project intense personal attention. In doing so, he again called on George Miller, who oversaw the management of the job, and Charles Young, who carried much of the responsibility for the design of the interior of the hall itself. Well staffed as he was, Pei intervened at critical points with the sort of deft alterations to the design that had so often characterized his technique. One such move involved the bracing of the glass for the conoid, the glass skirt for the south side of the building. The structural engineering was in the hands of Leslie Robertson, who had worked with Pei on the ill-fated housing project for Iran, among other projects. Well into the Dallas design, Robertson was struggling with how to brace the delicate trusses

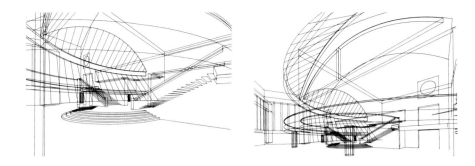

that were to support the glass of the conoid. The standard way to do so would have been to run heavier horizontal members through the trusses at regular intervals parallel to the roof line. At a meeting to review the matter, Pei looked at a drawing of the proposed horizontals, leaned over it with a pencil, and changed the horizontals to diagonals.

The angled supports instantly added to the visual interest of the framework, making the entire conoid look rather like the hull of a spaceship rocketing up out of the ground. But the adjustment also solved Robertson's problems with the structure. "It was perfect," said Robertson. "It was exactly what we wanted—and it worked."

Another example of Pei's refining of the design as it progressed was his alteration of the "dedication wall." The wall faced the staircase leading up to the lobby from the automobile entrance and was to bear the incised names of the major donors. Pei's first scheme for the wall was a semicircular recess that recalled the way he had inserted stair railings into the interior wall plane at the East Building. Drawings were prepared for his approval, but, just as he had with the bracing of the conoid, he then made a small change that had enormous impact. Looking over the drawings with his team, he extended the semicircle to create a three-quarter-round recess. Because it was *almost* round, but not quite, the shape gained a measure of tension. Pei's adjustment of his own earlier idea instantly produced a visual intrigue that the comparatively static half-round shape did not have and, in so doing, added to the dynamic composition of the curves on the floor above.

The fine-tuning of the symphony center extended to the artworks Pei had selected to embellish it. Although the symphony people had already approved a proposal by Eduardo Chillida, the distinguished Basque sculptor, to stand outside the main entrance, Pei took evident delight in surprising the board with an entirely different Chillida work that both artists had since agreed was more appropriate. The form of the new sculpture was unveiled at an outdoor press conference during a freak ice storm that hit Dallas in the spring of 1989, and although Pei had come dressed only in a thin raincoat and was limping from the effects of acupuncture recently undergone for leg pain, he joined Chillida on the site and grinned with pleasure as the sculptor pulled a seven-inch model of the work out of his jacket pocket for the benefit of the local television crews. In the end, Chillida's *De Musica*, a pair of fifteen-foot-tall, sixty-eight-ton Corten steel columns with branchlike protrusions, was duly erected to serve as a ceremonial gateway for visitors to the hall.

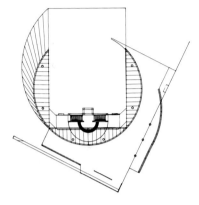

Pei drew on the ambiguities of German Baroque architecture as a source for the visual complexity of the Meyerson's public spaces. Computer-generated drawings (above) were used to test the effect.

Such changes were only one of the forces that drove the cost of the symphony hall steadily higher. The original estimate of $49.5 million was overtaken almost immediately as the real costs of the client's ambitions became clear. Building a twentieth-century hall that would compete with the best of nineteenth-century Europe, especially when it was designed by a famously demanding architect and an equally insistent acoustician, proved far more expensive than even Dallas in boom times had expected. Additional months and money were required when the original site had to be expanded. At least as important to the escalating cost as the site problems and the frequent design changes was the time spent on disputes between the city and the symphony over what was possible and what was desirable. These delays were compounded by the difficulty in coordinating the activities of the Pei and Johnson offices. To make matters worse, the Texas oil industry all but collapsed.

So rapidly did the cost of the building begin to rise in the mid-1980s that at more than one point the backers actually considered canceling it altogether. Disaster was staved off when Ross Perot offered to refloat the undertaking with a gift of ten million dollars on the condition that it be named for Morton Meyerson and dedicated to the employees of Electronic Data Systems. By the time the building opened, the official estimate of the cost stood at $81.2 million, but unofficial calculations put it even higher. The local press had great sport with the increases, which were widely described as scandalous (although no one ever suggested that any wrongdoing was involved). Stanley Marcus, for his part, insisted that it had been a mistake to set a price on the building at the outset. After all, he reminded the critics, virtually everybody involved was doing a symphony hall for the first time. "We were learning—and adding—as we went," he said.

Russell Johnson had another explanation. A rumpled, gruff man whose office garb includes work boots and an overfilled key chain dangling from his belt, Johnson is likely to pause in conversation for long periods with his eyes closed and then begin to issue complicated pronouncements about the trajectory of sound. Much as he clearly loves music and the challenge of housing it well, he has only limited sympathy for the people who most often pay for it. In Dallas, of course, the fear of cultural embarrassment was almost as powerful as the urge to create a great hall, putting social as well as professional reputations on the line. "The more prestigious the project," Johnson said, "the more people there are in positions of responsibility. It's normal in a project of this scale—but it's not easy, and Pei took advantage of it."

Johnson and Pei clashed over a multitude of issues. The long, narrow hall

Neither Pei nor his clients had ever attempted a building quite like the Meyerson Symphony Center. Their lack of experience added freshness to the architecture, but contributed to internal dissension among the backers and a steady rise in the cost of the project.

While Pei exploited the Baroque as a general stylistic source, he focused on the grand stairs and balconies of Charles Garnier's Paris Opéra as a specific example in presenting the design to his clients.

The inscription reads THE MORTON H. MEYERSON SYMPHONY CENTER

**Following pages: The freestand-
ing balcony gave concertgoers
sweeping views of the architecture—and of their fellow citizens.**

Johnson wanted struck Pei as an oppressive space. To break it up, the architect proposed a pair of large, space-defining columns, one at either side of the stage. Johnson objected that the columns would interfere with the sound. The columns went in. Pei wanted carpet on the orchestra floor. Johnson objected, saying it would absorb too much sound. The carpet was abandoned. Johnson insisted that the surfaces of the doors to the reverberation chamber be left bare. Pei countered that they should be camouflaged with a decorative screen. The screen went on. The biggest battle between the two experts was about the canopy intended to reflect sound from the stage out into the hall. Pei objected to Johnson's proposed version, saying to one collaborator that it looked like an extended tongue (and extending his own to illustrate the point). The battle raged until Meyerson finally stepped in. "I banged their two heads together until I heard a sound I liked," he said. The result was a movable canopy made of wood and steel.

For all his objections to Pei's demands, Johnson was remarkably gracious once the project was finished. "It moved at a very stately pace," he said. "But that's Pei's way of achieving excellence. And I hold that great architecture cannot be great if the architect satisfies every functional detail." Pei was not so charitable. In an uncharacteristically harsh judgment, he described Johnson to a *Newsweek* reporter as a man with "a good pair of ears, but no eyes." [5]

Pei may have had limited influence over the form of the hall itself, but he was determined that the surrounding spaces be done his way, and he pushed his clients' patience at almost every opportunity. In the original design, the exterior cladding of the building was to have been brick, but the drawings and models were prepared to make it look more like stone. When the funds were allocated, the clients were alarmed to learn that the money did not cover the elegant surface they had seen in the models, but they were loath to settle for brick and reluctantly embarked on ways to pay for limestone, an additional expense of roughly two million dollars. Having secured the limestone for the exterior, Pei explained how important it was that, if the interior finishes were not also going to be limestone (the clients would not go that far), the concrete substitute should match the stone in texture and color. So exacting were Pei's requirements for the concrete, though, that not a single contractor responded to the first call for bids. The one who eventually took the job had reason to regret it later. When his samples didn't satisfy the architect, they were sent back, and it happened often.

As so many of his previous clients could attest, such perfectionism had long since become a Pei trademark. In Dallas, there was much muttering about "the Pei factor" as a basic cost of doing business with the man. But here, as in so

Opposite: Among the many points of conflict between Pei and Russell Johnson were the movable acoustical canopy and the two columns flanking the stage. Above: Continuing his tradition of using sculpture as a counterpoint to his architecture, Pei selected a piece by Eduardo Chillida; here, one of its members is being lowered into place near the main entrance.

many of the earlier cases, the constant refining and pushing of the limits of the budget were done with the assent of the client—grudgingly at first, perhaps, but usually enthusiastically in the end.

There is no better example of the way Pei was able to convert his Dallas clients to his own purposes than the ornamental lighting for the public spaces. In the early spring of 1989, the building was already many millions of dollars over the original estimate, and the Dallas arts community was increasingly upset about the way the symphony people were soliciting donors who might otherwise have been expected to support other cultural facilities. Pei arrived in Dallas for what was to be a meeting on some final details, including the lighting for the lobby. The meeting took place in a construction shed on the site with several members of the client team, including Meyerson and Marcus.

Pei began the proceedings looking almost like a schoolboy about to deliver his first public-speaking assignment. His hands trembled slightly as he arranged drawings on the table before him, and he avoided the eyes of the people on the other side. With the help of Christopher Rand, the architect in his office who had been responsible for the lighting, he unrolled a number of drawings of the proposed lamps, which were to stand at either side of the grand staircase. The drawings showed a slim steel column topped by an onyx disc that was flanked by an assemblage of spiky shafts, the whole thing vaguely resembling a Navaho headdress. Meyerson, Marcus, and the others pondered the drawings and a cardboard mock-up that Rand had erected against one wall and murmured to each other about how attractive they were. At which point Pei began to speak. "As you remember," he said softly, "we have from the start been striving for an effect comparable to that of the Paris Opéra, something dramatic and entertaining with plenty of glitter. I hope you like what we have done."

The clients clearly did, but then came the inevitable question, about the cost. With what appeared to be some embarrassment, Pei answered: "Let's use a figure of $40,000 each." The clients stared at Pei, then at each other, and began to protest that the budget for fixtures had already been nearly exhausted, that donors were growing exasperated, and that the local papers were at their throats for being extravagant.

Pei, more confident now, explained in a smoothly apologetic tone that anything less would not do justice to the building they had all struggled so long to achieve. Abandoning the image of the Paris Opéra, he invoked the effect of the ornate lamps on the Alexandre III bridge over the Seine and suggested with an increasingly contagious enthusiasm that the ones for the symphony might even

become a symbol for the building—a logotype for their accomplishment.

After some further back-and-forth, Meyerson began to soften, finally declaring, "These aren't just lights, they are works of sculpture!" After a few more minutes of steadily cooling debate, Marcus turned slowly to Meyerson and said, "We've got to look for fresh money. I have a corporation in mind."

Clearly pleased with the outcome, Pei waited a barely decent interval. "Now that we're on the subject of lights," he said with what appeared to be considerable pain, "we should probably talk about some for outdoors." It would hardly be right, he explained, warming to his subject again, to have all the glitter inside this building without an appropriate "invitation" to passersby. "I don't want to go forward until I know that you approve, that you think it is necessary," he said deferentially. "But it's just a matter of adding a little." And then the ominous last word, "This, of course, is not the final design."

There was considerable rolling of eyes across the table, but by the time the meeting adjourned, the clients had agreed to the purchase of not two, but eleven of the lamps—two for the grand stair, two smaller ones for the side stairs, four for the lobby bars, one for the garage stair, and two for the forecourt—at a cost of roughly a quarter of a million dollars, for which no source had yet been secured. The triumph of the moment was not so much that Pei had got his way, but that he had been able to make the clients believe sufficiently in his commitment to *their* ambitions that they became the agents of his idea. They were not going further into the hole for Pei, they were doing it for themselves—and for art. To do less, Pei had persuaded them, would be to deny the best in themselves.

Not every obstacle fell to Pei's combination of dedication and guile. Just weeks before the opening, the architect discovered while in Paris (where he was giving his friend and former client Jacqueline Onassis a personal tour of the Louvre) that the travertine that had been ordered in Italy for the Dallas lobby floor had not yet been cut. Not to be frustrated at so late a date in such a major detail, Pei flew to Italy overnight and persuaded the stonecutters to finish at least enough for the main spaces; 120 metric tons were then airlifted to Dallas. On the construction site, workmen fell to joking about how Pei was going to make every Dallas tourist in Europe carry a slab of travertine home.

In a scene that recalled the days before the openings of the Fragrant Hill Hotel and the Louvre, Pei and his people were making refinements until the last minute. The architect himself supervised the trimming of a ficus tree for the garden facing the conoid. On the day before the opening, he was scampering about the building in shirtsleeves, the sweat running freely, alternately chatting

Funding the group of sculptural lights designed for the lobby (above) tested Pei's talents as a salesman. Getting them made took him to Italy (opposite and top), where he monitored the grinding of the translucent stone disks.

with visiting journalists and directing the installation of carpet to cover the portion of floor for which the travertine had arrived, but had not yet been installed. He was clearly exhausted, but also at his best.

For all the effort expended over nearly a decade, the Morton H. Meyerson Symphony Center was not without its flaws. There were some leftover spaces in the lobby, where, as in the East Building, the geometry had overwhelmed the logical flow of pedestrian space. The arch over the main lobby wall was spanned by a metal tie rod that seemed especially out of place. The ceremonial gate over the street level entrance—a device Pei had used in various forms from NCAR through the Choate Rosemary Hall Science Center—seemed slightly gratuitous against the authoritative composition of the building itself. And, as in the Dallas City Hall and the Kennedy Library, the back wall of the building was disappointingly bleak.

Perhaps the unhappiest element of the final design was the relationship between the public spaces and the interior of the hall itself. Finished in a delicate mix of exotic woods and fine fabrics, the "box" exuded the spirit of the intimate European halls of the eighteenth century—the effect for which Pei and Charles Young had so striven. But the contrast with the bold sensuosity of the spaces just outside the "sound lock" was mildly jarring. And here and there were traces of unresolved connections between Johnson's aural requirements and Pei's visual interpretation of them.

But if there was something of a continuity gap between the interior and the exterior, it was bridged by the excellence of the individual parts, which together made an ensemble worthy of the ambitions voiced in 1980 when the process began. Here was a building that contributed a monument to a city much in need of one and did so with an inviting combination of Modernist rigor and informed humanity. The addition of curves to the assured manipulation of angular forms Pei had used in the East Building had indeed created a baroque impression of sensual delight, of premeditated disorientation, without falling into rococo excess. Once again, as he had in virtually every building since the National Gallery, Pei had brought together the intellectual purity of geometry and the sculptural potential of people in motion to create a work of animated architecture. If his City Hall a few blocks away had been excessively masculine, the symphony center benefited enormously from just the right touch of the feminine.

To the enormous relief of the backers, even the musical people approved, writing with rare enthusiasm about the acoustics of the new hall. The music critic of the *New York Times* spent a week in Dallas listening to performances ranging

The constant intersecting of
curves throughout the building
creates the impression that there
is always something more to see.

from violin solos to choral works and declared in what amounted to a rave that "Dallas has not lost its shirt on this one." He went on to predict that, if Johnson's tuning devices proved effective, the Meyerson "might well develop into something close to the original dream."[6]

Shortly before the opening-night concert, Pei gave a small cocktail party for the members of the firm who had worked on the building. The setting—a nearby superdeluxe hotel in the mock-French-château mode—could not have been more inappropriate for the celebration of Pei's symphony hall. And the Pei people, many of whom clearly cared more for their work than their tailoring, could not have looked more out of place. But the atmosphere was strikingly like a family baptism. As the festivities began, a relatively new member of the Pei staff detached him from a conversation long enough to tell him earnestly that she thought the Meyerson Center was "a very mature building." To which Pei replied with a wide smile, "Ah, but did I have to wait this long?"

After about half an hour of banter about the years spent on the project, Pei tapped a spoon against a glass and called for quiet. He began slowly, noting that the building had gone on for so long that many of the original team members had been transferred to other projects and that others had come into it only recently "Nonetheless," he said, "all of you are part of it." There were some cast-down eyes and a few hugs, and then the people who had actually made the building set off down the street to consign it to the owners.

As the Meyerson Symphony Center neared its opening, Pei's third major work of 1989 was overtaken by events that even he could not control. The building was the Hong Kong branch of the Bank of China, a building that had been set in motion when Britain agreed to turn the colony of Hong Kong over to mainland Chinese control. The transfer was scheduled for 1997, and the bankers of the People's Republic were eager that they should have a building in Hong Kong that would stand as a monument both to the unification of the former colony with the mainland and to their country's reemergence as a full participant in international financial affairs.

The decision to ask Pei to design the building might at first have seemed improbable. Even though the Communist government had invited him to design

Recognizing that most people would arrive at the hall by car rather than on foot, Pei designed an underground garage that was linked to the lobby by a staircase with a suitably impressive view.

the Fragrant Hill Hotel, and in so doing buried any lingering animosity about his lineage, this was not a tourist facility, but a building intended as a symbol of the Communist government's financial power. Yet Pei's father had been the first manager of the same branch when he fled Canton in 1918 and had gone on to serve Chiang Kai-shek in the losing battle against the Communists. Here, suddenly, were some of the same Communists calling on an archenemy's son to do what he might rightly have expected to be asked to do by his father had the Nationalists won in 1949.

In a way, the call did come from his father. When planning for the building began, in 1982, the Chinese first sent emissaries to New York, where Pei's father, then eighty-nine, was living. They asked him if it might be appropriate for them to approach the son for such an undertaking. "That is Chinese," Pei told an English reporter, "very respectful, even though they were politically at odds. With one hand my father wanted to have nothing more to do with it, and with the other he thought it important for me to do it."[7] Tsuyee Pei did not exactly say yes, but he did not say no, either. After discussing the project at length with his father, Pei felt that he had been given tacit permission to accept the invitation. "It was a building my father would have wanted me to do," Pei said some years after his father's death. Despite the bitter experience of Fragrant Hill, he decided in the fall of 1982 to explore the Chinese offer.

Dealing with his own family history was only one of the challenges Pei faced in accepting the BOC commission. Although the tall office building has long been thought of as the quintessential American architectural form, it was not one that Pei had ever been much interested in. And despite a public impression to the contrary, he had done relatively few. Although it is still identified by many as a Pei building, the firm's best-known skyscraper, the Hancock Tower in Boston, was entirely Henry Cobb's. Pei was the principal partner on a number of other high rises, including the Wilmington Tower in Delaware (1963–71) and the Gateway in Singapore (1981–90). But he was closely involved in the design of only the Mile High Center in Denver, the Canadian Imperial Bank of Commerce in Toronto (1967–73), the Oversea-Chinese Banking Corporation Centre in Singapore (1970–76), which involved a revision of an existing design, and the Texas Commerce Tower in Houston (1978–82). The rest, including an enormous planning project in Singapore named Raffles City, were largely the work of his associates. "None was particularly memorable," Pei said of his own commercial towers, "but they were necessary to keep the office going."

What had most kept Pei away from the iconic American architectural form was its all-too-frequent lack of personal commitment on the part of the client. (As Pei put it, "When the lease runs out, someone else moves in.") Where the likes of NCAR and the East Building were designed as lasting facilities for their highly specialized clients, office buildings were rarely more than housing for transients. One of the things that drew Pei to the BOC assignment was that he felt it represented "the aspirations of the Chinese people" as the country was emerging from its long isolation. But beyond that was the bank's intention to remain in the building permanently.

There were, of course, other attractions. Not the least of them was the implicit competition with British architect Norman Foster's forty-three-story building for the Hongkong and Shanghai Banking Corporation, Hong Kong's leading colonial bank. Foster's building, which stood only two blocks from the site of the BOC tower, was a complicated mass of columns, trusses, and pipes that had set the international architectural community astir when it opened in 1985.[8] Pei was well aware that, even if the Bank of China goal was unstated, he had a responsibility to outdo Foster architecturally.

The Bank of China tower began with several strikes against it. The site, although located in the highly desirable Central District of Hong Kong, was tiny—a mere 90,000 square feet—and was hemmed in on three sides by highway overpasses. To make matters worse, during the Second World War the Japanese had established a military police headquarters on the spot and had tortured scores of prisoners there. Whatever the physical disadvantages of the site, no Hong Kong company would have considered building on ground with such a bloody past. The Bank of China managers were well aware of the site's grisly history, but that was one reason the price was relatively low, and there was no other comparable downtown location.

The site's small size virtually dictated a tall building. But there were no clear precedents in Pei's mind for a formal source, as there had been for Fragrant Hill. Indeed, Hong Kong in the early 1980s was a hodgepodge of thoroughly undistinguished towers erected more out of concern for financial return than aesthetic impact. The exception was Foster's bank, but its blatantly high-tech exuberance was hardly a starting point for the more restrained Pei. Nor was there much to look to at the time in the United States, where the historicist trend had been producing skyscrapers modeled on Art Deco predecessors and pieces of English furniture. Pei had never been comfortable attacking his colleagues publicly, but he had little use for some of their high-rise designs. In an ill-concealed swipe at some of his contemporaries, he said, "I can't believe the future of skyscrapers lies in second-rate Woolworth Buildings, looking backward for details." Nor was he content with merely refining or embellishing the best Modernist examples. "We've gone beyond that," he insisted.

The idea for the Hong Kong tower seems to have emerged almost fortuitously. During a weekend visit to the family's house in Katonah, Pei fell to toying with four small sticks, which he had bundled together. Having first aligned their ends equally, he began to slip each stick in sequence past the others. His son Sandi, who was to oversee much of the work on the building, noticed what his father was doing. "It was like watching the whole thing unfold in front of me," Sandi said later. Back at the office the following week, Pei asked his son to have the firm's model makers select a square shaft of wood, and divide it diagonally into four equal triangular pieces in a more refined version of the bundle with which he had experimented in Katonah. The model shop promptly did so, and Pei began to try various stepped combinations, finally lopping off the bottoms of all four at the same point to create a form rather like an attenuated spiral staircase.

To win support for the stepped form among the tradition-conscious Chinese, Pei invoked an image of the trunk of a bamboo pushing upward with each joint: a metaphor for the search for strength and excellence.

The form of a tall building in Hong Kong was only one of the necessary considerations for construction. Because of its vulnerability to typhoons, Hong Kong requires that buildings meet wind-resistance standards twice as rigorous as those in New York. Pleased with the unorthodox shape he had come up with, Pei had a hunch that it also would translate into a stable structure. To be sure, he took his four sticks to Leslie Robertson, the structural engineer with whom he had worked most recently on the Meyerson Center. Robertson made an extended series of calculations and concluded that Pei's form would indeed stand up under the demands of the Hong Kong code.

Robertson was not entirely surprised that Pei's formal idea had worked out structurally. Collaborating with Pei on a number of previous projects, he had come to appreciate the architect's sense of how buildings work. Robertson attributed it mostly to Pei's grounding as an engineering student at MIT, but he also said he felt Pei had an "intuitive" understanding of structure. "If you had put me and fifteen other architects together," Robertson said of the Bank of China tower, "we wouldn't have come up with this solution."

The solution was a major departure from conventional high-rise construction. Most tall buildings are constructed like enormous steel or concrete versions of the conventional column-and-beam system. To withstand typhoons,

The site for the Bank of China was an inhospitable one, ringed by highways and shadowed by a history of wartime atrocities.

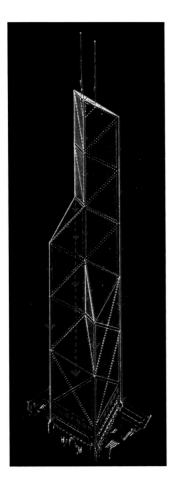

While visually striking as a sculptural form, the tower was also an engineering breakthrough. By using an enormous version of a conventional three-dimensional truss as the basic structure (above and opposite), Pei was able to transfer stress to the four corners of the building, making it far more stable than it would have been if built according to the column-and-beam method.

however, buildings in Hong Kong must be heavily braced with additional steel so that they are not twisted out of true, which would collapse their boxlike frames. The solution worked out for the Bank of China by Pei and Robertson, instead of relying on stiffening the two-dimensional sides of the standard box, used a three-dimensional frame, or space truss, whose members penetrated through the building itself. These members united the vertical planes of the four faces of the building and allowed wind loads to be transferred to the four corners, which were steadied with reinforced columns. In addition to bracing against wind, the trusses supported most of the weight of the building. Since the structure itself had become the bracing, less steel was required, making the building relatively easy to build. This was not a simple Modernist case of form following function, but of both proceeding simultaneously.

To make sure that was true, Pei and Robertson checked and rechecked the figures. Only when they were certain of the structural implications of the design did Pei formally accept the commission.

Much as the trapezoidal shape of the East Building's site had generated its triangular design motif, the compelling diagonals of the structural underpinnings of the Bank of China were intimately related to its aesthetics. Rather than leave the roofs of the ascending shafts flat, as might have been expected, Pei set them at an angle, adding to the sense of thrust as the building rose. The skin was to be a reflective glass. In true Modernist tradition, Pei chose to express the structural members that met the skin by highlighting them with aluminum cladding, creating facades of boxed X's. At seventy stories, the tower would be the tallest building in the world, outside the United States, and its strikingly abstract form—topped with a pair of broadcast masts—would make a dramatic vertical gesture in the heart of the city.

Lest his building suffer from the street-level ills of Cobb's Hancock Tower, which was an icon at a distance but proved an uncomfortable experience for pedestrians, Pei set the glass-and-steel portion of the tower on a base of stone. Although apparently inconsistent with the rest of the building, the base was in fact a deft solution to the problem Cobb had faced, for in the tight confines of the Hong Kong site, only the base would be easily visible from the street, maintaining a comfortable relationship with its existing masonry neighbors (including the old Bank of China building). Similarly, the base would be invisible from a distance, particularly from the harbor, so that the full sculptural impact of the tower at longer range would be undiminished.

As had so often been the case with Pei's buildings, the Hong Kong project was immediately embroiled in controversy. Not the least of it involved *fung shui* (pronounced "fung shway"), an ancient Chinese concept that is roughly translated as wind and water. In simplest terms, *fung shui* is a set of rules for surveying land based on such commonsense principles as not building on sand and not putting large windows in the north wall. But over the centuries, *fung shui* has evolved into a complex blend of practical advice and mysticism whose masters are said by their followers to be able to gauge a building's prospects for success or failure according to whether its shape and location are pleasing to supernatural forces. So popular and tenacious has the belief in *fung shui* remained in Hong Kong that certified practitioners can demand—and easily get—exorbitant prices to advise otherwise rational developers and architects on how to site and design their buildings. (The managers of the Hongkong and Shanghai Banking Corporation had been careful to have its plans approved by a *fung shui* master in advance of construction.)

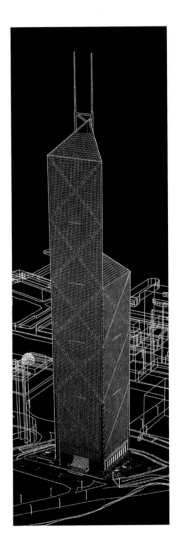

The Bank of China people, representing an officially atheistic society, were steadfastly opposed to the practice and refused to have the traditional analysis done. Not surprisingly, freelance advice began to proliferate almost as soon as the design was made public. As if the unhappy history of the site was not curse enough, the local geomancers noted that the masts atop the tower could be interpreted either as chopsticks held vertically in an empty rice bowl (a symbol of poverty) or as the sticks of incense used to memorialize the dead. Far worse were the X's made by the crossbracing that was to be expressed on the facades. Local authorities noted immediately that, at best, the X's evoked the mark traditionally drawn on a failing student's exercise by a calligraphy instructor. At worst, they suggested the custom of hanging a name tag around a condemned man's neck and slashing an X through it to signify that he was "finished."

Pei's clients persisted in ignoring the popular sentiment at the official level, but, acutely aware that their building was at least partly intended to symbolize the coming together of Hong Kong and the mainland, they arranged for a private consultation, which was attended by some junior bank officers. Pei, for his part, was not about to make an overt case for what his clients considered superstition, but he did agree to two symbolic concessions. Having been persuaded by Robertson that the structure of the building could still be "honestly" expressed without exposing the horizontal members on the facade, he agreed to conceal them behind the glass skin. The result, as it was explained to the Hong Kong community, was to transform the unhappy X's into "diamonds," a thoroughly benign form with no negative *fung shui* implications. For good measure, a

premature "topping out"—the traditional construction ceremony marking the erection of the final piece of framing—was arranged for August 8, 1988. According to *fung shui* experts, the date was the most propitious of the century. (The Chinese word *baat*, meaning eight, rhymes with *faat*, which means good fortune.) Nevertheless, construction workers on the site continued to defy their company's regulations and set up small shrines at the gate, regularly replacing the incense to keep the dragons at bay.

Despite the spiritual opposition, the building went up without mishap (except for the discovery during the excavation of a small geologic fault, which pleased the *fung shui* people but was rapidly secured) and close to schedule. The finished product was spectacular. Whether seen from across the harbor on the Kowloon Peninsula or from the mountain behind it, the building rose from the dreary agglomeration of Hong Kong high rises with a clarity and simplicity that were as impressive as its height. The tower's weakest points were where the angles of the tallest shaft seemed so narrow that it appeared almost unstable. But from every other aspect, Pei's building was as strong an urban symbol as anything since Cobb's Hancock Tower.

In a way, the Bank of China is not unrelated to what Pei had been developing in his work ever since the National Gallery: an increasing interest in architecture as movement. Just as the East Building and the Meyerson Symphony Center cannot be understood without moving through them, this tower cannot be grasped without moving around it. Indeed, the Bank of China solves one of the enduring problems of the modern skyscraper: its predictability. Most of the great tall buildings rely for their effect on their height and their surfaces, but their forms tend to be tediously repetitive. Pei made full use of the power of his reflective skin, but the real impact of the Hong Kong building is the result of its unexpectedness. Seen from different angles, the building presents a series of equally different profiles. This constantly changing composition is further animated by the distortion of the surface pattern created by moving around the building. As he did with the triangles at the East Building, with the courtyards at Fragrant Hill, and with the curves at the Meyerson Center, Pei made of this skyscraper an unceasing invitation to the eye. Yet the large scale and manifest rationality of the form keep the experience from being confusing. To drive the point home, one need only compare Pei's building to Foster's, which, once the novelty has worn off, is at once predictable and fussy, a conventional box concealed in fancy clothing.

The success of the Bank of China lay in more than its aesthetic impact. For Pei, who had developed such a reputation for expensive buildings, the Hong

Assembling the steel for the building's unorthodox structure required the skills of a special team of construction workers (above and opposite), who labored with minimal protection above the Hong Kong skyline.

Kong tower was a special triumph. The 800,000-square-foot Hongkong and Shanghai Banking building had cost roughly $650 million, making it the most expensive building ever erected at the time it opened. Pei's tower contained even more floor space—1.4 million square feet—but, at least partly because of the forty-percent savings in the amount of steel required by the innovative structural system he and Robertson had worked out, it came in at roughly one-fifth the cost.

As the building neared completion, every obstacle seemed to have been overcome. But in a tragic development well beyond questions of aesthetics and engineering, the symbolic importance of the Bank of China tower—both for Pei and for China—was brutally compromised.

In April of 1989, a wave of democratic fervor began to sweep the Chinese mainland. To the amazement of the rest of the world, Chinese students by the hundreds of thousands began to demonstrate against their government in mass rallies held across the country. The largest by far was in Tiananmen Square, directly in front of the Forbidden City in Beijing, where Pei had years before refused to build a high-rise hotel. For seven weeks, the demonstrations grew, and, incredibly, the authorities did nothing to stop them. But as the demonstrations continued into June, the government finally reacted, sending in convoys of troops. At first, the soldiers were stymied by the protesters, who by then included thousands of workers and other citizens as well as students. But on the night of June 3, the troops suddenly began shooting, killing large numbers of unarmed civilians. The massacre was followed by the imposition of martial law and a crackdown on dissenters throughout the country. In the wake of the crackdown, which included numerous executions of students and others who had participated in the demonstrations, the Hong Kong workmen who were putting the finishing touches on the Bank of China tower draped it with enormous banners that read in Chinese characters, "Blood must be paid with blood."[9]

The events in Tiananmen Square horrified Pei. After all, it had been largely as a gesture of national reconciliation that the Bank of China project had begun, and his decision to accept the commission was no less a personal gesture of his own across the generations. The impact of what he saw as a betrayal was intense. Although he had long since established a reputation for avoiding passionate gestures, especially in public, Pei felt strongly enough in this case to write an article for the *New York Times* condemning the violence.[10] What was even more remarkable was that he made it clear that he was speaking not just for himself, but for his wife. It was, he said, "a situation about which I could not be silent. My conscience demanded it."

Pei's design began as a tribute to his father and a gesture of reconciliation between contemporary and pre-Communist China. It ended under a cloud of political conflict and personal disappointment.

The piece, which was published on June 22, was entitled "China Won't Ever Be the Same." In it, Pei declared with uncharacteristic heat that he and Eileen had "wanted to believe that a more open and modern China was possible." The killing of students and citizens, he went on, "tore the heart out of a generation that carries the hope for the future of the country." Talking about the upheaval some weeks later, he said, "It wasn't so much the loss of life—so many precious lives—but the loss of respect. The people no longer respect the government. I haven't been able to rest. China is besmirched."

Pei's public declaration was not without real risks. He still had at least six months of work to do on the building, and he could not expect the client to take kindly to his action. His one hope for the tower he had designed very much in his father's honor was a conviction that "the time will pass, the building will stand. Out of the ashes, something may come."

Bitter as the experience of the Bank of China proved to be for Pei, he resolutely put it behind him. And as 1989 came to a close, there was much to do. Across from the firm's Madison Avenue office, work was under way on the Regent, a forty-six-story luxury hotel Pei had designed for a development group that included William Zeckendorf, Jr., the son of his first patron. There was the Wildwood office complex in Atlanta, one of several projects the firm had done for IBM since the loss of the commission for the company's New York headquarters in the wake of Hancock. An expansion of Mount Sinai Hospital in Manhattan was slightly behind schedule, but plans for Cleveland's Rock 'n' Roll Hall of Fame and Museum, a somewhat improbable commission for the classically oriented Pei, had been reactivated after a pause caused by fund-raising problems. There was also a center for research on the aging near San Francisco and the second phase of the Louvre. But one commission stood apart and seemed to sum up the point at which Pei had arrived in his professional life.

Among the many religious cults to have appeared in Japan following the Second World War is one known as Shinji Shumeikai, which is headed by a reserved older woman named Kaishu Koyama, known to the sect's three million followers as the *kaishusama,* or spiritual leader. In the early 1980s, the sect had commissioned Minoru Yamasaki, the Japanese-born architect of the World Trade Center towers in New York City, to design a temple in the wooded hills southeast of Kyoto.

As a complement to the main building, the matriarch wanted to add a tower that would house bells to summon worshipers. She decided to approach Pei and traveled to New York to meet with him.

Amid the nondescript Hong Kong jumble, the building provides an orderly architectural focus (opposite). The surrounding gardens and fountains (above) were intended in part to mitigate the disadvantages of the cramped and noisy site.

As Pei recalled the meeting, it took place on a day when he was distracted with work on the Louvre, and, partly because the brief conversation was carried on through an interpreter, he was not entirely sure what the self-effacing elderly woman was seeking. In any case, Pei had the impression that she was merely dropping in to explore a possibility as part of an extended visit to the United States. Pei recalled later that he declined "as politely as I knew how" and saw the lady to the elevator. Only later did he discover that the *kaishusama* had made the trip from Japan specifically to see him and had returned immediately after his rebuff.

Embarrassed by what he belatedly realized was his insensitivity to the matriarch's mission, Pei wrote to her and suggested another meeting on his next trip to Japan. It took place in early 1988, when Pei was on his way to inspect the progress on the Bank of China, and it went very differently from the one in New York. Struck by the simplicity of the program Mrs. Koyama presented, as well as the evident sincerity of her religious belief, Pei agreed to design the tower.

The form for the building emerged almost immediately, but from an unexpected source. In the mid-1950s, Pei and his wife had made a trip to Japan during which he had found in a Kyoto shop an ivory *bachi*, an object used to strike the strings of a traditional Japanese instrument. He was intrigued by the grace and elegance of the shape, which was narrow at the bottom and flared at the top. When he got back to New York after his meeting with Mrs. Koyama, Pei asked Eileen what had become of the striker. After much rummaging through closets, she found it, only to discover that the corners of the flared top had been broken off when it was packed away. Pei felt that the accidentally squared-off ends actually improved the shape for his purpose, "terminating" the curves at the top, and, after some alterations in the proportions, he presented the design to the matriarch, who accepted it immediately.

To help him with the execution of the design, Pei turned to Christopher Rand, who was working with him on the Meyerson Center. Together, they tuned and adjusted the details of the tower, reducing its height slightly (to two hundred feet) to avoid having to paint aircraft-warning stripes on it and lowering the opening that was to display the fifty handmade bells that made up the carillon. For the surface of the tower, the client had proposed a pinkish Korean granite. Pei approved the choice, but grew increasingly concerned that it would not work well with the white ribs of the nearby Yamasaki sanctuary. Rand remembered Pei finally going to the firm library and flipping through catalogues on the chance that a better color could be found. Pei settled on a paler substitute, but the supplier

Local geomancers at first objected to the patterns created by Pei's expression of the structure on the surface of the tower (opposite). The architect agreed to a compromise after being reassured by his engineer that it would not affect the overall integrity of the design. The insistent geometry of the tower (above) generated an unorthodox solution to the common skyscraper problem of formal predictability.

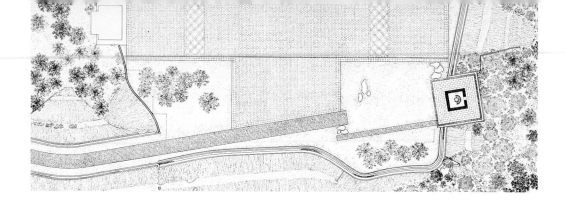

was an American company, and its quarry was in Vermont. Although shipping the new material to Japan would add a million dollars to the bill, Pei presented the alternative to the *kaishusama*, who agreed—and immediately wired the money.

In many ways, the bell tower was perfect for Pei. Here was a supremely simple sculptural form that was to be set in a landscape as part of a larger architectural composition. Moreover, it had been commissioned by a committed individual who was willing to give her architect unquestioning support. And it was informed by a high purpose. "Even though I didn't know much about the religion," Pei said, "it was a challenge to try to capture its spirit. It was a search for the sort of expression that is not at all technical." Consistent with so much of Pei's best work over the years, the tower was rigorously geometrical and in that sense totally rational. But it was also deeply romantic, touching Pei as perhaps only the wildness of the NCAR site and the historical significance of the Louvre had done.

It was a building that, for a number of reasons, Pei could not have done only a few years earlier. For one thing, the managing of the firm, not to mention its profitability, would not have permitted it. More important, however, he had not, working at the grand scale, been so able to set himself loose artistically. The bell tower had all the grace and freshness of a sketch done by a master who no longer needed to prove his merit to anyone, including himself.

In 1985, Pei had said to an interviewer, "Self-doubt is the most important thing to any creative artist. When you lose it, you are headed for disaster."[11] Although manifestly sincere, the remark was no less well crafted for its effect. Five years later, in talking about the bell tower, Pei conveyed the feeling that, if doubt had ever really plagued him, it had finally been overcome, if not replaced, by a sort of contentment. Not that he planned to stop working. The long list of projects in the office left no doubt of that. But, as he said, "I no longer feel obligated to keep the firm in high gear."

The change in the name of the firm to Pei Cobb Freed & Partners on September 1, 1989, was a tangible acknowledgment of that feeling, as well as a tribute—overdue in the eyes of some—to people who had contributed so much to the overall fortunes of the organization. (George Miller, who had overseen the Meyerson Center, and Michael Flynn, the firm's expert on curtain-wall construction who had wrestled the French into manufacturing the glass for the Louvre pyramid, were both elevated to the rank of full partner.) Given the fate of other firms as their founders have withdrawn, however, there was no guarantee that the success would endure, although Pei's highly skilled partners and their veteran support staff provided strong hope that it would.

The Shinji Shumeikai bell tower was classic Pei. Designed for a dedicated client, it was a simple, sculptural shape (above, a photograph of the model) and sited in a garden (top, dark square at extreme right).

The prospect of eventually losing Pei's unique combination of artistic skill, managerial savvy, and peerless salesmanship was, nonetheless, a source of concern to his professional heirs—and of eager speculation in the architecture world. (On hearing the news, the publication of the New York chapter of the American Institute of Architects immediately called to ask if Pei was retiring. He cryptically replied that "an architect never retires."[12]) While his partners each possessed special talents, none combined the qualities that had made I. M. Pei for so many years the unquestioned leader of the enterprise. Indeed, it was difficult to imagine any of them communing with a William Zeckendorf on wines, with a Walter Orr Roberts on atmospheric research, with a François Mitterrand on French history, or a *kaishusama* on religion, in quite the same way.

There were those who felt that Pei had, over the years, subconsciously arranged the succession that way, passing over potential heirs who might have perpetuated the Pei mystique but competed with the master. Indeed, the list of Pei alumni includes some intensely talented people who came to feel that they had only a limited future in the firm. It would not have been the first time a powerful person had made himself irreplaceable. "We shouldn't ever think that I. M. has wings and a halo," said a longtime admirer. But that was a view balanced by a widespread appreciation that Pei's firm itself was one of his finest creations.

Pei took pains to stage his withdrawal. "I couldn't just leave; it would not be fair to the firm, or to its clients," he said. "And furthermore, I don't intend to stop making architecture; I will simply be doing it in a different relationship with the firm. I no longer want to practice as I have. I want to enjoy life a bit more— and I want to do better work. I want to take on projects that were too small for the firm in the past. My physical capacities are receding; they must. To do my best work, I can no longer work at that pace."

Whatever his firm's future, its founder could, on the eve of a new decade, look backward on a career of unique accomplishment and forward to a period of rare, if risky, creative opportunity. As an architectural elder statesman who had reached the peak, where was he to go? It was a journey from which he did not shrink. But in a way, it led back to his beginnings as an architect. Having been swept up by Zeckendorf before he could make his mark as a designer— something he would be able to do only later and at the grand scale—he was now confronted with the chance to do the sort of totally personal architecture which his forty-plus years of extraordinary organizational success had largely denied him. "This is the kind of freedom I have been looking for," he said. "And now I think I have found it."

The commission for the bell tower coincided with an expansion of the partnership, which was documented in the fall of 1989 with a new office portrait. Seated, from left: James Freed, Henry Cobb, Eason Leonard, and Pei. Standing, from left: George Miller, Werner Wandelmaier, Leonard Jacobson, and Michael Flynn.

NOTES

The following citations refer primarily to printed sources in which material on I. M. Pei has appeared. Most of the quotations used in the text without footnotes were drawn from personal interviews with Pei and others conducted by the author between February 1986 and January 1990. In some cases where names have been omitted, the sources requested anonymity.

INTRODUCTION

1. Peter Blake, "I. M. Pei & Partners," *Architecture Plus*, February 1973, p. 53.

CHAPTER 1

1. Walton's remarks were prepared for a dinner on the occasion of the award to Pei of the Gold Medal of the National Arts Club, January 28, 1981 (I. M. Pei archives).
2. Pei during an interview for the television documentary *Ieoh Ming Pei* by Thomas M. C. Johnston and François Warin, Antenne 2, Caméras Continentales, Palm Production, Télé-Europe, 1986.
3. Peter Blake in "The Devil's Advocate and the Diplomat," *AIA Journal*, June 1979, p. 77.

CHAPTER 2

1. Two extremely useful sources for background on China during and following the period are John King Fairbank, *The Great Chinese Revolution, 1800–1985* (New York, 1986), and Jonathan D. Spence, *The Gate of Heavenly Peace: The Chinese and Their Revolution, 1895–1980* (New York, 1982).
2. The political setting of the time is colorfully described in Sterling Seagrave's *The Soong Dynasty* (New York, 1985).

3. Quoted in an interview with Pei in the MIT publication *The Tech*, March 5, 1985, p. 8.
4. Gropius's aims were detailed in the "Proclamation of the Weimar Bauhaus," issued in 1919. It read in part: "Let us create a new guild of craftsmen, without the class distinctions which raise an arrogant barrier between craftsman and artist. Together let us conceive and create the new building of the future, which will embrace architecture and sculpture and painting in one unity and which will rise one day toward heaven from the hands of a million workers like the crystal symbol of a new faith." For a brief history of the institution, see Frank Whitford's *Bauhaus* (New York, 1984).
5. Walter Gropius, "Architecture at Harvard University," *Architectural Record*, May 1937, p. 10.
6. Pei to Frederick S. Roth in a letter dated January 8, 1946 (Pei archives).
7. "Museum for Chinese Art, Shanghai, China," *Progressive Architecture*, February 1948, p. 52.
8. Ibid., p. 51.

CHAPTER 3

1. William Zeckendorf in *Zeckendorf: The Autobiography of William Zeckendorf* (New York, 1970), p. 97.
2. Ibid., p. 98.
3. Ibid.
4. Ibid.
5. Ibid., p. 70.
6. Ibid., p. 71.
7. Quoted in *Architectural Forum*, January 1950, p. 93.
8. "Small Office Buildings," *Architectural Forum*, February 1952, p. 108.
9. Zeckendorf, p. 170.
10. Ibid., p. 243.
11. The definitive source on

Moses, including his relations with Zeckendorf, is Robert Caro's *The Power Broker* (New York, 1974). His account of the United Nations saga begins on p. 771. See also Victoria Newhouse, *Wallace K. Harrison, Architect* (New York, 1989), p. 104.
12. Zeckendorf, p. 205.
13. Ibid., p. 208.
14. Ibid., p. 224.
15. I. M. Pei, "Urban Renewal in Southwest Washington," *AIA Journal*, January 1963, p. 69.
16. An account of the Society Hill project appears in Bacon's *Design of Cities* (New York, 1987), beginning on p. 264.
17. Memo, "To My Colleagues at I. M. Pei and Associates," August 1, 1960 (Pei archives).

CHAPTER 4

1. The interview was with William Marlin in *The Christian Science Monitor*, March 16, 1978.
2. Quoted by Lucy Warner in *The National Center for Atmospheric Research: An Architectural Masterpiece* (Boulder, 1985), p. 6.
3. Quoted by Henry Lansford in *UCAR at 25*, published in 1985 by the University Corporation for Atmospheric Research marking the twenty-fifth anniversary of the institution, p. 25.
4. The quote appears in "High Mountain Monastery for Research," *Architectural Forum*, January 1964, p. 84.

CHAPTER 5

1. The description is from *Common Ground*, by J. Anthony Lukas (New York, 1986), p. 195. Lukas paints a vivid picture of the social and political context of the downtown plan.

2. This quote and the two preceding are from the "Summary of Preliminary Meeting of the Committee on Arts and Architecture for the Kennedy Library," p. 10 (William Walton archives).
3. The quote appears in "He Loves Things To Be Beautiful," by Arthur Herzog, *New York Times Magazine*, March 14, 1965.
4. *Progressive Architecture*, January 1965, p. 39.
5. William Marlin, "Lighthouse on an Era," *Architectural Record*, February 1980, p. 85.
6. James S. Duesenberry, chairman of the Harvard economics department, as quoted by Michael Winerip in the *Harvard Crimson*, December 5, 1973.
7. Quoted by Marlin in "Lighthouse," p. 85.
8. Quoted by Mildred F. Schmertz in "Getting Ready for the John F. Kennedy Library: Not Everyone Wants To Make It Go Away," *Architectural Record*, December 1974, p. 98.
9. Ibid., p. 101.
10. Quoted by Marlin in "Lighthouse," p. 88.
11. Ibid., p. 86.
12. John Morris Dixon, "Pei's JFK Library: Inadequate Tribute," *Progressive Architecture*, January 1980, p. 50.
13. Edward Klein, "The Other Jackie O," *Vanity Fair*, August 1989, p. 146.

CHAPTER 6

1. *Goals for Dallas* (Dallas, 1969) covered issues ranging from urban design to the provision of health care and remains a model document for thinking about a city's future.
2. The cartoon, drawn by Bob Taylor, was sufficiently symbolic of the municipal debate that it was used as an illustration in Peter Papademetriou's article on

302

the building, "Angling for a Civic Monument," in the May 1979 issue of *Progressive Architecture*, p. 102.

3. A useful account of the City Hall's development appears in David Dillon's *Dallas Architecture: 1936–1986* (Austin, 1985), beginning on p. 98.

4. Ada Louise Huxtable, "One of Our Most Important Public Buildings," *New York Times*, November 28, 1976.

CHAPTER 7

1. Quoted in Robert Campbell, "Evaluation: Boston's John Hancock Tower in Context," *AIA Journal*, December 1980, p. 19.

2. Interview with the author, April 29, 1988.

3. Quoted in *Progressive Architecture*, October 1975, p. 40.

4. Quoted in *Progressive Architecture*, December 1975, p. 24.

5. Paul Goldberger, "A Novel Design and Its Rescue From Near Disaster," *New York Times*, April 24, 1988.

6. Robert Campbell, "It Was a Tower of Tribulation," *Boston Globe*, April 9, 1988.

7. The story was entitled "Gesturing" and appeared in *The Best American Short Stories of 1980* (Boston, 1980).

8. Interview with the author and Stanley Abercrombie. Quoted in "A Gentle Master Builder," *Horizon*, April 1978, p. 58.

CHAPTER 8

1. "A Step-by-Step Guide to Designing," by J. Carter Brown, *Washington Post/Potomac*, May 16, 1971.

2. "The Man Who Has Everything," *Vogue*, August 1978, p. 251.

3. "Many Partake of Culture But Few Study It," *New York Times*, September 13, 1988.

4. Quoted by Russell Lynes in "National Gallery's New Building Is Triangular Triumph," *Smithsonian*, June 1978, p. 48.

5. J. Carter Brown, "Masterwork on the Mall," *National Geographic*, November 1978, p. 692.

6. Quoted by Barbaralee Diamonstein, "I. M. Pei: 'The Modern Movement Is Wide Open,'" *ARTnews*, Summer 1978, p. 66.

7. Ibid., p. 65.

8. Robert Hughes, "Masterpiece on the Mall," *Time*, June 5, 1978, p. 62.

9. Ada Louise Huxtable, "Geometry with Drama," *New York Times*, May 7, 1978.

10. Christian Otto, "Washington—A New Centre for the Arts?," *Connoisseur*, August 1978, p. 324.

11. Martin Filler in "P/A on Pei: Roundtable on a Trapezoid," *Progressive Architecture*, October 1978, p. 52.

12. Colin Amery, "Inside the NGA," *Architectural Review*, January 1979, p. 22.

13. Richard Hennessy, "Prototype and Progeny," *Artforum*, November 1978, p. 71.

14. Allan Greenberg in a letter to Brown dated November 4, 1987 (Brown archives).

CHAPTER 9

1. William Marlin, "The Sowing and Reaping of Shape," *Christian Science Monitor*, March 16, 1978.

2. The remark was made to Thomas M. C. Johnston in his film *Ieoh Ming Pei*.

3. Pei to the author, June 18, 1988.

4. Quoted by Christopher S. Wren in "I. M. Pei's Peking Hotel Returns to China's Roots," *New York Times*, October 25, 1982.

CHAPTER 10

1. Paul Goldberger, "A Tough Architectural Job," *New York Times*, April 30, 1979.

2. Quoted by Joe Klein in "Beached Whale on the Hudson," *New York*, November 7, 1983, p. 30.

3. Ibid., p. 27.

4. Ibid.

5. Quoted by Maureen Dowd in "City's New Glass Palace Gets Hectic Last-Minute Polishing," *New York Times*, March 31, 1986.

CHAPTER 11

1. The incident is described by Ronald Koven in "Pei's Paris Pyramid," *Boston Globe*, August 7, 1988.

2. Quoted by Mark Stevens, "Pyramid Scheme," *Vanity Fair*, June 1988, p. 52.

3. Jean Dutord, "Appel à l'insurrection," *France-Soir*, January 26, 1984.

4. Bruno Foucart, "Le Grand Louvre et sa pyramide," *Le Quotidien de Paris*, January 26, 1984.

5. André Fermigier, "La maison des morts," *Le Monde*, January 26, 1984.

6. Henry Bernard, "Un gadget inutile," *Le Figaro*, January 28, 1984.

7. The statement was widely reported; the full text was published in *Le Monde*, February 3, 1984.

8. Quoted by Mary Blume in "It's Adieu to the Dingy, Difficult Louvre," *International Herald Tribune*, February 2, 1989.

9. Quoted by Richard Bernstein in "I. M. Pei's Pyramid," *New York Times Magazine*, November 24, 1985.

10. Claude Pompidou in an interview with Philippe de l'Estang, *Galeries*, May 1985.

11. Charles Jencks, "Symbolism and Blasphemesis," *Art & Design*, September 1985, p. 42.

12. Bruno Foucart in *Le Quotidien de Paris*, March 30, 1989.

13. Quoted by Edward Cody in "Louvre Pyramid Makes a Glowing Debut," *International Herald Tribune*, July 5, 1988.

CHAPTER 12

1. The most prominent use of the expression was by Paul Goldberger in his 1989 year-end architecture review, "Pei, Prince Charles—and Skyscrapers Everywhere," *New York Times*, December 24, 1989.

2. Quoted by David Dillon and Terry Box in "The Meyerson Center: Saga of a Symphony Hall," *Dallas Morning News*, August 6, 1989.

3. George Rodrigue in "I. M. Pei's Superhall," *D*, August 1982, p. 52.

4. David Dillon, "Pei Hits High Note with Concert Hall," *Dallas Morning News*, May 16, 1982.

5. The remark was quoted by Cathleen McGuigan in "The Perfectionist," *Newsweek*, September 25, 1989, p. 61.

6. Donal Henahan, "The Acoustics of Dallas's New Concert Hall," *New York Times*, September 12, 1989.

7. Quoted by Glenys Roberts in "A Chinese Puzzle," *Daily Telegraph*, April 1, 1989.

8. Stephanie Williams's *Hongkong Bank: The Building of Norman Foster's Masterpiece* (Boston, 1989) covers the building in detail.

9. William Stewart, "Fear and Anger in Hong Kong," *Time*, June 19, 1989, p. 22.

10. I. M. Pei, "China Won't Ever Be the Same," *New York Times*, June 22, 1989.

11. Interview with the author, August 7, 1985.

12. Quoted in *Oculus*, September 1989, p. 13.

BIBLIOGRAPHY

The following list includes, in addition to sources cited in the Notes, a selection of other material that may prove useful to a larger appreciation of specific aspects of I. M. Pei's life and work.

Abercrombie, Stanley. "A Gentle Master Builder." *Horizon*, April 1978.

Amery, Colin. "Inside the NGA." *Architectural Review*, January 1979.

Bacon, Edmund N. *Design of Cities*. New York: Penguin, 1987.

Bernard, Henry. "Un gadget inutile." *Le Figaro*, January 28, 1984.

Bernstein, Richard. "I. M. Pei's Pyramid." *New York Times*, November 24, 1985.

Blake, Peter. *The Master Builders*. New York: Knopf, 1960.

———. "I. M. Pei & Partners." *Architecture Plus*, February, March 1973.

———. *Form Follows Fiasco*. Boston: Little, Brown, 1977.

———. "The Devil's Advocate and the Diplomat." *AIA Journal*, June 1979.

Blau, Judith. *Architects and Firms*. Cambridge: MIT Press, 1984.

Blume, Mary. "It's Adieu to the Dingy, Difficult Louvre." *International Herald Tribune*, February 2, 1989.

Boesiger, W., and Girsberger, H. *Le Corbusier 1910–65*. New York: Praeger, 1967.

Bos, Michiel. Interview with Pei in *The Tech*, Massachusetts Institute of Technology, March 5, 1985.

Brown, J. Carter. "A Step-by-Step Guide to Designing." *Washington Post/Potomac*, May 16, 1971.

———. "Masterwork on the Mall." *National Geographic*, November 1978.

Bunting, Bainbridge. *Harvard: An Architectural History*. Completed and edited by Margaret Henderson Floyd. Cambridge and London: Belknap, Harvard University Press, 1985.

Bush-Brown, Albert. Introduction to *Skidmore, Owings & Merrill: Architecture and Urbanism 1973–1983*. Stuttgart: Gerd Hatje, 1983.

Campbell, Robert. "Evaluation: Boston's John Hancock Tower in Context." *AIA Journal*, December 1980.

———. "Learning from the Hancock." *Architecture*, March 1988.

———. "It Was a Tower of Tribulation." *Boston Globe*, April 9, 1988.

Carney, Thomas. "Big Daddy: William Zeckendorf Senior Is a Legend in New York Real Estate. His Son Also Rises." *Manhattan, Inc.*, December 1986.

Caro, Robert A. *The Power Broker: Robert Moses and the Fall of New York*. New York: Knopf, 1974.

Cody, Edward. "Louvre Pyramid Makes a Glowing Debut." *International Herald Tribune*, July 5, 1988.

Collier, Peter, and Horowitz, David. *The Kennedys*. New York: Summit Books, Simon & Schuster, 1984.

"**C**ounter-claims Filed in John Hancock Suit." *Progressive Architecture*, December 1975.

Curtis, William J. R. *Modern Architecture Since 1900*. Oxford: Phaidon, 1982.

Davis, William, and Tree, Christina. *The Kennedy Library*. Exton, Pa.: Schiffer, 1980.

Dean, Andrea. "Conversations: I. M. Pei." *AIA Journal*, June 1979.

Diamonstein, Barbaralee. "I. M. Pei: 'The Modern Movement Is Wide Open.'" *ARTnews*, Summer 1978.

———. *American Architecture Now*. New York: Rizzoli, 1980.

———. *American Architecture Now II*. New York: Rizzoli, 1985.

Dietsch, Deborah. "Space Frame Odyssey." *Architectural Record*, September 1986.

Dillon, David. *Dallas Architecture: 1936–1986*. Austin: Texas Monthly Press, 1985.

———. "Pei Hits High Note with Concert Hall." *Dallas Morning News*, May 16, 1982.

Dillon, David, and Box, Terry. "The Meyerson Center: Saga of a Symphony Hall." *Dallas Morning News*, August 6, 1989.

Dixon, John Morris. "Connoisseurs of Cast-in-place." *Progressive Architecture*, September 1974.

———. "Pei's JFK Library: Inadequate Tribute." *Progressive Architecture*, January 1980.

Dowd, Maureen. "City's New Glass Palace Gets Hectic Last-Minute Polishing." *New York Times*, March 31, 1986.

Dutord, Jean. "Appel à l'insurrection." *France-Soir*, January 26, 1984.

Eckardt, Wolf Von. *A Place to Live*. New York: Delacorte, 1967.

———. "The Architect Who Understands Social and Visual Dynamics." *Washington Post*, May 14, 1978.

L'**E**stang. Philippe de. "Claude Pompidou." *Galeries*, May 1985.

Fairbank, John King. *The Great Chinese Revolution, 1800–1985*. New York: Harper & Row, 1986.

Fermigier, André. "La maison des morts." *Le Monde*, January 26, 1984.

Filler, Martin. "P/A on Pei: Roundtable on a Trapezoid." *Progressive Architecture*, October 1978.

———. "Power Pei." *Vanity Fair*, September 1989.

Forgey, Benjamin. "East Wing Treasure." *Washington Star*, May 28, 1978.

Forsyth, Michael. *Buildings for Music*. Cambridge: MIT Press, 1985.

Foucart, Bruno. "Le Grand Louvre et sa pyramide." *Quotidien de Paris*, January 26, 1984.

———. "Pyramide, où est ta victoire?" *Quotidien de Paris*, March 30, 1989.

Gallery, John Andrew, ed. *Philadelphia Architecture*. Cambridge and London: MIT Press, 1984.

Goldberger, Paul. "A Tough Architectural Job." *New York Times*, April 30, 1979.

———. "Winning Ways of I. M. Pei." *New York Times*, May 20, 1979.

———. *The Skyscraper*. New York: Knopf, 1981.

———. *On the Rise*. New York: Times Books, 1983.

———. "A Novel Design and Its Rescue From Near Disaster." *New York Times*, April 24, 1988.

———. "Pei, Prince Charles—and Skyscrapers Everywhere." *New York Times*, December 24, 1989.

"**G**ood Luck, Mr. Pei!" *Progressive Architecture*, January 1965.

Goodman, Robert. *After the Planners*. New York: Simon and Schuster, 1971.

Gropius, Walter. "Architecture at Harvard University." *Architectural Record*, May 1937.

"**H**elix. the." *Architectural Forum*, January 1950.

Henahan, Donal. "The Acoustics of Dallas' New Concert Hall." *New York Times*, September 12, 1989.

Hennessy, Richard. "Prototype and Progeny." *ARTforum*, November 1978.

Herdeg, Klaus. *The Decorated Diagram*. Cambridge: MIT Press, 1983.

Hersh, Burton. *The Mellon Family*. New York: Morrow, 1978.

Herzog, Arthur. "He Loves Things To Be Beautiful." *New York Times Magazine*, March 14, 1965.

Heyer, Paul. *Architects on Architecture*. New York: Walker, 1966.

"**H**igh Mountain Monastery for Research." *Architectural Forum*, January 1964.

Hughes, Robert. "The Nation's Grand New Showcase." *Time*, May 8, 1978.

———. "Masterpiece on the

Mall." *Time*, June 5, 1978.

———. *The Shock of the New*. New York: Knopf, 1980.

Huxtable, Ada Louise. *Kicked a Building Lately?* New York: Quadrangle, 1976.

———. "One of Our Most Important Public Buildings." *New York Times*, November 28, 1976.

———. "Geometry with Drama." *New York Times*, May 7, 1978.

———. *The Tall Building Artistically Reconsidered*. New York: Pantheon, 1984.

———. *Goodbye History; Hello Hamburger*. Washington: Preservation Press, 1986.

Jencks, Charles. *Modern Movements in Architecture*. Garden City, N.Y.: Anchor Press, Doubleday, 1973.

———. *Symbolic Architecture*. New York: Rizzoli, 1985.

———. "Symbolism and Blasphemesis." *Art & Design*, September 1985.

———. *Architecture Today*. New York: Abrams, 1988.

"John Hancock Sues for Glass Damage." *Progressive Architecture*, October 1975.

Johnston, Thomas M. C., and Warin, François. *Ieoh Ming Pei* (film). Antenne 2, Caméras Continentales, Palm Production, Télé-Europe, 1986.

Jonsson, J. Erik. Preface to *Goals for Dallas*. Dallas: Goals for Dallas, 1969.

Kidder Smith, G. E. *A Pictorial History of Architecture in the United States*. New York: American Heritage, 1976.

———. *The Architecture of the United States*. Garden City, N.Y.: Anchor Press, Doubleday, 1981.

Klein, Edward. "The Other Jackie O." *Vanity Fair*, August 1989.

Klein, Joe. "Beached Whale on the Hudson." *New York*, November 7, 1983.

Koskoff, David E. *The Mellons*. New York: Crowell, 1978.

Kostof, Spiro. *A History of Ar-*chitecture. New York and Oxford: Oxford University Press, 1985.

Koven, Ronald. "Pei's Paris Pyramid." *Boston Globe*, August 7, 1988.

Krinsky, Carol Herselle. *Gordon Bunshaft*. New York: Architectural History Foundation, 1988.

Lansford, Henry. *UCAR at 25*. Boulder: University Corporation for Atmospheric Research, 1985.

Lukas, J. Anthony. *Common Ground*. New York: Vintage, 1986.

Lynes, Russell. "National Gallery's New Building Is Triangular Triumph." *Smithsonian*, June 1978.

McGuigan, Cathleen. "The Perfectionist." *Newsweek*, September 25, 1989.

"Man Who Has Everything, the." *Vogue*, August 1978.

Marlin, William. Interview with I. M. Pei in *Christian Science Monitor*, March 16, 1978.

———. "The Sowing and Reaping of Shape." *Christian Science Monitor*, March 16, 1978.

———. "Lighthouse on an Era." *Architectural Record*, February 1980.

"Museum for Chinese Art, Shanghai, China." *Progressive Architecture*, February 1948.

Newhouse, Victoria. *Wallace K. Harrison, Architect*. New York: Rizzoli, 1989.

Otto, Christian. "Washington—A New Centre for the Arts?" *Connoisseur*, August 1978.

Papademetriou, Peter. "Angling for a Civic Monument." *Progressive Architecture*, May 1979.

Pastier, John. "Bold Symbol of a City's Image of Its Future." *AIA Journal*, Mid-May 1978.

Pei, Ieoh Ming. "Urban Renewal in Southwest Washington." *AIA Journal*, January 1963.

———. "China Won't Ever Be the Same." *New York Times*, June 22, 1989.

Polshek, James Stewart. *James Stewart Polshek*. New York: Rizzoli, 1988.

Rodrigue, George. "I. M. Pei's Superhall." *D*, August 1982.

Rosenthal, Robert. "How UMass-Boston Finally Won Its Battle for the Kennedy Library." *Boston Globe*, June 12, 1977.

Roth, Leland M. *McKim, Mead & White, Architects*. New York: Harper & Row, 1983.

Russell, John. *Paris*. New York: Abrams, 1983.

Schmertz, Mildred F. "Getting Ready for the John F. Kennedy Library: Not Everyone Wants To Make It Go Away." *Architectural Record*, December 1974.

Schulze, Franz. *Mies van der Rohe*. Chicago: University of Chicago Press, 1985.

Scully, Vincent. *Modern Architecture*. New York: Braziller, 1979.

Seagrave, Sterling. *The Soong Dynasty*. New York: Harper & Row, 1985.

"Small Office Buildings." *Architectural Forum*, February 1952.

Smith, C. Ray. *Supermannerism*. New York: Dutton, 1977.

Spence, Jonathan D. *The Gate of Heavenly Peace: The Chinese and Their Revolution, 1895–1980*. New York: Penguin, 1982.

Spring, Bernard. "Evaluation: From Context to Form, I. M. Pei's National Center for Atmospheric Research." *AIA Journal*, June 1979.

Stern, Robert A. M. *New Directions in American Architecture*. New York: Braziller, 1978.

———. *Pride of Place*. Boston: Houghton Mifflin, and New York: American Heritage, 1986.

Stevens, Mark. "Pyramid Scheme." *Vanity Fair*, June 1988.

Stewart, William. "Fear and Anger in Hong Kong." *Time*, June 19, 1989.

Suner, Bruno. *Ieoh Ming Pei*. Paris: Hazan, 1988.

Tafuri, Manfredo, and Dal Co, Francesco. *Modern Architecture*. New York: Abrams, 1979.

"Texte des conservateurs, le." *Le Monde*, February 3, 1984.

Thorndike, Joseph J., Jr., ed. *Three Centuries of Notable American Architects*. New York: American Heritage, Scribner's, 1981.

"The Ties That Bind." *Oculus*, September 1989.

Trachtenberg, Marvin, and Hyman, Isabelle. *Architecture*. New York: Abrams, 1986.

Tuchman, Janice, and Gibb, Robina. "Architect's Vision, Bank's Visibility." *ENR*, October 13, 1988.

Turner, Paul Venable. *Campus: An American Planning Tradition*. New York: The Architectural History Foundation, 1984.

Walton, William. "New Splendor for China." *House & Garden*, April 1983.

Warner, Lucy. *The National Center for Atmospheric Research: An Architectural Masterpiece*. Boulder: NCAR, 1985.

Whitford, Frank. *Bauhaus*. New York: Thames & Hudson, 1984.

Williams, Stephanie. *Hongkong Bank: The Building of Norman Foster's Masterpiece*. Boston, Toronto, London: Little, Brown, 1989.

Winerip, Michael. "Harvard's Expansion to Kennedy Library Will Physically Split International Studies." *Harvard Crimson*, December 5, 1973.

Wiseman, Carter. "Pei's Convention Center Was Worth the Wait." *New York*, September 16, 1985.

Wren, Christopher S. "I. M. Pei's Hotel Returns to China's Roots." *New York Times*, October 25, 1982.

Wurman, Richard Saul, and Gallery, John Andrew. *Man-Made Philadelphia*. Cambridge and London: MIT Press, 1972.

Zeckendorf, William (with Edward McCreary). *Zeckendorf: The Autobiography of William Zeckendorf*. New York: Holt, Rinehart and Winston, 1970.

CATALOGUE OF WORKS

The following lists include all works executed or under construction as of April 1, 1990, by the firm of Pei Cobb Freed & Partners (and its predecessors, I. M. Pei & Associates and I. M. Pei & Partners). The time required to take these buildings and planning projects from conception to completion in most cases spanned several years, during which others were initiated. Accordingly, two dates have been included for each: the date planning began and the date of actual or estimated completion. The listings have been arranged chronologically according to the first date. Figures for square footage refer to construction gross area. Where the building type is not evident from the title, it has been included in parentheses.

In the early years of the Pei firm, as the text of this book makes clear, I. M. Pei himself was heavily involved in virtually every aspect of the work produced by his firm. With time, however, his colleagues began to assume more responsibility until, beginning in the 1970s, some were operating with almost total autonomy. These listings cite in parentheses the senior member or members of the firm ultimately responsible for overseeing a given undertaking. Some of the planning and development projects involved such a large number of people that credit should properly go to the firm as a whole, rather than to an individual, and therefore no name is given. Architectural works for which I. M. Pei was totally or primarily responsible are accompanied by illustrations. (All information supplied by Pei Cobb Freed & Partners.)

1

2

3

4

5

6

7

10

12

13

14

ARCHITECTURAL DESIGN

1. Webb & Knapp offices: New York; 43,322 sq. ft.; 1950–51 (I. M. Pei).

2. Gulf Oil Building: Atlanta; 50,000 sq. ft.; 1950–52 (I. M. Pei).

3. Franklin National Bank: Garden City, N.Y.; 171,000 sq. ft.; 1951–57 (I. M. Pei).

4. Roosevelt Field Shopping Center: Garden City, N.Y.; 1,150,000 sq. ft.; 1951–56 (I. M. Pei).

5. Pei residence: Katonah, N.Y.; 1,152 sq. ft.; 1951–52 (I. M. Pei).

6. Mile High Center (office building): Denver; 458,000 sq. ft.; 1952–56 (I. M. Pei).

7. Town Center Plaza (housing–community development): Washington, D.C.; 548,500 sq. ft.; 1953–61 (I. M. Pei).

8. May D&F Department Store, Courthouse Square: Denver; 504,000 sq. ft.; 1954–58 (Henry Cobb).

9. Denver Hilton Hotel, Courthouse Square: Denver; 1,008,955 sq. ft.; 1954–60 (Araldo Cossutta).

10. Luce Memorial Chapel: Taichung, Taiwan; 5,140 sq. ft.; 1954–63 (I. M. Pei).

11. Place Ville Marie (office complex): Montreal; 3,071,097 sq. ft.; 1955–66 (Henry Cobb).

12. University Gardens (housing–community development): Chicago; 548,650 sq. ft.; 1956–61 (I. M. Pei).

13. Kips Bay Plaza (apartment towers): New York; 1,216,290 sq. ft.; 1957–62 (I. M. Pei).

14. Society Hill (multi-building residential complex): Philadelphia; 1,044,250 sq. ft.; 1957–64 (I. M. Pei).

15. Washington Plaza Apartments—Phase I: Pittsburgh; 537,360 sq. ft.; 1958–64 (I. M. Pei).

16. Cecil and Ida Green Earth Sciences Building, MIT (science facility): Cambridge, Mass.; 130,493 sq. ft.; 1959–64 (I. M. Pei, Araldo Cossutta).

17. Chancellery for United States Embassy: Montevideo, Uruguay; 85,000 sq. ft.; 1960–69 (I. M. Pei).

18. East-West Center (research campus): Manoa, Hawaii; 225,500 sq. ft.; 1960–63 (I. M. Pei, Araldo Cossutta).

19. University Plaza (apartment towers): New York; 747,000 sq. ft.; 1961–66 (I. M. Pei, James Freed).

20. L'Enfant Plaza (mixed-use complex): Washington, D.C.; 1,364,000 sq. ft.; 1961–68 (Araldo Cossutta).

21. Newhouse Communication Center, Syracuse University (academic building): Syracuse, N.Y.; 71,100 sq. ft.; 1961–64 (I. M. Pei).

22. National Center for Atmospheric Research: Boulder, Colo.; 223,220 sq. ft.; 1961–67 (I. M. Pei).

23. Everson Museum of Art: Syracuse, N.Y.; 63,200 sq. ft.; 1961–68 (I. M. Pei).

24. Bushnell Plaza (apartment towers): Hartford, Conn.; 287,000 sq. ft.; 1961–70 (I. M. Pei).

25. Century City Apartments: Los Angeles; 842,398 sq. ft.; 1961–65 (I. M. Pei).

26. Federal Aviation Administration Air Traffic Control Towers (50 buildings): Various locations; 3,500–17,000 sq. ft.; 1962–72 (I. M. Pei).

27. National Airlines (TWA) Terminal, JFK International Airport: New York; 352,330 sq. ft.; 1962–70 (I. M. Pei).

28. Academic Center, State University of New York: Fredonia, N.Y.; 610,000 sq. ft.; 1962–71 (Henry Cobb).

29. Hoffman Hall, University of Southern California (graduate school building): Los Angeles; 88,000 sq. ft.; 1963–67 (I. M. Pei).

30. Wilmington Tower (office building): Wilmington, Del.; 210,500 sq. ft.; 1963–71 (I. M. Pei, Araldo Cossutta).

15

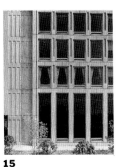

16

17

18

19

21

22

23

24

25

26

27

29

30

31

32

34

35

37

38

39

40

42

45

31. Cleo Rogers Memorial County Library: Columbus, Ind.; 52,500 sq. ft.; 1963–69 (I. M. Pei).

32. New College (academic campus): Sarasota, Fla.; 98,295 sq. ft.; 1963–67 (I. M. Pei).

33. Harbor Towers (apartment buildings): Boston; 1,339,500 sq. ft.; 1964–71 (Henry Cobb).

34. Camille Edouard Dreyfus Chemistry Building, MIT (academic facility): Cambridge, Mass.; 137,700 sq. ft.; 1964–70 (I. M. Pei).

35. John F. Kennedy Library: Boston; 113,000 sq. ft.; 1964–79 (I. M. Pei, Theodore Musho).

36. Christian Science Church Center: Boston; 693,550 sq. ft.; 1964–73 (Araldo Cossutta).

37. Tandy House (private residence): Fort Worth, Tex.; 18,750 sq. ft.; 1965–69 (I. M. Pei).

38. Polaroid Office and Manufacturing Complex: Waltham, Mass.; 365,000 sq. ft.; 1965–70 (I. M. Pei).

39. Des Moines Art Center Addition: Des Moines, Iowa; 21,300 sq. ft.; 1966–68 (I. M. Pei).

40. Dallas Municipal Administration Center (city hall): Dallas; 771,104 sq. ft.; 1966–77 (I. M. Pei).

41. Baltimore World Trade Center (office building): Baltimore; 421,550 sq. ft.; 1966–77 (Henry Cobb).

42. Fleishman Building, National Center for Atmospheric Research (headquarters facility): Boulder, Colo.; 4,318 sq. ft.; 1966–68 (I. M. Pei).

43. John Hancock Tower (office building): Boston; 2,059,060 sq. ft.; 1966–76 (Henry Cobb).

44. Third Church of Christ, Scientist and Christian Science Monitor Building: Washington, D.C.; 81,782 sq. ft.; 1967–71 (Araldo Cossutta).

45. Canadian Imperial Bank of Commerce/Commerce Court (office building): Toronto; 2,475,125 sq. ft.; 1967–73 (I. M. Pei).

46. Herbert F. Johnson Museum of Art, Cornell University: Ithaca, N.Y.; 60,000 sq. ft.; 1968–73 (I. M. Pei).

47. Wilson Commons, University of Rochester (multi-use campus facility): Rochester, N.Y.; 91,000 sq. ft.; 1968–76 (Henry Cobb).

48. 88 Pine Street (office building): New York; 571,000 sq. ft.; 1968–73 (I. M. Pei, James Freed).

49. National Gallery of Art—East Building: Washington, D.C.; 604,000 sq. ft.; 1968–78 (I. M. Pei).

50. Paul Mellon Center for the Arts, Choate Rosemary Hall School: Wallingford, Conn.; 76,000 sq. ft.; 1968–72 (I. M. Pei).

51. John Hancock Tower Garage: Boston; 3 acres; 1968–72 (Henry Cobb).

52. Bedford-Stuyvesant Superblock (neighborhood rehabilitation): Brooklyn, N.Y.; 13 city blocks; 1969 (I. M. Pei).

53. Collins Place (mixed-use towers): Melbourne, Australia; 717,000 sq. ft.; 1970–81 (Henry Cobb).

54. Oversea-Chinese Banking Corporation Centre: Singapore; 929,000 sq. ft.; 1970–76 (I. M. Pei).

55. Laura Spelman Rockefeller Halls, Princeton University (student apartments): Princeton, N.J.; 66,500 sq. ft.; 1971–73 (I. M. Pei, Harold Fredenburgh).

56. Ralph Landau Chemical Engineering Building, MIT: Cambridge, Mass.; 131,000 sq. ft.; 1972–76 (I. M. Pei).

57. National Bank of Commerce Center: Lincoln, Neb.; 309,576 sq. ft.; 1972–76 (James Freed).

58. Raffles City (hotel and office building complex): Singapore; 4,207,700 sq. ft.; 1973–86 (I. M. Pei).

59. Fine Arts Academic and Museum Building, Indiana University: Bloomington, Ind.; 115,000 sq. ft.; 1974–82 (I. M. Pei).

60. Chamber of Commerce of Greater Augusta (office building): Augusta, Ga.; 8,500 sq. ft.; 1974–77 (Henry Cobb).

61. AT&T Boardroom: New York; 1975–76 (Henry Cobb).

62. Augusta/Richmond County Civic Center: Augusta, Ga.; 192,700 sq. ft.; 1975–80 (Henry Cobb).

63. Commercial Plaza (office building): New Brunswick, N.J.; 125,600 sq. ft.; 1976–79 (Henry Cobb).

64. Johnson & Johnson World Headquarters: New Brunswick, N.J.; 421,130 sq. ft.; 1976–82 (Henry Cobb).

65. Johnson & Johnson Baby Products Headquarters Complex: Montgomery Township, N.J.; 269,400 sq. ft.; 1976–81 (Henry Cobb).

66. One Dallas Centre (office building): Dallas; 664,000 sq. ft.; 1977–79 (Henry Cobb).

67. Museum of Fine Arts— West Wing (addition and renovation): Boston; 366,700 sq. ft.; 1977–86 (I. M. Pei).

68. Akzona Corporate Headquarters: Asheville, N.C.; 140,400 sq. ft.; 1977–81 (I. M. Pei).

69. One West Loop Plaza (office building): Houston; 577,000 sq. ft.; 1977–80 (James Freed).

70. 499 Park Avenue (office building): New York; 264,350 sq. ft.; 1977–81 (James Freed).

71. Sunning Plaza (office and apartment complex): Hong Kong; 457,000 sq. ft.; 1977–82 (I. M. Pei).

72. Gem Plaza (bank and office building): Dayton, Ohio; 261,600 sq. ft.; 1977–81 (James Freed).

73. IBM Office Building: Purchase, N.Y.; 764,239 sq. ft.; 1977–84 (I. M. Pei).

74. Texas Commerce Tower (office building): Houston; 2,054,600 sq. ft.; 1978–82 (I. M. Pei).

46

67

54

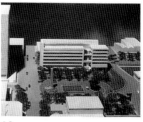
68

48

55

49

56

71

50

58

73

52

59

74

81

88

82

90

84

92

85

93

87

94

96

75. Texas Commerce Motor Bank (drive-in bank): Houston; 20,413 sq. ft.; 1978–80 (Harold Fredenburgh).

76. One Galleria Tower (office building): Oklahoma City, Okla.; 294,500 sq. ft.; 1978–81 (Henry Cobb).

77. Mobil Exploration and Production Research Laboratory: Farmer's Branch, Tex.; 337,000 sq. ft.; 1978–83 (Henry Cobb).

78. ARCO Tower (headquarters–office building): Dallas; 1,375,240 sq. ft.; 1978–84 (Henry Cobb).

79. Sixteenth Street Transitway Mall: Denver; 13 city blocks; 1978–82 (Henry Cobb).

80. Charles Shipman Payson Building, Portland Museum of Art: Portland, Maine; 62,790 sq. ft.; 1978–83 (Henry Cobb).

81. Wiesner Building, MIT (academic arts and media facility): Cambridge, Mass.; 111,429 sq. ft.; 1978–84 (I. M. Pei).

82. Texas Commerce Center (bank, athletic and parking facilities): Houston; 1,200,000 sq. ft.; 1978–82 (I. M. Pei, Harold Fredenburgh).

83. Warwick Post Oak Hotel: Houston; 604,623 sq. ft.; 1979–82 (James Freed).

84. Fragrant Hill Hotel: Beijing; 396,791 sq. ft.; 1979–82 (I. M. Pei).

85. Jacob K. Javits Convention Center: New York; 1,688,860 sq. ft.; 1979–86 (I. M. Pei, James Freed).

86. Pitney Bowes World Headquarters: Stamford, Conn.; 812,337 sq. ft.; 1979–86 (Henry Cobb).

87. World Trade Center (office building): Miami; 1,161,500 sq. ft.; 1980–86 (I. M. Pei, Harold Fredenburgh).

88. Gateway Towers (office complex): Singapore; 1,398,720 sq. ft.; 1981–90 (I. M. Pei).

89. Columbia Square (office building): Washington, D.C.; 842,680 sq. ft.; 1981–87 (Henry Cobb).

90. Morton H. Meyerson Symphony Center: Dallas; 485,000 sq. ft.; 1981–89 (I. M. Pei).

91. First Interstate Bank Tower at Fountain Place (formerly Allied Bank Tower: office building): Dallas; 1,877,838 sq. ft.; 1982–86 (Henry Cobb).

92. Bank of China (office building): Hong Kong; 1,430,465 sq. ft.; 1982–90 (I. M. Pei).

93. IBM (entrance pavilion): Armonk, N.Y.; 9,148 sq. ft.; 1982–85 (I. M. Pei, Theodore Musho).

94. IBM Office Complex: Somers, N.Y.; 1,174,468 sq. ft.; 1983–89 (I. M. Pei, Theodore Musho).

95. First Interstate World Center (office building): Los Angeles; 1,710,000 sq. ft.; 1983–89 (Henry Cobb, Harold Fredenburgh).

96. Mount Sinai Hospital Modernization and Extension: New York; 909,000 sq. ft.; 1983–90 (I. M. Pei).

97. Grand Louvre Phase I—Cour Napoléon and Richelieu Wing Connections (museum expansion and renovation): Paris; 669,490 sq. ft.; 1983–89 (I. M. Pei).

98. Commerce Square (office complex and courtyard): Philadelphia; 1,155,249 sq. ft.; 1984–88 (Henry Cobb).

99. Jacob K. Javits Convention Center Plaza (public park): New York; 1.1 acres; 1984–88 (James Freed).

100. Central Terminal Complex, JFK International Airport (expansion and modernization): New York; 3,000,000 sq. ft.; 1984–95 (Henry Cobb).

101. Potomac Tower (office building): Rosslyn, Va.; 415,000 sq. ft.; 1985–89 (James Freed).

102. Choate Rosemary Hall Science Center: Wallingford, Conn.; 43,000 sq. ft.; 1985–89 (I. M. Pei).

103. Los Angeles Convention Center (expansion): Los Angeles; 2,500,000 sq. ft.; 1986–93 (James Freed).

104. Creative Artists Agency (headquarters building): Beverly Hills, Calif.; 75,000 sq. ft.; 1986–89 (I. M. Pei).

105. Credit Suisse, First Boston (office building): London; 750,000 sq. ft.; 1986–91 (Henry Cobb).

106. The United States Holocaust Memorial Museum: Washington, D.C.; 250,000 sq. ft.; 1986–92 (James Freed).

107. JFK Library Extension: Boston; 24,000 sq. ft.; 1987–90 (Theodore Musho).

108. First Bank Place (office building): Minneapolis; 1,300,000 sq. ft.; 1987–92 (James Freed).

109. 1299 Pennsylvania Avenue (office building; renovation of historic theater): Washington, D.C.; 700,000 sq. ft.; 1988–91 (James Freed).

110. Shinji Shumeikai Bell Tower: Shiga, Japan; 215 feet high; 1988–90 (I. M. Pei).

111. Johnson & Johnson World Headquarters Child Care Center: New Brunswick, N.J.; 24,500 sq. ft.; 1988–90 (Henry Cobb).

112. 2600 Grand Avenue (office building): Kansas City, Mo.; 491,680 sq. ft.; 1988–91 (Henry Cobb).

113. International Trade Center: Barcelona; 1,250,000 sq. ft.; 1988–91 (Henry Cobb).

114. Regent Hotel: New York; 400,000 sq. ft.; 1988–92 (I. M. Pei).

97

102

104

110

114

1. Southwest Washington Renewal Plan: Washington, D.C.; 552 acres; 1953–56 (I. M. Pei).

2. Washington Square East: Philadelphia; 16 acres; 1957–59 (I. M. Pei).

3. Erieview General Neighborhood Renewal Plan: Cleveland; 163 acres; 1960.

4. Erieview I: Cleveland; 96 acres; 1960.

5. Downtown North General Neighborhood Renewal Plan: Boston; 400 acres; 1961 (Henry Cobb).

6. Government Center: Boston; 64 acres; 1961–62 (I. M. Pei, Henry Cobb).

7. Weybosset Hill: Providence, R.I.; 55 acres; 1961–63.

8. Market-Mohawk Urban Renewal: Columbus, Ohio; 60 acres; 1962.

9. Bunker Hill: Los Angeles; 136 acres; 1962–63 (Henry Cobb).

10. Central Business District General Neighborhood Renewal Plan: Oklahoma City, Okla.; 500 acres; 1963–64 (I. M. Pei).

11. Central Business District Project I-A: Oklahoma City, Okla.; 125 acres; 1963–66.

12. Kendall Square: Cambridge, Mass.; 40 acres; 1965.

13. Christian Science Center: Boston; 25 acres; 1965–70 (I. M. Pei, Araldo Cossutta).

14. Kiryat Sir Isaac Wolfson: Jerusalem; 8 acres; 1966–67.

15. Harvard Medical Area: Boston; 200 acres; 1970–71.

16. St. George Place: Staten Island, N.Y.; 36 acres; 1970–74 (James Freed).

17. Yonkers City Center: Yonkers, N.Y.; 7 acres; 1971–72 (I. M. Pei).

18. Raffles International Center: Singapore; 160 acres; 1971–72 (I. M. Pei).

19. Lafayette Place Downtown Study: Boston; 5 acres; 1973.

20. Parque Urbano/Torre Real Madrid: Madrid; 2.5 acres; 1973 (Henry Cobb).

21. Midtown East Station: New York; 7 blocks; 1973–74.

22. Honiron: Honolulu; 27 acres; 1973–74 (Henry Cobb).

23. Squaw Valley Development Concept: Squaw Valley, Calif.; 100 acres; 1974 (Henry Cobb).

24. Collyer Quay/Raffles Square Development: Singapore; 3 acres; 1974–75 (I. M. Pei).

25. Broad Street Mall: Augusta, Ga.; 10 acres; 1974–77 (Henry Cobb).

26. Nathan Road Development Plan: Singapore; 12 acres; 1975–76 (I. M. Pei).

27. Orchard Road Development Plan: Singapore; 5 acres; 1975–76 (I. M. Pei).

28. Singapore River Master Plan: Singapore; 40 acres; 1975–76 (I. M. Pei).

29. Downtown Development Concept: New Brunswick, N.J.; 100 acres; 1976 (Henry Cobb).

30. Al Salaam Project: Kuwait; 28 acres; 1976–79 (Harold Fredenburgh).

31. Dallas Centre: Dallas; 9 acres; 1977 (Henry Cobb).

32. The Galleria: Oklahoma City, Okla.; 15 acres; 1977–79 (Henry Cobb).

33. The South End Plan for Civic and Community Initiatives: Stamford, Conn.; 350 acres; 1980 (Henry Cobb).

34. United Engineers/Robertson Quay Development Concept: Singapore; 30 acres; 1980–82 (I. M. Pei).

35. Raffles City: Singapore; 8.5 acres; 1981–86 (I. M. Pei).

36. Collins Place: Melbourne, Australia; 3.3 acres; 1982 (Henry Cobb).

37. Mission Bay: San Francisco; 195 acres; 1982–84 (James Freed).

38. International Design Center: Long Island City, N.Y.; 10 acres; 1983 (I. M. Pei, Harold Fredenburgh).

39. Playa Vista Concept: Playa Vista, Calif.; 957 acres; 1984–89 (Henry Cobb).

40. Jacaranda Park: Plantation, Fla.; 188 acres; 1987–89 (Henry Cobb).

41. Wildwood: Atlanta, Ga.; 200 acres; 1987–91 (I. M. Pei).

INDEX

Numbers in *italics* denote pages upon which illustrations appear. Unless otherwise noted, all buildings and projects cited are by I. M. Pei and/or his architectural associates; specific attributions may be found in the Catalogue of Works.

Aalto, Alvar, 97

Abbott, Richard, 48

Adams, Henry, 25

Aetna Casualty and Surety Company, 149–50

AIA Journal, 61

Albini, Franco, 97

Alsop, Joseph, 164

American Academy of Arts and Letters, 12

American Institute of Architects, 69, 148, 189, 301; Medal, 12, 38

Architectural Forum, 52

Architectural Record, 41, 103, 113

Architectural Review, 182

Aron, Jean-Paul, 251

Art & Design, 252

Artforum, 182

AT&T headquarters, New York City (Johnson and Burgee), 151, 152, 213

Atlanta: Gulf Oil office building, *52*; IBM Wildwood office complex, 294

Bacon, Edmund, 64

Bader, Ian, 240, 253, 272

Balladur, Edouard, 253–54, 255

Bank of China, Hong Kong branch, 12, 26, 29, 263; architectural evaluation, 292–93; background of project, 286–88; design process, 288–91; plans for, *290, 291*;

Tiananmen Square protest and, 293–94; views of, *289, 295–99*

Bank of China, Shanghai branch, 30, 31, 33

Barcelona, 264

Barnes, Edward Larrabee, 11, 77, 152, 264

Bauhaus, 11, 37, 40, *41, 42*

Beaubourg, *see* Centre Georges Pompidou

Beaux-Arts tradition, 34–35, 36, 40, 41, 71, 238

Beijing, 29, 30, 190, 191, 193; American embassy, 205; *see also* Fragrant Hill Hotel

Beijing Institute of Architectural Design, 206

Bell, Jack, 50

Belluschi, Pietro, 77, 96

Bérégovoy, Pierre, 253, 255

Berenson, Bernard, 157, 159, 164

Bernini, Giovanni Lorenzo, 232, 239

Bernstein, Leonard, 101

Biasini, Emile, *231*, 232–33, 235, 237, 239, 240, 249, 250, 254, 259

Black, Eugene, 99

Black, Leicia, 20, 165

Blackall, Clarence H., 145

Blake, Peter, 10, 27, 152

Bleicken, Gerhardt, 149

Boston, 94; Christian Science Center, 146; Copley Square, 145, 147, 148; Harbor Towers, 68; *see also* Hancock Tower; Kennedy Library

Boston Globe, 140, 150

Boston Navy Yard, 114

Boston Public Library (McKim, Mead & White), 145

Boston Society of Architects, 148

Boulder, Colo., 73, 75, 76; *see also* National Center for Atmospheric Research (NCAR)

Boulez, Pierre, 251, 255

Brancusi, Constantin, 260

Breuer, Marcel, 11, 25, 40, *42–43*, *94*, 100

Brown, J. Carter, *159*–63, 165–66, *167*, *177*, 183, 205, 254, 259

Bruce, Ailsa Mellon, 157

Bunshaft, Gordon, 62, 97

Burchard, John, 123, 148

Burgee, John, 57, 151, 152, 213

Bushnell Plaza, Hartford, Conn., 68

Cabell, Earl, 122

Calder, Alexander, 180

Cambridge, Mass., 95–96, 101, 102–4, 113–14, 147

Campbell, Robert, 140, 150

Canadian Imperial Bank of Commerce, Toronto, 146, 287

Canton, 30

Carey, Hugh, 223

Caro, Anthony, 15–17, 181

Centre Georges Pompidou, Paris (Piano and Rogers), 162, 229, 230–31, 251

Chabaud, André, 240

Charles, Prince of Wales, 259

Charles V, King of France, 231, 257

Chen Cong-zhou, *193*, 201, 205

Chiang Kai-shek, 287

Chiang Kai-shek, Madame (née May-ling Soong), 33, 38

Chillida, Eduardo, 273

China: Communist government of, 32, 137, 189, 191, 286–87; Pei's early life in, 28–

33; Pei's plans to return to, 38, 45; Pei's return visits, 189–90, *192*; Tiananmen Square demonstration, 293–94; *see also* Bank of China; Fragrant Hill Hotel; Shanghai; Suzhou

Chinese architecture, 44–45, 185, 189–90, 192, 206; gardens and, 192–94, 201–2

Chirac, Jacques, 252, 253, 254, 255

Choate Rosemary Hall School, Wallingford, Conn., 158; Mellon Center for the Arts, 13, *158*, 166–67; Science Center, 158, 263, *266*, *267*, 272

Christian Science Center, Boston, 146

Chunking, 38

Cleveland: Rock 'n' Roll Hall of Fame and Museum, 294

Cobb, Henry, *301*; as autonomous designer, 70, 71, 139, 153, 209; Boston renovation plan, 94; Denver projects, 57, 58; early contacts with Zeckendorf, 51, 52–53, 54, *55*; at Graduate School of Design, 43, 44; Hancock Tower, 139, 140, 145, 146–47, *148*–49, 151–53, 210, 251, 287, 290; Kennedy Airport, expansion, 263–64; Place Ville Marie, 61–62

Colbert, Jean Baptiste, 232

Coliseum, New York City, 211

Columbus: Cleo Rogers Memorial County Library, 94, 168, 177

Concertgebouw, Amsterdam, 267

concrete, use of, 63–64, *80*, 89, 128–29, 130, 178, 257–58

Connaissance des Arts, 250

Connoisseur, 182

Convention Center Development Corporation (New York City), 212, 223–24, 225, 226

ACKNOWLEDGMENTS

For giving me the opportunity to write this book, my sincere thanks to Paul Gottlieb at Harry N. Abrams, Inc.; for her insightful, energetic, and unflagging editing, Margaret Donovan; for his elegant design, Samuel Antupit; for his patient shepherding of the project, Sterling Lord; and for their teaching over the years, Professors Eduard Sekler at Harvard, George Collins at Columbia, and Vincent Scully at Yale.

I would also like to express my special thanks to I. M. Pei, who submitted with patience and understanding to an undoubtedly trying regimen of interviews over nearly four years, and to his longtime secretary Leicia Black for her unfailingly cheerful help throughout. I am indebted to Susan Sherman at Abrams and to Janet Adams, Director of Communications at Pei Cobb Freed & Partners. My further thanks to: Daniel Adler, Theodore Amberg, Ian Bader, Edward Barnes, Emile Biasini, Peter Blake, Constance Breuer, Carter Brown, Anthony Caro, Lo-Yi Chan, Helen Chillman, Henry Cobb, Araldo Cossutta, Charles Dey, David Dillon, Michael Flynn, Ulrich Franzen, Harold Fredenburgh, James Freed, Thomas Galvin, Cecil Green, Ralph Heisel, Leonard Jacobson, Russell Johnson, Erik Jonsson, Richard Kahan, Zhang Kai-chi, Robert Kliment, Edward Kosner, Michel Laclotte, Donald Lamm, Thomas Leavitt, Jean Lebrat, Eason Leonard, Edward Logue, Paul Marantz, Stanley Marcus, Paul Mellon, Morton Meyerson, George Miller, Preston Moore, Theodore Musho, Chester Nagel, Jacqueline Onassis, Michael Ovitz, William Pedersen, Chien Chung Pei, Eileen Pei, Liane Pei, Li Chung Pei, T'ing Chung Pei, Cesar Pelli, Adolf Placzek, James Polshek, Christopher Rand, Walter Roberts, Jaquelin Robertson, Leslie Robertson, James Rogers, Amy Segal, George Shrader, Jing Shu-ping, Stephen Smith, John Starr, John Sullivan, James Tilghman, Rebecca Tucker, Bartholomew Voorsanger, William Walton, Werner Wandelmaier, Daniel Waterman, Yann Weymouth, Kellogg Wong, Tom Woo, Stephen Wood, King-lui Wu, Charles Young, and William Zeckendorf, Jr.

PHOTOGRAPH CREDITS

The author and publisher gratefully acknowledge the firm of Pei Cobb Freed & Partners for providing the majority of photographs and illustrations; all material not identified here came from that firm. We also thank the photographers and institutions named in the following credits for permitting the reproduction of works and for supplying images where necessary. (Credits in the main section are arranged by page and those in the catalogue section by figure.)

Pages 1, 2: © Marc Riboud; 3: Robert C. Lautman; 4–5: © Marc Riboud; 6: © Steve Rosenthal; 7: © Paul Warchol; 8–9: © Samuel N. Antupit; 14: Evelyn Hofer; 16: Sandi Pei/Pei Cobb Freed & Partners; 20, 21: Bob Adelman; 22: Courtesy *Look* magazine; 26: Dennis Brack/Black Star; 30: The Bettmann Archive; 33: *China Today;* 34: Courtesy Mark Valter, Reprinted from *Grand Oriental Hotels: From Cairo to Tokyo 1900–1939*, The Vendome Press, New York; 35: The MIT Museum; 40, 41: Courtesy of the Frances Loeb Library, Graduate School of Design, Harvard University; 42, 43: Courtesy Constance Breuer; 45: Courtesy of the Frances Loeb Library, Graduate School of Design, Harvard University; 46: John Loengard, *Life* magazine © Time Inc.; 51 top: Ezra Stoller © Esto; 52: Edgar Orr; 54, 55, 57: Ezra Stoller © Esto; 62 top: Courtesy *Look* magazine; 63 top: Joseph W. Molitor; 65: Robert Damora; 66: Frank Lerner; 67: Robert Damora; 69: George Cserna; 80: National Center for Atmospheric Research/National Science Foundation; 81–89: Ezra Stoller © Esto; 91 bottom: Ezra Stoller © Esto; 94 top: Robert Damora, bottom: George Cserna; 95 top: George Cserna, bottom: Robert Damora; 96, 97: Courtesy William Walton; 99: Aerial Photos International; 100, 105, 106: © Nathaniel Lieberman; 107–10: Mona Zamdmer; 111, 112: © Nathaniel Lieberman; 117: Aerial Photos International; 119: © Nathaniel Lieberman; 120: Ted Musho, renderer/Pei Cobb Freed & Partners; 128: © Bob Taylor, reprinted from the *Dallas Times Herald;* 129 top: Mel Armand Associates, bottom: Balthazar Korab; 131: Mel Armand Associates; 132, 133: © Nathaniel Lieberman; 134: Dennis Brack/Black Star; 137: Mel Armand Associates; 138, 141: © Steve Rosenthal; 142: Robert Damora; 143: © Steve Rosenthal; 144: Ted Gorchev; 145: Model Shop; 149: William Ryerson, *The Boston Globe;* 151: © Steve Rosenthal; 158 top and bottom: Joseph W. Molitor; 159: Dianah Walker, Courtesy Pei Cobb Freed & Partners; 160 bottom: Ed Gaida; 161 left: George Leavens, Courtesy Pei Cobb Freed & Partners, right: Russell Hamilton, Courtesy Pei Cobb Freed & Partners; 169: Ezra Stoller © Esto; 170: Robert C. Lautman; 171: Allen Freeman, Courtesy National Gallery of Art, Washington, D.C.; 172–74: Ezra Stoller © Esto; 176: Allen Freeman, Courtesy National Gallery of Art, Washington, D.C.; 178: Steve Oles, renderer/Pei Cobb Freed & Partners; 179 left: John Nicolais, Courtesy Pei Cobb Freed & Partners; 179 right, 181, 182: Ezra Stoller © Esto; 183: Ronald Reagan Library; 184: © Inge Morath, Magnum Photos, Inc.; 191 top: © Nathaniel Lieberman; 195: © Marc Riboud; 196: C. C. Pei/Pei Cobb Freed & Partners; 197: Taisuke Ogawa; 198 top left and right: © Marc Riboud, bottom left: Taisuke Ogawa, bottom right: © Marc Riboud; 199: Taisuke Ogawa; 200: © Marc Riboud; 205: C. C. Pei/Pei Cobb Freed & Partners; 207: © Marc Riboud; 217–20: © Nathaniel Lieberman; 221: © Samuel N. Antupit; 222: Peter X/Pei Cobb Freed & Partners; 224: © Samuel N. Antupit; 225 top: © Nathaniel Lieberman; 225 bottom–227: © Samuel N. Antupit; 228, 230: © Marc Riboud; 232 top: Photo Chevojon, bottom: Musée Condé, Chantilly, Ms. 65/1284 F°10v°, Photographie Giraudon; 241: © Serge Hambourg; 242: Koji Horiuchi, Courtesy Pei Cobb Freed & Partners; 243: Alfred Wolf; 244: James L. Stanfeld © 1989 National Geographic Society; 245: Koji Horiuchi, Courtesy Pei Cobb Freed & Partners; 246: © Marc Riboud; 247: Diede von Schawen; 248: © Marc Riboud; 252, 255, 256 top: © Marc Riboud; 256 bottom–258: Alfred Wolf; 260: Leonard Jacobson/Pei Cobb Freed & Partners; 261: Koji Horiuchi, Courtesy Pei Cobb Freed & Partners; 262: © Marc Riboud; 264 top, 265: © Paul Warchol; 266, 267 top: © Steve Rosenthal; 275: © Nathaniel Lieberman; 276, 277: © Paul Warchol; 278: Peter Cook; 279, 280: © Paul Warchol; 281: Frank Ribelin, Courtesy Tasende Gallery, La Jolla; 283 bottom: © Samuel N. Antupit; 285: © Marc Riboud; 286: © Samuel N. Antupit; 289: © Marc Riboud; 295–97: Ian Lambot, Courtesy Pei Cobb Freed & Partners; 298: John Nye, Courtesy Pei Cobb Freed & Partners; 299: © Marc Riboud; 300 bottom: © Nathaniel Lieberman; 301: © Serge Hambourg

CATALOGUE

Figures 1–3: Ezra Stoller © Esto; 5: Robert Damora; 6: Ezra Stoller © Esto; 7: George Cserna; 13: Joseph W. Molitor; 14, 15: George Cserna; 16: Frank Lerner; 18: James Y. Young; 19: George Cserna; 21: Robert Damora; 22, 23: Ezra Stoller © Esto; 24: Zaremba; 26, 27: George Cserna; 30: Robert Damora; 31: Balthazar Korab; 32: George Cserna; 34, 35: © Nathaniel Lieberman; 37: Ezra Stoller © Esto; 38: Hutchins Photography, Inc.; 39: George Leavens, Courtesy Pei Cobb Freed & Partners; 40: © Nathaniel Lieberman; 42: National Center for Atmospheric Research/National Science Foundation; 45: Ezra Stoller © Esto; 46: © Nathaniel Lieberman; 48: George Cserna; 49: Ezra Stoller © Esto; 50: © Nathaniel Lieberman; 52: George Cserna; 54: Kouo Shang-Wei; 55: George Cserna; 58: Kouo Shang-Wei; 59: Barry Rustin; 67, 68: © Steve Rosenthal; 71: Peter Aaron © Esto; 73: © Steve Rosenthal; 74: Richard Payne; 81: © Steve Rosenthal; 82: Richard Payne; 85, 87, 88, 90: © Nathaniel Lieberman; 92: John Nye, Courtesy Pei Cobb Freed & Partners; 93: © Steve Rosenthal; 94: © Wolfgang Hoyt; 96: Dan Cornish © Esto; 97: Koji Horiuchi, Courtesy Pei Cobb Freed & Partners; 102: © Steve Rosenthal; 104: Dan Cornish © Esto; 110, 114: © Nathaniel Lieberman